SO-CBR-968

Homeward Bound

Memoirs of a Foster Child

By

Dante Drummond

Ta Ta Dee!
What a delight
to know you! Keep up the
art!
      Dante

Copyright © 2015 by Dante Drummond
All rights reserved. No part of this book may be reproduced,
scanned, or distributed in any printed or electronic form without
permission.
First Edition: April, 2015
Printed in the United States of America
ISBN-13: 978-1-6331-8326-1
ISBN-10: 1-6331-8326-2

Faith

When you walk to the edge of all the light you have
and take that first step into the darkness of the unknown,
you must believe that one of two things will happen:

> There will be something solid for you to stand upon,
> or, you will be taught how to fly

© Patrick Overton
1975, 1997

Homeward Bound

Table of Contents

Prologue

Part 1
Early Childhood

Part 2
Arizona

Part 3
California Dreaming

Epilog

Me and Mom

Prologue

Katharine Hepburn

She started out as Katharine Hepburn. I saw her on TV and instantly fell in love. She was strong, powerful, confident and independent . . . just how I wanted to be. Like so many other foster children before me, I took a stand. Rather than feel weak, alone and afraid, I made the decision to identify with a powerful person and claimed Katharine Hepburn to be my mother. Well, she *looked* like my mother, or at least the way I remembered her years ago, in 1954 when I was six years old – the last time I'd seen her. It made me feel proud to tell people that Katharine Hepburn was my mother. How *lucky* they must think I was to have a mother of such substance. I told them that she was going to come to get me someday soon . . . maybe even swoop down like Superman and rescue me. So much better than being a lost child like I felt I was.

Because I was so convincing in my stand, some people who didn't know the movie star's history believed that I was the daughter of Katharine Hepburn. Others, especially adults, looked at me as if I were delusional. I'm sure it was particularly disturbing when they saw in my face that I believed it to be so. So it went year after year . . . . Where was my mother? Why hadn't she come to claim me? What was taking her so long? It seemed a mystery that no one really wanted to talk about.

The answer came many years later in 1968, on a late Sunday afternoon in Santa Maria, California – across the country from where I had last seen my mother in Newport News, Virginia. I was nineteen years old, and was outside on the lawn downstairs from my apartment, having a barbeque with friends. When the phone rang upstairs, I unfurled my long, lanky legs and took the stairs two at a time to answer it. In those days people always

1

answered their phone.

Out of breath, I grabbed the receiver and was shocked to hear my father's voice. It had been almost a year – a very eventful year, I might add – since I had last seen him in Tucson before running away from home and hitch-hiking to California. After exchanging surprised greetings with my father, he paused and said: "I've found your mother, she wants to say hello." I was stunned. At that moment my long quest was over – here on the phone was my mother.

Her voice was tight as she desperately tried to contain her emotions long enough to speak – to say: "Hi Baby, this is your Mother." After fourteen years of waiting, I couldn't believe my ears – this was my mother speaking. I didn't know what to say. I leaned against the wall for support and then slid down onto the carpeted floor, tightly cradling the phone buried in my ear. No point in trying to be strong and brave or pretending not to be affected by the siren song of her voice.

We seemed to melt together into the phone line as it became the umbilical cord connecting us to one another again. There was such emotion . . . both of us crying – the conversation becoming more intense by the minute – promises from me to come to Virginia . . . promises to visit my mother.

It didn't even matter that she wasn't Katharine Hepburn.

Part 1

Early Childhood

The Driftwood Shack

In balmy St. Petersburg Florida, just a block from the beaches of the Gulf of Mexico, sat the dilapidated red-stained wooden "Driftwood Shack." It couldn't be missed leaning there on the palm-studded commercial corner like a precarious house of cards. Its unique character – not to mention the big roadside cage filled with monkeys strategically placed at the store's front corner – compelled the curious tourists to stop to see what it was all about. Upon entering the store they were greeted by baby alligators in a shallow screened-in tank, surrounded by a veritable smorgasbord of interesting souvenirs such as exotic colorful shells, coral, starfish, and driftwood lamps and furniture my father created out of pieces of washed-up wood he gathered from the isolated beaches nearby.

As a young girl of six, it was my contribution to the oddities of the Shack to go out and capture colorful chameleons that we would keep in a fish aquarium next to my father's art studio. I even made it into the local newspapers – a picture of me posing with chameleons leashed and pinned to my shirt to entice the tourists to buy them. We'd fetch a good price too. We would pick the lizards from their leafy aquarium nest and send them home with the tourists in customized little glass milk bottle prisons. They were quite a hit.

In a way, my adventures at the Driftwood Shack began as traumatically as these lizards' days there ended. Just a few months earlier I was living in Virginia with my mother and step-father, Charlie. One day during one of their many vicious fights, Charlie ripped me from my screaming mother's arms, flung me into the backseat of his Chevy and while fending off my hysterical mother, whisked me off in the car. He drove for hours with me kicking the back seat, screaming and throwing fits until I finally fell asleep from total exhaustion.

In the middle of the night, after driving all the way from Newport News to St. Petersburg, Charlie got out of the car and yanked me from my sleep in the back seat and marched me up to a dark beat-up old house. He then banged on the front door and pushed me into the legs of the tall startled man who appeared there. At first I thought my step-father Charlie was going to get into another fight like he usually did, but instead he just yelled at the man, saying really mean things about me as I stood by crying. The tall man looked down at me and draped one of his long arms in front of me as if to protect me, and just when I thought Charlie might punch him in the face, to my disbelief he turned and stomped back to his car, got in and drove off – never to be seen again . . . *leaving me alone there with that man!*

I would soon find out that the tall stranger was Walter Cole Sauer, my biological father. He tried to introduce me to his wife, Valora, who stood back behind him, but the baby boy in her arms was screaming and crying louder than I was! As the shaken adults tried to calm us children down, I'm sure that they were hoping that this fragile, traumatized waif in the doorway was just part of a midsummer night's dream. I remember I was trembling so hard I couldn't stop and I kept crying and calling out for my mother. It was a strange house and the people in it were strange too! It didn't help that they began arguing with each other about what to do with me, given that my showing up on their doorstep in the middle of the night was a complete surprise to them. I couldn't help but wonder what was going to happen to me.

After calming me down with some milk and cookies, the strangers unfolded an Army cot in the living room and brought me a pillow and covered me up with a soft bright colored blanket with long-legged pink birds on it. But still it was hard to settle down and sleep that night. As I lay sobbing and restless, that man who was my father slept right there on the nearby couch, probably making sure I didn't run screaming out the door.

The new morning daylight seemed to soften the trauma of the night before and revealed a whole new set of peculiar and interesting surroundings. As I woke up and quietly peeked out from under the covers I saw that the interior walls of the living room were painted beautiful bright colors of turquoise, yellow and blue. The artist had painted murals of sea creatures all over them – complete with mermaids. My father was still asleep on the couch, but I could hear rustling in the next room and could smell food, and I was hungry! As I cautiously walked into the kitchen I saw Valora making breakfast and the baby sitting at the table in a high chair. Valora greeted me with a smile and introduced me to the resident pet walking around on the counter. Cindy was a friendly domesticated little monkey wearing a frilly pink dress and a diaper, and was apparently allowed full run of the house.

After breakfast my sleep-deprived father and his wife, with a now happier baby Curtis in her arms, toured me around the house and then through the adjoining store. I was already on sensory overload before I set eyes on the alligators and the monkey cage, but was unprepared for what came next. We ventured out to a small building in a fenced-off area behind the house marked with a big sign that said "Employees Only." This was my father's art studio. As we entered the large, sunlit room with all the art supplies and colorful paintings, I let out a scream. There in the midst of the art were . . . well . . . *bodies*! There were even detached arms and legs and hands laying scattered on the floor and hanging from a clothesline across the back of the room. Thankfully, it happened that my newly-acquired parents designed storefront windows and this was where they kept the mannequins. My father repaired the bodies and painted on glamorous faces while Valora designed the wigs. It was a surreal sight!

This day was really my first chance to size up my father, as the night before had been a screaming blur. He was a tall, lanky, red-headed man with a gentle smile and a slow Southern way about him. His wife and baby were red-heads too, both quite curious as to what to make of *me* – as if I were the strange wild creature that was allowed to come into the house. For them life at the Driftwood Shack would never be the same . . . nor would mine.

Across the Bridge

It was a summer night in Florida a year or so later. The air was warm and humid. The stars were all there in their glory and the moon shone down on me with its soft protective glow. At the young age of eight I had come to welcome the celestial moon as one of my only constant companions. I would often talk to that glowing globe, sharing my hopes and dreams and fears – sometimes praying in its direction as if it were my portal to the ear of God. I had to believe that He was listening.

I stood there that night at the entrance to the Cory Causeway, looking up at its inclining mass of wood and steel with all its light poles jutting up in a row like giant inverted fish hooks – their metal skirts directing light down onto the wooden planks and passing cars below. I found the sight to be quite intimidating, especially knowing that I had to traverse it at night alone. But like a lost dog, I had good homing instincts and knew that this was the bridge I needed to cross to get back home to my new-found family. I was sure the earlier events of the night had all been a big misunderstanding, but then here I was and what else could I do?

As I ventured onto the pedestrian section of the bridge, the cars running over the wooden planks were so noisy that at first I had to put my hands over my ears. My heart was racing wildly and the added assault on my ears didn't help. I noticed that once in a while cars would slow down after passing me as if they were going to stop, but I kept walking as fast as I could with my head held down in my usual determined, strong-willed fashion. I knew this bridge: it would incline up, over and then down the other side where it joined the busy street with the smoked fish stand and then on to Mr. Peterson's gas station. I would then make a left turn and go up a couple of blocks to the street where my house, the old Driftwood Shack, stood in all its glory.

After several minutes walking on the bridge, a car stopped ahead of me and someone got out. I didn't want to talk to anyone and kept walking as fast as I could. Then I saw *another* car stop and *those* people along with the others were yelling across the barriers trying to coax me into their car, offering me a ride across the bridge and to my home. My experience was never to trust strangers and I already knew about getting into a car with someone I didn't like. As I continued to walk on I glanced back again and saw that a police car had pulled up behind the other parked cars. Well, I knew to stay away from *them* – policemen always meant trouble. I kept walking and pretty soon the police car drove up and parked just ahead of me and the policeman got out and started walking toward me. I tried to ignore him at first and wouldn't talk to him and just kept on walking. I just wanted people to leave me alone so I could get home. I didn't *need* a ride! His voice was kind, but firm and persuasive enough for me to begin to realize that I had no choice but to get into his car so that he could take me home (this would be my first experience of getting chauffeured by a police officer, and the only time I got to ride up in the *front* seat). After I calmed down a bit and saw that the policeman wasn't a threat, I found the experience to be interesting – even fun – and directed him to my house.

When we arrived we found the Driftwood Shack to

be dark and quiet except for the stirrings of the monkeys outside in their cages, awakened by the approach of the police car. We sat and waited in the parked car while the policeman asked me a lot of questions about what had happened that night. I recounted that the evening had started out to be very special. My father, step-mother and three-year-old little brother and I were all going to go to the drive-in theater together. This was always a big treat for us. My father would drive the station wagon onto the big cleared field with the massive two-story white screen in the front. We had visited there often enough to know which of the fifty or so speakers worked best and would drive the car up to one of our favorite spots and hang the metal speaker on the partly opened window of the driver's side.

One of my favorite things about going to this outdoor movie was getting to visit the concession stand. They had set up a fenced-in children's play area where they had all kinds of jungle gym equipment and I was a real jungle gym expert by then. We would all go together, buy cokes and popcorn and then take them back to the car to watch the movie. Sometimes people would bring fold-up chairs, put them out on the lawn area in front of the concession stand and sit there instead of in their cars. It was quite a busy social scene with children everywhere running around the lawn and playing in the fenced-off area until the movie started, at which time we were told to come and quiet down and watch.

This particular night had started off like any other, all of us excited and happy about going to the movie, though we did have one little unfortunate incident on the drive there. I hadn't closed the back door of the car all the way and they almost lost me going around a curve as the door swung open with me holding onto it . . . but all ended well and I didn't fall out.

Once we arrived at the drive-in theater safe and sound, we set up and made our trek to the concession stand.

After my brother and I played around the children's area for a bit, we all went back to the car together with our refreshments and settled in. It was a really boring romantic movie and my little brother Curtis went to sleep. I was fidgety and my parents suggested I go back over to the fenced-in area and play quietly on the jungle gym equipment for a while, but to be sure to come back as soon as the movie was over. This really pleased me. I was happy to go. Of course I had to take the slow way around and wandered about checking on what other people were doing in their cars. There sure seemed like a lot of kissing going on, but then my parents were kissers too.

I took my time with this exploration and then arrived at the concession stand area and found some other kids who had probably been just as bored as I was. After playing for a while, I could see that the movie was over and people were putting their chairs away, coming back and forth to visit the bathroom and getting into their cars to leave. The other kids had all left the playground area. Even though I knew I should be getting back to the car, I continued to play for a little while longer and then finally made my way back over to the car, taking my time and checking out the scene along the way. When I arrived at the place where I thought the car had been, the space was empty. By then most of the cars were lining up and leaving the field. With people still coming and going to and from the concession stand and with all the cars weaving about, there was a lot of confusion and dust. I looked around for my parent's car, but it was nowhere in sight. I became panicked and started to run in and out between the cars and people, calling out for my parents. They were nowhere to be found. I ran back to the concession stand and they were not there either. I couldn't imagine that they would go home without me, but I couldn't find them anywhere. I was shaking all over, but what other choice did I have but to walk home . . . which involved walking across the bridge.

As I sat in the police car in front of the Driftwood Shack with the policeman writing down my story, my parents drove up. My father leapt out of the car, looking completely frantic and raced over to the police car. He was so relieved to see me sitting there. I guess I had caused quite a scare. The policeman and I then got to hear *his* story. He and Valora had packed up the car and waited for me to return. Since I did not come back right away, they decided to play a little joke on me and go park down behind the concession stand . . . more to teach me a lesson about not coming back to the car in time when the movie was over. Of course they expected to find me there, but we somehow missed each other – I must have already decided they weren't coming back and had left to walk home. They too had panicked and searched the field and bathrooms for me, but we must have been looking in different places trying to find each other.

The bottom line was that at last I was home safe and sound without a scratch. Just one exciting adventure of my young life – with many more yet to come.

Gulf Beaches Elementary

Looking back I realize I must have been pretty confused by the time I had entered first grade at the Gulf Beaches Elementary school in St. Petersburg. I was six years old, and had just come to live with my father, step-mother and little brother, Curtis, only a week or so before. Later in life I was told that my mother and step-father had taken me out of first grade in Virginia some time earlier with the excuse that they were sending me to live with my biological father. Months had passed before school board officials discovered I was still living at home and showed up at our house to question my parents about it. Perhaps that visit was what sparked the big fight between my parents and the awful car ride with Charlie that ultimately landed me in Florida, where I was scholastically behind all the other kids. Even so, I somehow managed to finish first grade at the new school in St. Petersburg.

So after a wild summer with little or no supervision hanging around the Driftwood Shack and around the beaches of the Gulf of Mexico, I started second grade. A few weeks into it, I remember that I really had to struggle to keep up with the other kids – I was in over my head. One day my teacher, Mrs. Bedford, along with the principal and another teacher, took me into a back room to test me and ask me a lot of questions. There was a big discussion between them. I sat close-by and watched them huddling together talking about me, turning and looking at me every now and then. Although I could see that the decision wasn't unanimous, it was finally agreed that I would be put back into first grade again.

Even at that very young age, this was a horrible embarrassment and the kids would tease me relentlessly – especially when we all lined up by grade levels after recess and lunch when the second-grade kids would call out my name from across the lines. I was already having trouble navigating my life changes and trying to keep up with the others in school. Teasing by the resident bullies didn't help my advancing behavioral problems. Also, as you might imagine, my placement back to first grade would have a ripple effect throughout the rest of my school years, causing me the shame of always being older and taller than anyone else in my grade level and the challenge of trying to meet the high expectations of my new teachers.

At the Gulf Beaches school I remember spending a great deal of my recess time hidden and sulking deep within a big clump of sprawling palm bushes at the corner of the school yard playground. This was the first secret fortress of many I would construct in my childhood years to come.

By next year the school officials, along with my father and step-mother, were trying to figure out what to do about me. I was completely unfocused and starting to act out – I even stole money from my teacher's desk. While my home life was anything but stable, now my school life had taken a turn for the worse.

Luckily for me around this time my second-grade teacher, Mrs. Bedford, took a personal interest in me. She encouraged me to start drawing and to get involved with art projects such as mosaics with colored glass. I seemed to have an aptitude for art and began to get comments and positive feedback from teachers and other students. I even entered an art contest and won two tickets to a children's play. This made me feel better about myself, and Mrs. Bedford's interest in me and my art became a bonding experience for us both. Because she didn't have any children of her own and saw that I was going through some challenges, I think she really wanted to nurture me in some way. Perhaps she thought that spending time with me could offset my quirky home environment and make a positive impact on my life. Close to the end of the second grade, Mrs. Bedford set up a private meeting with my father and step-mother and made a surprising proposal: after the school year was over I would come to live with her and Mr. Bedford for the summer. Years later Valora would tell me that she and my father were relieved that they would no longer be fully responsible for the day-to-day care of the "wild child" that I was becoming and they were happy for me, that I would have the care and influence from someone upstanding like Mrs. Bedford. While I'm sure that Mrs. Bedford's heart was in the right place, I can tell you now that she had no idea what she was getting herself into.

When I was a Child . . .

So there I was at eight years old, having already lived with multiple family members in multiple cities. I now know that when I was born my mother and father were young and inexperienced in life and were divorced soon after my birth. My mother loves to recount the story about how she and my father lived in a little upstairs studio apartment in Newport News, Virginia – right across the street from the police station. In 1948 when her labor with me began, a couple of the policemen from across the street came over and helped my father ease my very pregnant mother (and me) down the narrow staircase in a chair and then drove us to the nearby hospital in a police car. My mother also likes to share how I was born a breach baby and came out "ass backwards!"

My mother told me that she was only eighteen at the time I was born and that she had lived a very sheltered life. And that her parents knew my tall red-headed father, recently returned from the War and now working at the local ice cream store, and they liked and trusted him so much that they allowed her to go out on a date with him to see the movie "Bambi." How innocent. It was her very first date ever. According to her, however, the next thing she knew, after the movie my father convinced her to *cross the state line to get married that night!* I can only imagine what a shock it must have been for her parents when she called them at home that night to tell them that she wouldn't be coming home because *she was married* and was going to spend the night with her *husband*! My mother said that they not only couldn't believe it, they even sent the police to her hotel to confirm that the marriage was valid – which they did.

My parents' marriage didn't last long. I was told by my father's sister that my father left us shortly after I was born and my mother and I lived with his parents for six months. Then in a letter from my mother's mother (Nana) years later, I learned that when I was about eight months old he sent for me and my mom to come live with him in Connecticut where he was working with his sister. Not long after we moved there, my dad contacted Nana to tell her that my mother was sick and would she please come to pick me up and take me to stay with her until my mother was well again. I'm not sure what was wrong with my mother, but my Nana did pick me up and took me home to live with her and my grandfather, Gus. There I would remain until I was five years old.

They lived in a nice little raised brick house in nearby Hampton. Gus was a train engineer and Nana did not work outside of the home. I have pictures of me standing by the makeshift rope swing, hanging from a low branch of their backyard tree. I was old enough then to develop good memories of living there with my mother's parents. One of my favorites is when they surprised me with my own Bambi. My memory is that Nana told me that we were going to take a walk to town by way of the overgrown dirt alleyway behind our house – a pleasant walk that we often took together. I recall that she held my hand as we took one step at a time down the steep back porch stairs. There was an old shed at the corner of the yard where Gus kept all of his lawn equipment. Nana walked me up to it and bent down facing me with her finger over her lips. She slowly opened the door and motioned for me to peek inside. It was dark in there and I was a little afraid that something would jump out at me. I told her that I couldn't see anything. She told me to look way to the back. I looked, and after waiting for my eyes to adjust to the darkness, noticed something white and fuzzy lying on a bed of straw in the back corner. I looked up to my Nana with surprise and waited for an explanation. She whispered to me that it was Bambi. This Bambi was a little lamb. She said that Mary had a little lamb and now I had one too!

And just like Mary's little lamb, Bambi would become my best friend and follow me all around the yard whenever I went down there to play. As Bambi got older and started to grow horns, he started to get rough with me – chasing me around the back yard to butt me. I found the easiest way to escape him was to quickly crawl under the house. (I found the cat down under there too!) Soon after that Bambi was sent away to a farm, or at least that is what they told me. Years later when I was reunited with my Nana I asked her if we ever ate Bambi for dinner. When she answered no, I found that to be a great relief!

Aunt Elsie's Farm

Nana's sister Elsie and her husband, Herbert, owned a farm in the countryside just a few hours from Newport News. It was in this little farming community named after its only general store, Kents Store, that my mother was born. I always looked forward to going to the farm. My Aunt Elsie was a tall sturdy no-nonsense woman who had a sweet spot for me. I loved to visit her and see all the farm animals. Gus and Nana would take the weekend off and we'd drive for what seemed like forever to reach the old country road. Then after another long drive past fields of green for as far as the eye could see, we came to the dirt driveway leading to their farm. I would squeal and laugh with glee as I watched the canine welcoming committee consisting of three excited farm dogs come *racing* up to the car – barking, jumping and chasing alongside us as we drove up the driveway with the dirt cloud trailing behind us. My grandfather would be watching out to not run over some free-roaming animal along the way. Then once we parked behind the house where the barn, chicken coop and corral were, Elsie would come running out of the back door all smiles, wiping her hands on her apron, and give us hugs. Uncle Herbert would come out from the barn all happy to greet us, slapping Gus' back. It was quite the scene – dogs barking, chickens and geese squawking and fluttering around – it was as if they hadn't had company in months!

After all the kissing and hugging was over, the first thing we would do was to get washed up at the well behind the house. I can still remember Uncle Herbert drawing up the dripping wooden bucket of pure cool water from the deep dark well. We would then drink the water from a tin ladle – it tasted as sweet as Heaven. Once washed up we would all pile into the house for lunch, family style, sitting around the big kitchen table. There would be ham, green beans, corn and fresh baked bread. Everything smelled so good! The peach pie for dessert was my favorite. Even though everything was so delicious, I could hardly contain myself long enough to just sit still, and listen to the animated talk of the adults – I wanted to go outside and explore the farm yard, the barn and see all the animals. Going to the corral to see the old gray horse was always one of my favorite destinations. He was kept safely behind the fence, so I couldn't ride him, but only touch him when I was in the arms of an adult. I also loved all the cats and dogs. Every picture I have of me from the farm has some kind of animal in it. You can see that they must have liked me as much as I liked them.

I was never bored at the farm. When we weren't outside with the animals, Auntie Elsie had lots of children's picture books that she would read to me while I sat on her lap. Also, I loved to play with her red tin can full of buttons. They were every imaginable shape, color and size – red ones, blue ones, silver and gold. I would spread them all out on the brightly colored linoleum floor and sit there and quietly entertain myself. At night I got to sleep with my Nana. They would keep a pot under the bed so if we had to go to the bathroom in the middle of the night we didn't have to go all the way out to the outhouse. I had so much fun at the farm that I never wanted to leave.

Back with Mom

When I was almost five, my grandfather Gus had a heart attack and died. With her husband gone, Nana – who was almost fifty years old by then, had to find work to help support herself. I guess the only choice she thought she had at the time was to give me back to my mother. She reluctantly sent me to live in Newport News again, only this time with my mother – who by now had not only landed herself another husband, but had a son! He was almost two years old and his name was Clifford, though everyone called him Cliff. I later found out that my mother and Nana had been on the outs with each other because Nana didn't want anything to do with mother's husband Charlie Coleman and wouldn't let him or my mother near her house. I hadn't even been told that I had a brother.

My step-father Charlie was a tough guy. He owned a termite extermination company, and was really abusive when he drank. I remember that he wasn't home much during the night time, but when he did come home he would often be drunk and take out his frustrations on my mother, brother and me. I learned to know him as a mean and angry man – at least *most* of the time. Up until then I had been pretty spoiled and sheltered by my grandparents. This would no longer be the case in Charlie's house. *I'm sad to say that it was there that my childhood nightmares began.*

My new home, however, was located in a nice neighborhood with a lot of children and an elementary school close-by within walking distance. It was an old two-story Victorian-style home, part of a row of houses on the street that were lined up just a few feet from each other. They were so close you could even jump from one porch to the other. I'm sure that in its day the house had been lovely, but it had fallen into disrepair.

I remember that I liked to play on the elevated front porch, high at the top of the stairs. I could sit in the porch swing and see all the neighbors passing by. I eventually made some friends from the neighborhood and they would come over and we would sit on the porch steps eating watermelon, singing songs, or making little people out of gathered sticks and leaves. Sometimes when it would get really hot my mother would fill up the big metal wash tub in the backyard and we would play in the water or make mud pies. We had an overgrown alley in the back just like the one at my Nana's house and it was full of sweet smelling honeysuckle bushes. My friends and I would pick the flowers and suck out the sweet juice from inside and then pretend we were smoking them like cigarettes, blowing our smoke into the wind like glamorous movie stars.

On rainy days there was a back, glassed-in sun porch downstairs to play in. My mother kept a big trunk there – full of frilly bright colored crinolines, hats, and shawls that I was allowed to play with. I would set the small child-sized table up for an afternoon high tea with my doll and stuffed animals. Occasionally a friend would stop by to visit and my mother would bring down cookies and lemonade. At first it all seemed fine there at Charlie's house.

I had a little bedroom to myself downstairs between the parlor and the house furnace – away from where my mother, Charlie and Cliff slept upstairs. It was pretty scary down there at night by myself all alone. Upstairs was where the family spent most of their time. The little eat-in kitchen was upstairs in the back, and I can remember my mother standing there next to the counter making me apple butter sandwiches at lunchtime. But there was a big rotted hole in the wood floor just in front of the sink, so we all had to walk around it and be careful not to put our foot into it. The house bathroom was at the top of the stairs and it had a matching hole in the floor under the old raised claw-foot bathtub. If we were very still while taking a bath we would sometimes get to see a little mouse creep out from under the tub. The first time I saw it I got all upset, but then after a while I got used to it.

Unfortunately my mother seemed to be gone a lot of the time. Since she didn't work, I'm not quite sure where she was. I have very few memories of her from that period. Charlie was also at work during the day and spent a lot of nights out at the bar. My savior during those times was my Black nanny, Lilly – who came in on weekdays. She was a big strong stocky woman with shiny dark chocolate skin and hair – such a contrast to my fragile and pale freckle-skinned mother. Lilly seemed to come across to everyone else as a tough force to reckon with, but to me she was gentle, kind and tolerant. When I was upset, she had a way of grabbing me and holding me tight to her big soft bosom and rocking me until I wasn't afraid anymore. I don't know what I would have done without Lilly looking out for me and standing up to my step-father on my behalf.

I remember one day during the weekend when Lilly wasn't there, I was playing with stick dolls outside on the front porch of the house. My mother and Charlie were upstairs, and as usual I could hear them yelling at each other and my mother crying. I was starting to realize that this was the norm, but it was always unsettling to me. It made me want to climb somewhere deep inside of myself and hide, to make it all go away – something I was learning to do a lot by then.

As the noise intensified and my mother started screaming I made the mistake of opening the front door. As I stood at the bottom of the stairs with the door open I saw, as in a nightmare, my mother coming down the stairs. She was slumped over, grabbing the rail and half sliding, half falling, crying hysterically, her face and dress red with blood. My step-father was yelling down at her from the top of the stairs threatening to hit her again, a hammer raised in his hand. When my mother looked down and saw me standing there she screamed for me to run, but my feet wouldn't move and all I could do was stand there frozen to the spot. The next thing I knew, her body came crashing down into mine, somehow lifting me up and pushing me through the front door and out onto the porch – slamming the door hard behind us. The glass in the door shattered as we ran down the steps and away from the house. I think the broken glass must have landed on Charlie, because when I turned to see if he was coming after us, I saw him inside through the door where the window used to be, looking surprised and mean – blood on his face.

My injured mother and I made it next door to our neighbor Eleanor's house. Eleanor had already heard the disturbance and called the police. I vividly remember staring into the wet, bloodied face of my mother as she and Eleanor and I all crammed in together under the couch trying not to make any noise as my step-father kicked and pounded at the locked front door trying to get in.

Then I heard dogs barking and men outside shouting at Charlie . . . they even knew his name. Charlie was yelling like a crazy man, shouting back at them, calling my mother names and saying he was going to kill us all. Thank Heaven the men out there with Charlie were policemen and they arrested him right then and there. Later, as she held me tight, I buried my head in Eleanor's skirts as we stood there on her front porch watching the ambulance driving away with my mother.

Eleanor took care of me at her house while we waited for my mother to return home. When my mother finally returned several days later with a big bandage on her head, she seemed different – very quiet and staring into space. She was never quite the same after that, with some parts of her memory missing. My Nana came to visit for a little while to take care of us and I could tell that she was frustrated with my mother. A few weeks later Charlie came home all apologetic. He said that it was the alcohol making him crazy and he would quit drinking. It didn't take long for my mother to take him back and the nightmare just started all over again.

The Exterminator

I had been living with Mom and Charlie and their son for about a year and it wasn't going well, but by then at least the chaos had become familiar. I attended to my mother's bedside occasionally when she was feeling sick and I soon found out why – she was pregnant. After my sister Frances was born, my step-father seemed to become even more hostile towards me. He would refer to Cliff and Fran as *his* children – leaving me to believe that I didn't belong with *his* family.

I remember all of us standing around outside of the house on one of those warm, sultry mornings when the humidity was high and the air fell over us like a thick wool blanket. It was a good day for me so far because my mother had allowed me to wear my favorite yellow Sunday dress – the one with the big bow at the waist. I ran around the front yard twirling and showing it off to my mother and Lilly. My three-year-old brother Cliff was there too and Lilly held his hand tightly while also cradling my new baby sister in the soft folds of her body like a prize football. Everyone seemed in a strange mood that morning – all edgy and anxious as if in anticipation of something about to happen. My mother was especially nervous, though attentive to me – grabbing me by the hand and crouching down to talk sweetly to me about what a good girl I was, while straightening the bow on my pretty dress. I loved it when she paid attention to me. While my little sister slept in the protective arm of Lilly, my brother was fidgety and wanted to be with his mother. Lilly tried to divert his attention away from us by pacing him around – having him smell the fragrant honeysuckle bush on the other side of the yard. You could tell from his annoying whine that he wasn't interested.

Then, without warning, Charlie came bolting out the front screen door carrying that old suitcase I had seen in our attic, upstairs next to my parent's room. He rushed down the porch steps and quickly threw the suitcase into the trunk of the car and slammed down the trunk. He turned around to face us and from that point everything got wild and crazy. People started wailing and my mother grabbed me tight and hung on as if for dear life! I was really confused and frightened by all this behavior. *What was going on?*

The next thing I knew I was being lifted up in the air and pulled out of the arms of my mother. Charlie had me now, and I started kicking and screaming – expecting another beating when I hadn't done anything wrong! Fending off my hysterical mother, he managed to get me over to the car and threw me into the back seat. He paused long enough to point his finger in my face and holler: "stay put"! By then I was bawling, my mother was hysterical, and Lilly was frantically holding onto my terrified screaming brother – herself shaken and in tears. After a quick yelling match between my mother and Charlie, he hopped into the driver's seat of the car and off we went – with Mother running after the car crying: "My baby! My baby!" I was screaming from the back seat of the car, arms outstretched back to my mother as she slowly disappeared into the distance.

I'm not sure how long I cried and threw fits in the back seat of the car, while Charlie angrily gripped the wheel and stared ahead at the road. At one point I remember him yelling at me to shut up and throwing coins in the back seat, promising me that we were going to go buy some candy with it. (I guess that was one of the ways he had stopped me from crying in the past.)

We drove for a long time before we stopped. I had cried myself into exhaustion and fallen asleep. When I woke up it was night time and we had pulled over alongside a dark road. Charlie told me to get out of the car and go pee in the bushes. When I got back into the car, he got in the back seat beside me and we ate an apple butter sandwich together and drank water from a jug he had brought. As we were eating he put his arm around me and stroked my hair softly, saying how terribly sorry he was for taking me away from my mother, but that I was going to have to go live with my real father for now. Well that was confusing, because by then I had been led to believe that Charlie *was* my father. I didn't know who my father really was, since he had left when I was a baby. I remained thoroughly confused – and my mind flashed back to the things I must have done wrong for Charlie and my mother not to want me to live with them anymore.

I remembered there had been that time not too long ago when I was walking home from school and a nice old lady on the next street had invited me inside for cookies and Kool Aid. She was so nice that I couldn't resist her invitation. Once inside she talked to me a lot and whenever I started to leave she would give me more cookies and Kool Aid. What was a kid supposed to do? Sometime later when I finally left, I was hurrying home when I encountered Charlie driving down the street in his car. He said he had been driving around the neighborhood frantically looking for me after he was told by Lilly that I didn't return home from school. He was what we called "spitting mad" and he told me to *get in the car*! When we got home he literally threw me onto my bed and gave me such a beating that I threw up the cookies and Kool Aid. After he left the room and slammed the door I remember laying there crying in my bed, watching the pink Kool Aid vomit run down the wall beside my bed. Several days later the vomit began to smell and I got in trouble all over again for not telling my mother about it sooner so she could have it cleaned up! *Maybe that was why they were sending me away. I had been a bad girl.*

~

Now sitting there in the dark car, eating our apple butter sandwich, Charlie went on to say that since my mother and Charlie had a new baby girl, he would have to "make some changes" and it would be better for me to go live with my father. So once again he had made it clear – my new baby sister would take my place in the family, so they didn't want me to live with them anymore. Tearfully I asked Charlie when I would be able to come back home to see my mother and brother and friends again. "Real soon" he said.

Charlie continued to hold me in his arms, gently rocking and comforting me there in the car, holding my head close to his chest with his hands. He could be so kind and gentle at times like this when we were alone, stroking my head and body while I hugged him back and stroked his mysterious body in return. It was only at these times that I felt that he really *did* love me – as he was so kind and affectionate – not mean and yelling and hitting people like he usually did.

As Charlie and I sat there in the back seat of the car, another car pulled up behind us on the road, its lights blaring in on us. Charlie quickly fixed our clothes and got out of the car. I could hear a strange man's voice outside and tucked myself deeper into the back seat. A flashlight lit up the car and then for a moment was directed right at my face! I heard an exchange of voices again and my stepfather being ordered to "*stay clear of the car*".

The car door opened and a big bulky man got into the back seat and sat down *right* next to me! He smelled like cigarettes and looked very scary and official in his uniform and I knew right away that he was a policeman as I had seen them at our house several times before. He told me not to be afraid, but I was already afraid because I knew that policemen meant trouble. He asked me if my step-father had hurt me in any way and I said no. He asked me a lot of other questions too, but I just denied any wrong-doing – as Charlie had already told me a long time ago what he would do to me if I was to tell. I think the policeman must have been suspicious because he then started pleading with me, telling me that everything would be alright if I just told him what my step-father had done to me there in the back seat. Again I just told him we were eating a sandwich and denied any wrong-doing, thinking of all the trouble I would get into if I told.

The policeman got out of the car and there was a lot of yelling going on back and forth outside between him and my step-dad. I could tell that the policeman was really mad because he was talking to Charlie as if he were Charlie's father! A few minutes later Charlie slid back into the driver's seat of the car looking rattled and angry. He sat there fuming with his shoulders all hunched over and his hands firmly gripping the steering wheel. I could tell that he was "spitting mad" – and I huddled even deeper into the seat. We slowly drove off, and the policeman pulled out behind us and followed in his car for a long time down the highway. Charlie drove on in silence, staring ahead at the road, looking as if he was out to kill somebody.

We drove on and on in silence, and eventually I settled down and fell back to sleep again. It was in the wee hours of the morning that I was awakened by Charlie jerking me out of the back seat and marching me up to an old dark shack. We had arrived at my father's house in St. Petersburg Florida.

~

My mother would apologize to me 50 years later for Charlie's behavior – saying that things were different in those days – that there were no safe houses where women and children could go. She explained that she was fearful of my step-father and his vengeance, yet felt like she had nowhere else to go, she would just go back to him and hope that things would change. Well things changed alright. It changed me – and the way I would forever view others. I learned that the world was not a safe place and the people in it could not be trusted or relied upon – even if they were the people you loved.

Looking back I'm sure that going to live with my artist father and step-mother in St. Petersburg when I was six years old helped me to get over some of my fears and to eventually blossom into a free spirit. With very little adult supervision, I spent most of my days that first summer in the same faded yellow bathing suit, wandering alone in the nearby fields of sandy palms searching for lizards and critters and combing the beaches of the Gulf of Mexico. I became headstrong and independent – a strong-willed, angry little girl who didn't like people telling her what to do.

Thankfully, with the help of Mrs. Bedford's encouragement and support I somehow would manage to get all the way through the second grade at the Gulf Beaches Elementary School.

The Teacher's House

It was the summer of 1957 and I had been living with my "real" father at the Driftwood Shack for almost three years before I was off to have yet another new life adventure. My step-mother, Valora, drove me with my little sack of clothes to my teacher Mrs. Bedford's house in Largo, Florida, which was a small quiet town just north of St. Petersburg. My first memory of arriving there is that the house sat on a wide corner with lovely green grassy lawns, fruit trees and beautiful flowering gardens. The left side of the yard was a fabulous pallet of colors – bright reds, pinks, yellows, and oranges. This was the first time I had seen these colorful zinnias. This wonderful paradise of lush flowering gardens was a testimony to Mr. Bedford's skill as a landscape architect.

The house was a contemporary design and in pristine condition – the complete opposite of the Driftwood Shack. Mrs. Bedford, who by then I was told to call Ruth, was waiting at the front door. When she opened the door and welcomed us, I could see all the way through the living room into the dining room and out the glass floor-to-ceiling window to the backyard gardens. It was a beautiful sight, like being in the Garden of Eden.

Once inside, what caught my eye right away was a large fish aquarium framed and built right into the wall of the living room! It was amazing with bright-colored fish leisurely swimming from one side to the other. It had a very calming effect on me as I stood there mesmerized by it while Valora and Mrs. Bedford talked. Valora seemed very impressed by my new home and on her way out to the car commented to Mrs. Bedford: "Watch out – she might never want to leave!"

As Mrs. Bedford was showing me around the house, she let her dog in from the backyard. He was a Shepherd mix named Shotzie – which means Sweetheart in German. Indeed he was an absolute sweetheart and we had an instant connection to one another. The only picture I have from this time of my childhood is one of Shotzie and me playing next to the Bedford house. I am looking happy and very prim and proper with my new haircut and new clothes, complements of Ruth Bedford.

Her husband came home from work and we met for the first time. There was something about him that reminded me of Charlie Coleman, perhaps because they were both tan and about the same height and build. But he seemed much nicer and I hoped that he would like me. The Bedfords were both kind and made me feel like a special guest in their house. But I wasn't sure just how long I'd be there.

Over time, as I tried to settle in and become accepted into the Bedford household, the reality of the situation hit me. I soon discovered that living there was going to take a lot of work and patience – from me and from them too. Unlike the lifestyle I was used to at the Driftwood Shack, I was not free to come and go as I pleased; there was much more structure and rules, responsibilities, expectations and accountability. I had to get up early every morning, eat what they considered a "healthy breakfast" (which often included shredded wheat, which I hated) – and go to bed early at night. I had to study a lot more too – even in the summer! It was another whole new world for me – *once again.*

You would think I would have rebelled against all these strictures, and believe me I had my moments of fit-throwing and refusals to conform, but they talked me through it and reasoned with me. I could see that the Bedfords cared about me and my future and that made a difference in my perception of things. All in all we got along pretty well together, so much so that I not only stayed with them that summer, but then on into the fall. I started third grade at the nearby Seminole Elementary School, even though Mrs. Bedford still taught at the Gulf Beaches School in St. Petersburg. I suspect she thought that my returning there would be too complicated for both of us – especially with my having to face up to the resident bullies again, given the history of my failure. At Seminole School I could have a whole new start. It was also farther away from my parents, who may not have been the best influence on me – though they never came around to visit anyway.

It was there at Seminole School that I first remember learning to sing. There were tryouts for the school choir with each kid standing up next to the piano and singing solo. It started out at first with the musical scale d*o re mi fa so la ti do* and then followed with a short song piece. When I got up to sing, the auditorium had quite a few students in it and they were all talking to each other. When I started to sing the scale, the kids stopped talking and turned to look at me. I found this to be really embarrassing – either I was really loud or really good or maybe even really bad, I'm not quite sure which – but I did get their attention and was accepted into the choir.

I liked playing on the Jungle Gym equipment at the new school. I had plenty of practice from when I attended the Gulf Beaches Elementary School, but here the monkey bars were higher and I discovered that kids would challenge each other by each swinging from the opposite ends, coming together in the middle, and forcing one or the other off. Well, I took to *that* right away and became the overnight *winner and champion,* as I was one of the tallest kids and had long arms and legs to gain momentum and hold onto the challenger. Also, I soon figured out that if I wasn't feeling so great some days, I could go to the nurse's office and they would be really nice to me and let me lie down there and rest for a while and I didn't have to sit through the boring class instruction. It was not long before my teacher put a stop to that.

It was while I was at this new school that I discovered snakes! One of the boys brought in a garden snake in a box one day and I was hooked on them from then on. I was so thrilled and fascinated that I immediately set out on a mission to find a snake of my own. Fortunately for me, *and* Mrs. Bedford, I never found one!

I had a girlfriend at school named Mary who lived out in the country and I got to spend the weekend at her house one time. I remember one night as we lay in bed listening to the noisy frog chorus coming from the nearby pond, I became homesick for Nana, Aunt Elsie and the farm in Virginia. It made me cry to think of them and I wondered if they ever thought of me.

Speaking of the farm, our third grade class went on a field trip to a ranch a few miles from the school. I was finally going to get to ride on a horse! I watched some of the other kids ride around the corral as I waited anxiously for my turn. Then when the horse came back, I was motioned to stand by the horse next to the man that was lengthening the saddle stirrups for me – my legs were much longer than the other kids. I think it was just shooing away a fly, but the horse kicked me and knocked me down. The first thing that happened was that the cowboy started hitting and kicking the horse which was really upsetting to me. There was quite a commotion which ended up with me being picked up and whisked away by the cowboy and my teacher. I remember they put me into the front seat of a nearby truck and *pulled my pants down* to see if my leg was broken! That was extremely embarrassing and I didn't even get to ride the horse! The doctor later stated that I was lucky that it was not higher or lower on my thigh or it would have broken my leg. I limped around for a week and ended up with a nasty bruise in the perfect shape of a horse shoe!

One of my fondest memories of the Bedford house was that Christmas. We had a wonderful morning together like a real family – opening up presents and drinking hot chocolate. Most of my presents were games, books and puzzles. After all the presents were opened, Mrs. Bedford told me to go next door to get a box from the neighbor, but I was *not* to look into the box before I brought it home. She then made a call to the neighbor to let her know I would be coming over. I went next door and the neighbor met me at the door and handed me a big long box. After walking through the hedge and into our backyard, I stopped and looked around to see if anyone was watching and quickly lifted the lid and took a peek inside. All I could see was some frilly wrapping paper and I caught a glimpse of something pink. I quickly closed the box and once again looked around to see if anyone had seen me. Once inside Mrs. Bedford asked me if I had peeked inside the box and I said no. I don't remember if she caught me in my lie or not, but I do remember opening the box to the most beautiful doll I had ever seen in my life! She was a pink ballerina that stood about eighteen inches tall and had long thin arms and legs (like me) that could bend at the knee, ankle, elbow and wrist. She had beautiful *pink* hair, a *pink* ballerina dress, *pink* stockings and *pink* satin ballerina slippers. That Christmas day had to be one of the happiest days of my life!

However by the spring of the next year things were not going as well. Somehow I had gotten on the wrong side of Mr. Bedford and I could see that there was a strain between us. There was an unfortunate incident when he thought I had stolen some money. One day while Mr. and Mrs. Bedford waited in the car, I ran into the grocery store to get some bread. When I paid the lady at the counter, part of the change she gave back to me fell from my extended hand and through a crack in the counter. There was some confusion and the checker expected me to try to get it out – instead of getting it out herself or giving me the change again. Since the store was busy with people lined up behind me, my attempts to find the change that had dropped failed, so I ended up just leaving. I handed over what money I had to Mr. Bedford, hoping he wouldn't notice that some was missing. *That was my mistake.* Later when I got home there were questions about the change. I explained in detail what had happened. My pockets were then searched, and I'm sure that what occurred next was a lesson in what could be the consequences of stealing.

I was sat upon a chair and Mr. Bedford sat across facing me and questioned me about the money, while Mrs. Bedford paced around the kitchen. Once again I told him about the story of how the change fell into the crack in the store counter and I couldn't get it out – but he didn't believe me. He gave me a good whack on the side of my right thigh and asked me again, where did I put the money! I was really shocked that he would hit me and started to cry and looked for support from Mrs. Bedford. I told them that *I didn't steal the money*, and started my explanation over again – and received another whack. This went on for a few more whacks before Mrs. Bedford stopped him. (Ironically, two days later we were invited to go to a fancy swim event at a country club and I remember Mrs. Bedford trying to give excuses for the bruises on my leg.) *Things seemed to go downhill from there.*

Looking back, I expect that the whacking incident really had something to do with what had happened a week earlier when Mrs. Bedford was out of the house one night, a rare occasion for her. Mr. Bedford and I were left alone and as I was sitting at the dining room table doing my homework, he came in and suggested that I come into the living room to sit on his lap and read to him from my school book. That seemed totally out of character for him, and at the age of nine, given my experiences with Charlie Coleman, I knew what his subtle suggestion meant. I was older and wiser, so would have no part of it. But then he said it was just an innocent request and demanded that I come over and sit down with him. So I sat down next to him on the chair, not on his lap, and started reading my book. The next thing I knew he was touching me and pulling me up onto his lap – this ended with me eventually getting up and running into my room, crawling into the far corner under my bed with Mr. Bedford down on the floor trying to persuade me to come out and warning me to never tell Mrs. Bedford of the incident. He eventually left, and I stayed in my room for the rest of the night. Neither of us spoke of it again, but it hung over our heads. I thought several times of telling Mrs. Bedford, but I didn't think she would believe me.

Then shortly after the money incident, Mr. Bedford

had an accident out in the garden and seriously cut his hand on a garden tool. Mrs. Bedford and I were inside the house when he came in holding his bloodied hand and grimacing in pain. She quickly wrapped his hand in a towel and then had me wait at home while she rushed him to the hospital. They must have had plenty of time to talk that day because by the time they came back home there had been a decision made *for me to leave*. I could tell something was wrong by the way they were cold and distant to me when they came home – and I later overheard Mrs. Bedford on the phone in her bedroom making arrangements with someone to take me away. At the time I thought I would only be going away temporarily during the time Mr. Bedford was at home convalescing, but that wasn't the case.

My step-mother, Valora, much later in life and in her harsh manner, commented: "once she got pregnant with her own child she didn't want you anymore." I didn't know anything about Mrs. Bedford being pregnant and I suspected there was more to it – with Mr. Bedford being behind it – though I never spoke to anyone about our encounter until years later. I was too ashamed.

~

Perhaps Mrs. Bedford knew more than I thought. Fourteen years later when I was twenty-four, I went back to Florida to visit my family. I was very excited to find out that Mrs. Bedford was still teaching at Gulf Beaches Elementary School and I wanted to see her and thank her for all she had done for me.

It was late in the afternoon after school was out when I arrived and found Mrs. Bedford sitting alone in her quiet classroom. I was so excited to find her there and rushed in and told her who I was. It was heart-wrenching to see that she didn't meet my excitement with her own. Instead she just sat there rather surprised with a forced smile on her face, looking up at me from across her desk. It was as if she had dreaded that something like this would happen some day and here I was. I wanted to run around the desk and hug her and tell her again that it was *me* – as if maybe she didn't understand – but something in her face and behavior told me not to.

I waited for a response, but when there was none I tried to gather my wits about me and started telling her about my life – how I was married now and how everything had eventually turned out fine, thanks to her help along the way. She still sat there very quiet and pensive, as if now that I had finished telling her the story I should go. I thought I certainly must have done something shameful for her to act in this hurtful way. With only silence and a steadfast stare from her I turned to go, hoping that she would stop me somehow with her words. Then, remembering that Valora had told me she had heard she had a daughter, I turned around and made a cautionary plea with her *that she should look out for her daughter – and that Mr. Bedford could not be trusted.* With that comment I could see the anger boiling up in her face and knew I had to leave. Today I wish I had stayed and confronted her – had it out with her – setting the story straight.

In my late twenties when I first started relaying my personal history for the first time, a therapist planted an ugly seed in my head . . . she said that maybe I could have provoked that intimate suggestion from Mr. Bedford – given my early childhood experience with Charlie Coleman. This thought has haunted me ever since.

Writing about this now is still very painful for me. I know that Mrs. Bedford had high hopes for me and was instrumental in creating a positive change in my life. I can't help but feel, even now so late in life that it was me that somehow changed all of that, and that I am a bad person because of it. These kind of shameful feelings have followed me through life, leaving me with a feeling of deep sadness.

What's a Social Worker?

It wasn't Valora or my dad who came to pick me up from the Bedford House. When the front door opened, it opened to a stranger. She was a short, chubby woman with a big smile and glasses that perched on her nose. She was all dressed up in a suit and holding a clipboard. Even though I had all my personal belongings packed, I had to sit in my room with the door closed while Mrs. Bedford and the lady talked in the dining room. When it was time to go, Mrs. Bedford gave me a big hug and wished me well – sending me on my way . . . with a smile on her face . . . just like that. I felt very sad and confused.

I was expecting the lady to drive me straight home to the Driftwood Shack, back to my family, but we went to a diner for a coke instead. She explained in a calm and friendly voice that she was a "social worker" and that her job was helping children who were away from their families to find another home. I was pretty surprised and said that didn't apply to me because I already had a home, she just needed to take me there – to the Driftwood Shack. She said that for the time being my family was not able to take me in and I would be "placed" with a nice "foster" family in a nearby town who were eagerly awaiting my arrival. *What was she saying? What was a foster family? Why couldn't she just take me home to my father? What did she mean that my family was not able to take me in? No answers! I just sat there red-faced and furious. It seemed I kept getting passed around like a hot potato. It was a wonder I didn't bolt right out the door and make a run for it.*

After a short drive across town with panicky thoughts racing through my head and no answers, I found myself standing in the living room of another new family – arms folded, all moody, pouty and confused. I was feeling a little sick to my stomach as the social worker introduced me to the Utterback family. They could see that I was shaken and spoke soft and quiet as if they were sympathetic to my situation. The husband and wife were both tall and skinny like me and they had an equally tall and skinny son named Danny who was around eight years old, just a couple of years younger than I was. I stood around waiting for the Utterbacks to wind up business with the social worker and was then shown about the house and to my new room – which was as neat and clean as they come. Once past the formalities, we all settled in and proceeded to move on into the next chapter of our lives . . . whatever that might be. I was pretty mad at the world by then and especially didn't like the fact that I had to share a bedroom with a *boy*! Where was my father? He needed to come get me.

~

Danny Utterback and I went to the same school together, so he was able to show me the ropes. We took the bus to school together. It was the first time I had ever traveled on a big city bus without the benefit of an adult. I remember riding down the wonderful tree-lined street that led to the school, looking out the window and taking in the joy of the sparkling morning sun shining through the arbor of heavy green leaves. It reminded me of Virginia. The school was so different from all the others I had attended. It was in an established part of town, and was in a large old building several stories high. The first day I remember climbing up lots of stairs to reach the classroom and once there I found it to be glorious. Wow! It was *huge* in comparison with any classroom I had seen before. It had a high ceiling, lots of windows and light bouncing off the gleaming hardwood floors. You could see out the window to a colorful canopy of trees surrounding part of the room and peer through the windows down to the people on the sidewalk far below. This was really an exciting place to be! My new third grade teacher came to greet me and she was warm, kind and welcoming – just like Mrs. Bedford used to be. I wondered . . . might I end up living with her too?

As the months went by I became more acclimated to my new family and surroundings. Danny and I became great friends and he introduced me around to all the kids at school and in our neighborhood. My new parents seemed very understanding of me and were generally patient and tolerant of my occasional unexpected moods and defiant outbursts of behavior. Danny and I would occasionally get into heated arguments, but remained buddies in the end. While I was the older of the two, Danny took on the protective role of the big brother, and I for the most part let him.

After about four months of living with the Utterback family, a most unexpected thing happened. There was a telephone call from my father! After a long conversation behind closed doors between the Utterbacks and my father, they called me in and told me my father was on the line. Can you *imagine* the joy of me getting to talk to my father after a year and a half! He sounded so excited and happy to talk with me, and to give me the great news . . . . I couldn't believe my ears! He and Valora and Curtis, now five years old, were packing up and leaving St. Petersburg to travel across country to Tucson Arizona! And the best part? They were going to come get *me* and *take me with them!!!* Oh wow! I was so excited that I was *screaming* with joy! My father went on to tell me that Tucson was where all the cowboys and Indians lived. I then remember asking him if we could get a horse! He said he wasn't so sure about that, but "we would see."

After his call I could only jump up and down and dance around the house singing and shouting that I was going to live with my *dad* and the cowboys and Indians in *Tucson Arizona* – and we were going to *get a horse!!* The reaction from the Utterbacks seemed more of reserved surprise than anything else, although Danny was jumping around with me, obviously impressed and excited that I was going to get to see real live cowboys and Indians and ride on a horse!

A week later, just as scheduled on that very special day, my father, step-mother and little brother Curtis drove up in that big, long Ford station wagon packed to the gills – though no monkeys or alligators, just one confused old cat. Everyone was in a happy mood with lots of hugging and kissing and laughing going on. I was in Heaven. But my elated emotions soon turned to that of conflict – thrilled to see my father and family (wow had Curtis grown!) but sad to leave the happy and loving Utterback family. It was especially hard to leave Danny – and I didn't know whether I should be laughing or crying and so I was doing a little of both at the same time.

Mr. Utterback had been standing back, watching over the reunion scene and at one point he smiled and nodded to my parents and came up to me and took me by the hand and walked me away from the others. He bent down and looked square into my wild excited eyes until he got my full attention, and I calmed down. His words were measured, quiet and kind – and he said, "We have enjoyed having you come to live with us and we want you to know that you will always have a home with us and can come back and visit us anytime you want." We hugged and parted, and off I went into the sunset heading for Tucson Arizona with my *real family* . . . the tears flowing down my face.

Part 2

Arizona

The Desert House

I was ten years old. The trip across country from Saint Petersburg Florida to Tucson Arizona – with me wedged in the back seat of the Ford station wagon with the miserable yowling cat and the rest of my family in the front seat – does not stand out as anything special in my memory. Although I was excited about being back with my dad and his family after almost two years of living with other people, I mostly remember long stretches of desert and roads that seemed to go on f o r e v e r! Are we there yet? When are we going to get there?

One memory I have of the trip is when Valora mentioned her mother had passed away during the time I had been living with the Bedfords and the Utterbacks. I was really surprised by this and upset to know that I would never see her again. I remembered how she was so kind to me when she would come to visit us. She would sing children's folk songs to me while we did the dishes together. When I started to cry, Valora said: "Oh, didn't you *know* she had *died*?" With that comment, I cried even harder. *How would I have known she had "died" – and what else had happened while I was gone?*

The other memory I have about our cross-country trip is after we stayed overnight at a motel and in the morning went to a nearby restaurant for breakfast. The restaurant had a big sprawling lawn in the front of it and my little brother and I had a great time running and jumping and rolling around on the grass. What *freedom* after being cooped up in the car and a motel room! After Curtis had been rolling around on the grass for a while, all of a sudden he jumped up and started screaming and frantically dancing around and swatting himself. My parents and I ran over to see *what* was wrong with him. Apparently he had rolled over an ant hill and was covered with red stinging ants. We all started brushing the ants off of him and off of ourselves. Then Valora rushed my screaming brother back through the restaurant to the bathroom – surprising all the patrons having their early morning breakfast.

Poor Curtis, there was always something going on with him. I was told that the main reason my dad and step-mother were moving from Florida to Arizona was because he was prone to illness and they thought the dry climate would be good for him. Valora especially would hover around him, giving him special attention and making sure he was always comfortable and as happy as possible. This of course had a grinding effect on me – and I have to admit that I felt put off and jealous considering that this was *my* family too. Why was it I wondered, that no matter where I went I was always the outsider coming in? *Would I ever really fit in anywhere?*

~

Valora likes to tell the story of how we came by our first house once we arrived in Tucson. She would say, "I will never forget our first house in Tucson . . . we rented it from an old American Indian woman who squatted and peed right there on the ground in front of us! I could never get over that!" I remembered the old Indian woman. She looked just like the ones I had seen on the Lone Ranger TV show. She was dark skinned, had braided hair and wore a long faded turquoise and yellow dress – a costume unlike any I had seen in real life before.

The house was about ten miles south of downtown Tucson – off of what was then called the Old Nogales Highway, which went from Tucson down to the Mexican border. To get there, suddenly in the middle of the Sonoran Desert, you would turn off the highway onto an obscure dirt road that led to a little old single-story adobe house that backed up to the San Xavier Indian Reservation – the homeland of the tribe known as the *Tohono O'odham* Nation. We could only see desert from our house and the surrounding area, but I found out later that there was a National Historic Landmark – the beautiful 1700s San Xavier Mission, just a few miles away.

Our new desert house had two bedrooms – each with its own bath. The bigger bedroom on the left was claimed by my parents and brother. The living room separated the two bedrooms and I got the one on the other side of the house with a bathroom that was useless because it was unfinished and full of stored construction materials. Who knew what else was hiding in there? Once we moved into *that* house, you could say that we had officially traded in the Florida Driftwood Shack's alligators and monkeys, for Arizona's rattlesnakes and javelinas.

And just like that, our introduction to the Wild, Wild West started on the first night we were in that house. I remember it was dark outside and we were having dinner in the kitchen when we heard a loud commotion in the backyard. We didn't *dare* open the door to see what it was, and waited for my father to run and get his flashlight as we peered out the back window to see what we could see. It was pitch-black out there and I couldn't see a thing, but could hear loud nasty snarling and growling that sounded like some kind of awful *monster*! When my father finally directed his flashlight beam to the source, we all screamed and jumped away from the window with fright! There *was* indeed a monster in our back yard! In fact there was a whole *herd* of monsters in our back yard and they were viciously fighting with each other over our garbage!

The "monsters" were four adult and two baby javelinas. Javelina look like Wild Boars, but technically they are a "collared Peccary." They stand approximately 19 inches tall and weigh somewhere between 30-55 pounds. They can be very vicious and have been known to kill humans and their hunting animals. It wasn't a very pleasant welcome wagon for our little family from Florida, but it was indicative of things to come.

I personally had a couple of other run-ins with javelina – in broad daylight. We had a big front porch on the house and one day I ran out to play and came face to face with a rather small javelina about to climb up on the porch. We both froze in our tracks, stared at each other in shock, and then, as if in a synchronized dance step, turned and ran in opposite directions! I never ran out of the house again without looking both ways. Another time I was out playing in the yard and heard a lot of snorting and rustling in the bushes at the back of the property. I knew what must be coming and quickly ran inside. Sure enough, minutes later a herd of javelina came out of the bushes, headed toward the house.

I remember my parents would leave me alone in the house when they went off to town looking for work. At first they left me with my little brother to watch, but after an accident of making Jello and spilling boiling water on him (and having his skin blister and fall off) they decided I wasn't babysitting material anymore and started taking him with them.

You might think I must have been lonely and bored left alone out there in the middle of the hot desert without any neighbors or people to talk to, but I entertained myself by exploring the land . . . and I found that there was a lot to explore. I liked to think of myself as a little warrior in those days, and without my parents' knowledge I would climb the fence to the Indian reservation each day to go and see what I could find. Fortunately, I never ran into any Indians as most of their housing was somewhere far away. Besides I tried to stay fairly close to my house in case my parents would come home during the day. Sometimes my dad would work at home and so I wouldn't go onto the reservation on those days, but would entertain myself by digging in the yard or would hunt for critters, or build a fort. Sometimes I would write a play for my brother and me to perform or help my dad with his creative art work.

My dad had given me a book on desert creatures and I was a quick study. Even though I learned to love snakes in Florida, I knew to stay clear of them in the Arizona desert. That's not to say that I wasn't *fascinated* by them and would see them quite frequently on my travels. Rattlesnakes and sidewinders were my favorite snakes to observe. Rattlesnakes would mostly just lay there all coiled up, staring at you. You could see a little flicker of a tongue every now and then, but I was quiet and still and kept my distance, and fortunately none ever took a flying leap at me. The sidewinders were fun to run after because they were fast and would slither off quickly down the desert floor in a sideways direction. But I made sure I never caught up with one.

The most intriguing of all the desert creatures I encountered was a big slow-moving Gila monster. I knew well enough to keep my distance from this ugly creature as I had read in my book that these two-foot-long beaded lizards were the most poisonous of all. But hey, I was an adventurous girl, so of course I was fascinated and given that I had a big long traveling stick . . . had to tease it *just* a little bit before leaving it alone.

Since there were no other children to play with, the critters of the desert became my friends and daily entertainment, and I would come home with all sorts of things. I especially liked to catch the intimidating looking, but harmless "horny toads." They had squat, flat, toad-like bodies and thorn-like projections at the rear of their heads. They looked pretty mean, but they were no match for me. They liked to bury themselves in the sand and sometimes I would just come along and snatch them up before they had time to think about it. Once I would catch one, I would hold the three-inch lizard flat in my palm until it calmed down and then I gently rubbed its spiked head. It would just lie there as if it was asleep. They never put up much of a fight, although I read somewhere that they spit blood out of their eyes. I can't say that ever happened with me.

Once I found a prize lizard and brought it home and kept it in a big box as a pet for a couple of weeks. It was big and scaly and had a beautiful bright blue tail. I thought it looked like a dragon. I called him "Bluie." When I was in Florida collecting chameleons around the Driftwood Shack, I would tie a string around their little bodies and walk around with them. They were fun and harmless – and didn't hurt when they would nip me with their fine little teeth. But when I tried to pick up Bluie it bit me so hard I thought it would take my finger off! I guess it was a good thing it wasn't poisonous. This gave me a whole new respect for what I was dealing with in the desert. I let Bluie go that day.

~

The most bizarre creature encounter came several months after we had lived in the Desert House. My parents must have had a big evening planned for that night and dropped off my five- year-old brother and me at the movies in town. I'm not sure they knew what was playing. We went in and sat down inside the theater and began watching the film. On the screen we saw the name of the movie was "Horrors of the Black Museum." Now this *was* an horrific movie – about torture, violence and sadism. I remember it started out with a beautiful woman getting ready for a party; a box was delivered to her door. She opened it and inside was a lovely pair of opera glasses. She ran to the window and put them up to her eyes and with a click knives came out of the glasses and poked out her eyes. Though shaken, somehow my little brother and I got through *that* part. But soon after that there was a scene where a man was peacefully sleeping in his own bed and a guillotine came down and cut off his head! My brother and I screamed and ran out of the theater room shaking and weeping. There was no one in sight in the lobby. I tried to console my brother, but he just cried and wanted our parents, but we had to wait. We sat there for what I remember to be about an hour – hugging each other, totally traumatized, until my parents finally came back to pick us up. They thought we were just over-reacting and tried to explain that it was all just pretend – actors playing a part in a movie, nothing real at all. Nevertheless, I remember that long drive home with me curled up alone as usual in the back of the Ford station wagon trembling with fright, and my weeping brother snuggled up all cozy between our parents in the front seat.

Once we arrived home I went crying to my bedroom, which was on the opposite side of the house from where my parents and brother slept. My step-mother came in and talked to me for a while until I calmed down. After she left, I put my black and white stuffed dog over my neck so the guillotine wouldn't come down and cut off my head. Every shadow in the room had the potential of someone lurking there ready to jump out and do me harm. I tried to be brave, but the scenes from the movie just kept running over and over in my head.

Then I heard a noise coming from the other room. Since my parents had already gone to bed, I figured it must be the cat. I tried to ignore it, thinking maybe my parents were right that I was just being silly after all. Then I thought that maybe it would be a good idea to go *get* the cat and bring it back to my bed to comfort me. I quietly crept out of my bedroom and crossed through the living room. I could hear the noise was coming from the kitchen so I turned and started to go in that direction. As I turned . . . there in the doorway of the kitchen stood a creature – the symbol of every horror I had manifested from the movie. I screamed as loud as I could and ran to my parent's room and jumped under the covers and continued screaming and crying under the covers. My parents and brother were upset with my behavior and tried to get me to stop screaming and tell them what was wrong, but I couldn't speak. All I could do was cry and *try* to speak, but no words would come out.

After my parents finally quieted me down, I was able to get the words out: "a skunk!" Well, then they were relieved and laughed and said no, there was no skunk in the house – I must have seen the cat. And besides if it was a skunk it would have stunk up the whole house by now! Nevertheless, I insisted that it was a skunk and my father went out into the dark house to see what he could find. He came back with the cat and told me again that it had just been the cat I had seen and that my mind must have been playing tricks on me because of the influence of the movie. I insisted to the point that he reluctantly went back out to take another look. After a while went by he came back in the bedroom smiling. My step-mother and little brother and I were all huddled together on the bed and felt relief seeing the smile on Dad's face. Had he slayed the demon? He came over to me and leaned over and took my hand. He told me to be very quiet and that he wanted me to come with him so he could show me what I had seen. *Well, I have to tell you, I wasn't about to go anywhere!* However, after a minute or two of convincing, he prevailed and we quietly walked out to the kitchen together, my dad leading the way.

When we got to the kitchen my dad put his finger to his lips and quietly walked over and slowly opened the cabinet door under the kitchen sink. As I cautiously peeked inside, there in the very back corner of the cabinet was a little huddled-up *skunk* the size of a kitten. I think it was more scared than I was. My dad explained that the door from the kitchen must have been left open to the outside and the skunk had found its way in. Who knows, maybe the whole *skunk family* had been in there earlier! My dad boarded off the area, setting up a fence made from chairs leading out from the kitchen sink cabinet to the back door, so the animal could get out.

I finally got to sleep that night, snuggled up tightly next to my parents and little brother in their big cozy bed. By the next morning . . . the little skunk demon was gone.

~

While I can remember riding on a school bus, I don't remember much about the school I attended for a short time while we lived out in the desert. Perhaps it was a summer school because we made that trip out West in the summer of 1958. The school bus trips were very memorable because the kids riding on the bus with me were all so different from me. While I was tall, white-skinned and freckled, they were all short, dark-skinned and spoke a language unknown to me. Most of them were shy and seemed reticent around me, looking down or quickly away when I looked at them, but I could see from the corner of my eye that they would study me intensely once I looked away. Some would just sit there and stare at me like they were spitting mad at me about something. I don't ever remember making any friends on the bus. Now I realize that the kids were probably all of Native American or Hispanic origin. But whatever their background, they weren't very friendly and seemed afraid or angry. I think we all wondered what I was doing there. (When I asked her, my elderly step-mother could shed no light on that era of school time for me either. We figured that perhaps I went there for only a short time and was then taken out and never went back.)

Valora did remember, however, that after we arrived in Tucson and got settled into the desert house, she was hired as a sales clerk at a department store in town. I remember that too because once she got that job my family stopped leaving me alone so much at the Desert House and started taking me with them into town in the mornings. After the seemingly long ride they would drop me off at the local historic Armory Park to spend my day there entertaining myself. For me this was much more fun and interesting than hanging out alone in the desert. There were lush green lawns, a playground and lots of people to watch and talk with. In those days people weren't so worried about leaving children alone with strangers around.

My early experiences at Armory Park included taking it upon myself to single-handedly try to save the little naked, freshly-hatched baby birds that had fallen out of their nests in the tall stalky palm trees around the park. I would gently pick them up, cup them in my hands, and like a skilled paramedic would rush them over to the hospital nest I had made for them in a nearby hollow tree. There I would try to feed them bugs and bread from people's sandwiches that I had retrieved from the garbage. Of course these attempts had a disastrous outcome as the little birds all ended up dying anyway, so it wasn't long before I sadly gave up on my heroic efforts to save them.

One day while in the park, I met some older kids who were playing around on the elevated stage of the Grand Memorial band shell. They were dancing and swinging each other around while I stood by and watched. I persuaded one of the boys to swing me around too, but when he let me go I was really dizzy and stepped off the bandstand – falling about three feet onto the hard paved surface below. I caught my fall with my hands but still landed with a hard jolt. I let out a loud scream. All the big kids rushed over to the edge of the stage to peer down at me, so I tried not to openly bawl like a baby in front of them. My right arm really hurt, but I didn't want them to think I was a sissy so I just got up and kind of laughed it off and went to sit down on one of the park benches for a while – holding my arm and rocking myself. The big kids left soon after that (probably because they didn't want to get into trouble). By then my bruised arm was really starting to ache badly and after a while I was pacing around the park in pain.

Several hours later, when my father and step-mother

finally came to pick me up at the end of the work day, I was there waiting for them, pretty upset and miserable with my aching arm. I didn't hold back the tears then and cried like a baby when I saw them. I'm sure now that this injury must have come at the worst time imaginable for my parents . . . I heard them arguing between themselves trying to figure out what to do. I heard them saying that they didn't have the money to pay for a doctor. Nevertheless, they found a hospital and X-rays were taken and sure enough the bone above my right wrist was cracked, though fortunately not broken. Still it was just one more bothersome episode for my parents.

Well, that cast on my arm may have slowed me down some, but not by much! Once the pain went away I found that the cast could come in pretty handy. I could bat soft balls with it and hide things in it, and once I even clunked my little brother over the head with it. The once sterile and pristine white cast ended up black and grungy by the time they sawed it off of me. (I heard later that the hospital and doctor never did get paid.)

Old Tucson Studios

After dropping off my step-mother at work and me at the park and my brother who knows where, my father, who made his living as an artist, would make his rounds about the town of Tucson looking for work. He would find jobs doing sign painting, mannequin refinishing, odd jobs – or anything else that would come along. While at the desert house he painted a beautiful large mural of a desert scene including scenes of the amazing Saguaro cactus with their arms uplifted to the bright blue sky. Then, perhaps as a peaceful tribute to the Indians around us, he carved and painted a magnificent proud, life-sized Indian chief out of a big tall block of wood. This took some doing and once finished he placed the Chief out on the Nogales Highway at the entrance of the little dirt road leading to the Desert House.

As luck would have it, one day a man saw the Indian on the side of the road and contacted my father about work. Now this wasn't just *any* man, and what he was doing out there on the road to nowhere is still a mystery to me. Perhaps he was on his way to Mexico or perhaps someone he knew had seen my dad's Indian statue and told him about it and he had to come to see it for himself. Nevertheless, the rest is history and his visit would change our family's life forever.

The man who responded to the proud carved Indian chief along the highway was Robert Shelton, a movie producer and the Director of Old Tucson Studios. *According to Wikipedia, Old Tucson was built in 1939 by Columbia Pictures for the movie "Arizona" starring William Holden. The idea at the time was to construct a movie set replica of what the town of Tucson would have been like in the 1860s. The construction crews then set to work and built more than 50 buildings in 40 days, including a grand old church and a fully functional Main Street, complete with stores and businesses.*

After the completion of the movie "Arizona" in 1939, the site remained dormant for several years until the filming of "The Bells of St. Mary's" in 1945, starring Bing Crosby and Ingrid Bergman. Other early movies filmed on set included "The Last Round Up" with Gene Autry; "Winchester" with James Stewart; and "The Last Outpost" with Ronald Reagan. The 1950s saw the filming of "Gunfight at the O.K. Corral" with Burt Lancaster and "Cimarron" starring Glen Ford. About the time my father became involved at Old Tucson in 1959 they were filming "Rio Bravo" with John Wayne, Dean Martin, Ricky Nelson, Angie Dickinson and Walter Brennan.

Bob Shelton had leased the Old Tucson Studios site from Pima County and was attempting to restore the aging facility to be reopened as both a film studio and a theme park. He was looking for an artist with diversified skills to help him to pull the whole idea together. My father and Bob Shelton worked out a deal and my father found himself in his dream job for years to come – working in his element, as the "Art Director" of a film studio and theme park, making movie sets, props and tourist attraction displays.

I remember driving that long drive with my dad through the Sonora desert in the quiet early mornings on our way to his work at Old Tucson. After dropping off my step-mother and little brother in town, it was great to have my father to myself. He was an enthusiastic teacher and self-styled philosopher, and we would talk about all kinds of things, and witness some interesting sights together on our trip through the desert. For instance, we would be driving along and there would be the sudden appearance of a road runner bird challenging the speed of our car. We would also see other desert creatures like coyotes, jack rabbits, hawks, owls and snakes, and my dad would make up all kinds of stories about them. He was a real story-teller.

Once we arrived at Old Tucson my dad would go to work in his studio and I would be off for adventure, spending my day hanging around the sets or tourist attractions or combing the surrounding desert for critters of interest. After a while I had become a regular with the staff and all the people who worked there at the rides, stores and restaurants – especially the ice cream parlor. There were always cowboy ballads playing on the speakers overhead on Main Street and after a while I learned all the words to songs like Marty Robbins's "Cool Water" and "El Paso."

My dad helped create historic exhibits of what life used to be in the late 1800s, such as a fully equipped school room, post office and jail. He even made a dummy prisoner for the jail cell – an old prospector sleeping off a wild night on the town with a rat under his bed for effect. There was also a large dedicated museum displaying old household items, toys, clothes, jewelry and equipment that were used back in the time. My dad even went so far as to build a replica of an actual-size Indian village complete with a teepee and an Indian man standing alongside his pinto pony.

One of the favorite theme park attractions was a real stage-coach ride that would circle around the outside of the town, with a surprise visit from a band of masked bandits on horseback who would pretend to hold them up. There was a train ride around the park and a roped burro-train ride through town, led by a real cowboy on his mule. The most popular tourist attraction was the live gunfight shows on Main Street every hour on the hour. Sometimes my dad would dress up and play a gunslinger in these shows. Once I got used to the idea, I thought it was pretty cool to watch my father being shot down dead in a gun fight battle. Not every kid had a father who was a wild West gun slinger!

When we got to my dad's work early in the morning, usually before everyone else, my favorite first thing to do was to go out to the horse stables. It was out away from the town and I had to run a bit of a distance and down a deep gully road and up the other side to reach them. While there were rarely any horses there, there was always that little group of about a half-dozen little burros that were kept as part of the tourist ride down Main Street. I would climb over the fence into their corral and ride them, or just sit on them pretending I was sharp shooting like Annie Oakley. The sturdy little donkeys were pretty good-natured and were used to having people riding them all day. They were quite docile and tolerant of me, not putting up much of a fuss with all my shenanigans. They had very distinct personalities, and I got to know them pretty well and would bring them sugar cubes when they were all teamed up there at the Main Street corral waiting for customers to ride them. Their ears would perk up when they saw me.

I remember one morning I arrived early at the stables and found one of the burros lying down, away from the others. At first I thought that maybe she was dead, but then I noticed something really icky and strange was coming out from her behind. All alone there on that early misty morning I stood transfixed in awe, watching the birthing of a baby burro. Of course the first thing I had to do was to run and tell my father! They named the little guy "Boo Boo" – I'm sure that the pregnancy seemed to have been unexpected. He was the sweetest little thing and would run free down Main Street alongside his mother at the back of the roped little burro train. The tourists loved it!

Every now and then the studios had a special event like a visit from a movie star, or a filming of a movie. During those times there would be special livestock and horses brought in and kept at the stables. One early morning I ran out to the stables as usual . . . down the gully and up the other side. As I emerged, from the gully I saw men there with horse trailers and a line of beautiful, shiny, movie horses tied to the post. My sudden appearance from the gully apparently spooked the horses, and they started rearing up and one of the prize horses broke loose from its post and ran out into the desert and one of the men had to get on another horse and go out after it. Boy, did I get into a lot of trouble that time! I was *permanently* banned from going to the stables and considered myself even lucky to be able to hang out at Old Tucson anymore after that!

I remember a rodeo performer and wrangler by the name of Tom White would come out to Old Tucson to work with the actors and their horses. He brought with him a rare breed of animal indeed – in fact one of the first of its kind . . . a trained zebra. I have heard that zebras are worse than a mule with their wild, stubborn and untrustworthy nature and that they have rarely been trained or put to work in their native land in Africa, much less as a cow pony in the wild West. Tom, however, was able to train it and use it as a cow pony for rodeos and shows. The zebra's name was Ribbons and Tom fed him cigarettes instead of sugar as a reward for his tricks. I read a magazine article that Ribbons developed a taste for tobacco, which helped Tom domesticate him. Tom was very protective of Ribbons, being one of a kind and all, and he rarely let anyone ride on him. So I felt quite special when he let me sit on Ribbons and take a quick, supervised ride around the Main Street corral. I later got a kick out of seeing a special article about Tom White and Ribbons in the March 10, 1961 issue of Life Magazine.

Out on the desert things always seemed to look closer than they really were – at least this was my experience. For instance there was a small mountain close by the Old Tucson Studios and one early morning after just arriving, my little brother Curtis and I decided to walk to it. We didn't clear this with my dad because we figured we would be back by lunch time anyway. We took our time and found plenty to do along the way. We kept thinking we would reach the mountain any time, but we walked and walked and it still looked about as far away as when we had started. After a while we started to get tired and bored with the idea of walking to the mountain and turned around and started back to Old Tucson. We walked and walked and started getting worried when we couldn't see the town. We walked some more and about the time we started to get really panicked we heard horses off in a distance. A couple of young adults came riding up to us on horseback – or I should say we were standing in the direction where they were riding, and then they saw us there. We stopped them and told them we were lost and asked if they could help us get back to town. They said they were not allowed to let us ride the horses and pointed in the direction of town and rode off as if we were not their problem.

Again we walked and walked until we started to get scared that we would never find it. The sun had been burning down on us for hours by now and my little brother was really mad and yelling at me for getting us lost in the desert – especially since I had never gotten lost in the desert before! At about the time we had both come to tears, we heard a car horn beeping in the distance. We followed the sound and came upon a road. The beeping sound got louder and louder and then we heard our father calling our names! We yelled and ran with what strength we had toward his voice, waving our arms. When he saw us he was so relieved he stopped the car and jumped right out and ran over and hugged us. He had a big jug of water in the car for us and we drank it and then with what water was left, poured it over our heads. Our dad seeing we were safe and sound really gave us a harsh talking to on the way back to Old Tucson. It turned out that fortunately for us someone in town had seen my brother and me walk out into the desert that morning. That was not an unusual sight, so they hadn't said anything to my dad until later when he started desperately searching for us and asking around. At the time I thought it was too bad I never got to that mountain because it would have been fun to climb. When I think back now to all the big predators and dangerous animals there in the desert – like mountain lions, coyotes, javelena and snakes, I realize how lucky we were not to have encountered them.

Old Tucson still stands today, though much of it has been rebuilt. There was a huge fire in April of 1995 that practically destroyed the entire town and my father's work. It's unfortunate that so much was lost, including the only copy of a short film history of Old Tucson Studios.

Transitions in Tucson

With both Valora and my dad employed, our financial outlook was getting brighter. We packed up and left the Desert House and moved into a more normal house in a nice little neighborhood in town. Sadly, I had to let all my desert pets loose to go back to their natural habitat. The proud Indian Chief beside the highway found a new home at the Old Tucson Studios.

Later in life, try as she might, Valora could never remember the street name of that second Tucson house – probably because we didn't stay there very long. But while we were there my brother and I found it so exciting to live in a neighborhood with children our age. We had been so friend-deprived living out in the middle of the desert. The house in town was small and had black tiled cement slab floors. I remember this well because one night when my parents were out, my brother and I had the great idea to move out all the living room furniture and soap down the floor to play on. Once we soaped the floors we slid across them on our bottoms, sliding from one side of the room to the other – kicking off from the walls – laughing and screaming all the time. We had great fun and we both remember it to this day. You can only imagine the surprise when our parents came home and saw what we had done. I don't recall getting into any trouble for it. After all, they had to admit that the floor was clean.

I remember while we were in this house that my dad built a children's puppet stage and made several hand-held puppets out of Paper Mache and cloth. There was the usual hero, the damsel in distress and villain, along with a couple of other characters. My dad wrote a script and my brother and I would help him act out with the puppets and cue his lines. After all the time and work he put into it, the puppet show somehow never was accepted by the local theater. I have no one left to ask why. My dad then started acting in plays. They were mostly children's plays at first. I would help him with his lines at home and when I got to go to the theater with him at night or on weekends for rehearsals, I would know all the parts and could stand in for the absent actors. I loved that! Sometimes the director would have to tell me to get off the stage when I overplayed my character.

Another memory I have of this house is when it was announced that we were going to have a lunar eclipse, my dad sat us all down one night and read something out of the Bible about the world coming to an end when there was a red moon. I remember my dad being rather dramatic about it and it nearly scared me to death. I thought that by morning I might be dead and I had never thought about dying before. When I was in my bed that night and Valora was in my room, I anxiously asked her about it. She didn't even try to deny it. So I spent most of the night awake and panicked – thinking the world was going to end. I was so thankful when I woke up to the light of the day. My dad and Valora thought it was pretty funny when I explained to them that I had been up all night waiting to die.

Everything seemed to be going along fine there in Tucson – although I still have no memory of school. Could I have just blanked it all out? School was always such an awful experience for me, that it's possible. It seemed that I was always starting a new school in the middle of the school year. The teacher would stand me in front of the classroom and introduce me to the whole room of kids. I found this grossly humiliating as it seemed to define me for the remainder of the school year. Not only was I older than my classmates, but I was tall and skinny and lanky and freckled and red-haired and even had a funny name! I lost on all accounts – not to mention that I was a social disaster.

As we settled into things at the second Tucson house, Valora apparently started to get suspicious as to what my father was up to while he was gone all day at work and then part of the nights too. He was a charming and handsome man, standing 6'2" tall and with his flirtatious manner couldn't help but attract the ladies to him – especially when he was all decked out in his gun slinger costume at Old Tucson. My step-mother knew him all too well and figured that something must surely be up.

I can attest to at least one lady I knew who was especially attracted to my dad. Her name was Barbara and she worked as a tour guide at the Old Tucson history museum. Occasionally when I went to work with my dad during the summer, I would run to find him and see them together having a cigarette break or something. Barbara seemed nice enough and was always sweet and pleasant to me, so I liked her. Little did I know that someday she would play an important role in my life.

Valora had always been a jealous woman and the arguments between her and my father grew worse. Suddenly something serious must have happened between them and there was a decision made that they were going to pack us all up and leave Tucson to go back home to Florida! Sure enough, they checked us out of school and we all took off down the highway. We drove as far as Deming, New Mexico before they must have gotten their senses back and we stopped there, without going to Florida.

We took up residency at an old cinderblock motel in Deming. It was so hot I thought we would bake there. The highlight was that there was a big public pool in town where everyone would go. My brother and I loved it. Fortunately, after a couple of months in Deming, things seemed to get better between our parents and we headed back to Tucson – with the idea that they could hopefully get their jobs back. We found out that unfortunately our house had been rented out, though Valora told me that we couldn't have afforded to live there again anyway, since they had spent most of their savings making that impromptu trip and staying at the motel. Fortunately, Bob Shelton re-hired my father at Old Tucson Studios – so they at least still had *that* income to fall back on. Valora on the other hand, had to find another job. She wasn't so happy about that and blamed it all on my father. At that point, school was out of the question until we could find permanent housing.

In the meantime, we ended up renting a little one bedroom apartment and the four of us lived there for a while, all cozy and together – listening to the thunder and downpour of the monsoon season breaking over the desert. The arguments between my parents continued to rumble too and I remember lying on my makeshift bed on the living room floor with my head under the covers and a pillow over my ears, not wanting to hear what they were saying because it was just too disturbing. According to my step-mother – my father was a "no good lazy good-for-nothing womanizer" – who couldn't make a decent income to support his family in the style that we deserved and that he had promised her. And I, on the other hand, was a "stupid little brat" who just sat around all day and didn't do a damned thing worth mentioning. It was no surprise then that after a short time had passed, I found myself packed up and moving out again . . . this time right alongside my father!

Dad and I moved into a little one-room cottage (or I should say a converted garage) behind an old lady's house somewhere there in Tucson. My dad would go away to work in the morning and sometimes not get home until late at night. I was told that I just had to hang in there and find a way to make-do for a while – and everything would work itself out in the end. Live for Today was my father's philosophy. Planning for tomorrow seemed a bit beyond his comprehension.

Since I wasn't in school, I found myself spending a lot of time with the old lady at her house listening to her read the Bible to me. Sometimes she would even feed me lunch. I think she liked my company, and I could do things for her around the house. She gave me a little Bible to take home to read, and I would lie in bed at night waiting for my father to come home, trying to make some sense of it with all that "begotten" stuff. Reading the Bible was the only thing that kept my mind off the fear of being alone at night. Even though I knew that the old lady was right there in the front house, I would still get really scared in the cottage alone. There was a dividing partition between the main room and the kitchen and I was always afraid that something or someone was lurking behind it. At times I would really work myself up into a full-blown panic attack. Perhaps this was still the lingering result of that movie, "The Horrors of the Black Museum," we saw while living at the Desert House. But then I would hear my dad's old Ford station wagon coming from a block away and would be so thrilled and relieved when he would return home. Once he was home I felt safe and secure and all my fears would go away.

One night my dad came home with a woman. She had been laughing as she came in the door, but was shocked and became indignant when she saw me lying there, as I don't think her plans had included me. She got spitting mad at my dad for not telling her I lived there with him, and she made him take her right home. I can only guess that my dad was thinking it was late and dark and maybe she wouldn't notice someone sleeping in the next bed!

I remember only about a month after we moved into the cottage, my dad packed us up again. (This was starting to feel like a trend). Oddly enough, I was surprised that we ended up at the house belonging to my dad's friend, Barbara – the tour guide from Old Tucson Studios. I wondered what in the world we were doing there, but as always she was very sweet and welcoming to me when we arrived, introducing me to her three children. I had a feeling that maybe my dad had met them before as the children seemed to recognize him. The first to be introduced was Barbara's fourteen-year-old daughter, Dawn – who I found out later was suffering from Cerebral Palsy. Like me, she was tall and gangly, but seemed to be having difficulty controlling her body movements and wasn't particularly interested in meeting me. Her sister, Sharon – who was twelve, about my age – was obviously the ruler of the roost and seemed to step in as her sister's main care-giver. I was then introduced to Barbara's son, Brian, who was about ten years old. He was a bit shy, but was nice and seemed happy to meet me. Barbara told me she also had an older teenage son, but that he lived somewhere else with his father.

To my dismay my father left – actually snuck out during the introductions and left me there with them . . . and *didn't come back*! I thought he was going out to the car to get his stuff, but when he didn't come back and I heard the car driving away, I was told, sympathetically, by Barbara that everything was going to be just fine and that I was going to stay with them there "*just a little while*" until my dad was able to find us a new place to live and get his life back together again. Well this was devastating – and "just a little while" took on a whole new meaning as not long after that I was registered for school and started living there for what seemed like "permanently and forever" to me! (Actually it ended up being about six months, but living with a whole new family with lots of kids, especially one with special needs, was quite a challenge for me.) There was always something brewing. They had added an extra twin bed in the kids' room and we were all jammed in there like sardines, and had to learn how to get along.

The first thing I had to do was learn the pecking order. I found out that as I expected, Sharon, the twelve-year-old was in charge of the household. She was smart and mature beyond her years and took on the mother/care-giver role. She was quite good at it actually and seemed to have a whole organized working system in place. Her mother, Barbara, was out of the house working most of the day. She had recently met a new boyfriend who was a pilot so when she wasn't working she would go away on excursions with him and would sometimes be gone for days at a time. Given my independent ways, it was unlike me to answer to authority, but I grew to admire and respect Sharon and decided to go ahead and let her be in charge, taking my customary place in the pecking order . . . at the bottom. Thankfully, I never had to take on the duties of care-giver for Dawn or Brian as I found that *my* telling *them* what to do would not be tolerated by any one of the three of them! I did, however, have duties allotted to me in the household. I was told by Barbara early on that we kids were all old enough to take on responsibility and fend for ourselves and so we did just that and took on the day-to-day household duties together.

My duties were more or less assigned to me based upon the process of elimination. The first thing they discovered was that I couldn't cook, so that was eliminated right away. So, I ended up with the prize house-cleaning duties like cleaning the nasty little bathroom that everyone used and doing the smelly piled-up laundry – washing it in the old ringer washing machine out on the back porch and hanging it up to dry in the back yard or under the porch overhang when it rained.

While the four of us troopers were able to manage the day-to-day routine most of the time while Barbara was away, the biggest challenge for us was food – as in, there wasn't any, or at least not enough to feed four growing kids. Every now and then Barbara would come home at night and bring food and cook us all dinner which was glorious. Other times she would show up and drop off a carful of groceries that included canned goods and big burlap bags of rice, flour and beans – like feeding an army. Then she would take off and go away on her latest excursion with her boyfriend.

There were times, however, when there just wasn't anything decent to eat in the house and as growing adolescents we seemed to be hungry all the time. I can remember once during a long stretch of being without food, I rifled through the cabinets and finding nothing to eat, opened the refrigerator to find only a half-full bottle of catsup and a bright refrigerator light glaring up at me. Wait! What was that in the back corner, there in the little box? I was *really* hungry and ready to eat just about anything so I took it out and opened it to examine its contents. Wow! What luck! I felt I had just hit the jackpot to find *chocolate* hidden away in the refrigerator! Well, it *looked* like chocolate and it *smelled* like chocolate, and I *loved* chocolate! I had never heard of the brand, Ex-Lax chocolate before. But then I was hungry and didn't care *what* they named it and gobbled down the whole bar before anyone could come in and see that I had found it. Well, I don't think I have to explain the details of what happened later that night and the next day!

But we were all strong, resilient kids and without much money or food in the house, we had to be resourceful. As the new addition to the family I was taught all kinds of new skills. Besides cooking and sewing and household cleaning, I was amazed to be advised by Sharon that if I was very careful I could walk into the drugstore or supermarket and find just about anything I wanted, and then walk out with it . . . without paying. She told me that this new skill was called "shoplifting" and that it was especially useful for getting food and cosmetics. To learn this skill I went into the drug store with Sharon one day and pointed out the things that I wanted, then I let her take over, and the next thing I knew we were walking out of the store with them hidden in her jacket. On the way home we laughed about how easy it was to get away with it without being caught. When we got home we laid out all our little treasures on the bed to examine them. *What a racket!* Not long after that, Barbara – who actually did come home once in a while – saw our cosmetics in the bathroom and she demanded that we tell her where we had gotten the money to buy them. Well, we had some explaining to do, and this emerging skill was then quickly nipped in the bud!

Soon after that, I thought I was pretty smart getting a job at the school cafeteria. All I had to do was clean up and wipe down the tables at lunchtime and I got a free lunch! Boy, that was generous of them – and it helped to know that I could look forward to at least one healthy meal during the day, at least on school days.

My older foster sister, Dawn, had to have someone pick her up in the mornings because she went to a special school. Sharon, Brian and I would walk to school, which was only a few blocks away. While Sharon and Brian always seemed to get there just under the wire, it wasn't uncommon for me to be late for school in the mornings. Although I tried to get there on time, it seemed that there was always so much I needed to do at home before I could leave. I still didn't quite have the system down like the others. I was in the sixth grade now and tried my best to charm the ladies at the front desk to whom I had to answer when I checked in late. Sometimes my excuses had real merit and they began to realize the unusual conditions we had at home. They also noticed that I had a real problem with clothing as it was starting to get cold and my summer clothes were no longer appropriate for me to wear to school. The one pair of sandals I owned were already too small for me with my toes curling over the front of the shoes. Sometimes when it was particularly cold, Barbara would let me wear her tennis shoes to school, but they were also a size too small and my feet would be killing me by the end of the day. Barbara told me that my father was going to send money for school clothes real soon, but that it just hadn't happened yet.

My condition must have struck a chord with Gladys and Irene at the front desk. They knew that sometimes I wouldn't get breakfast in the mornings, and as an incentive to get me to school on time they started to award me with a doughnut and a carton of orange juice or milk if I got there early enough to eat it before the bell rang. Well that seemed to work, and I would look forward in the mornings to their smiling faces and a doughnut. Of course that was our little secret and I kept it to myself, not telling Sharon or Brian about it because they might want a doughnut too and then there might not be enough for me. I learned that an important element of the survival-of-the-fittest was to sometimes be selfish.

The front desk ladies' brigade did more than just give me doughnuts. They put out the word to some of the teachers and one day when I came in there was a whole big box of stuff waiting for me! There were hair curlers and shampoos and lotions and sweaters and other warm clothing items as well. I thought I had just died and gone to heaven!

Several months later a man came to our school and I was taken out of class and brought into the principal's office to meet him. Unfortunately, I had been in that office before and knew the principal all too well, so I was apprehensive. The man was introduced to me as some kind of County social worker. I didn't quite get the whole thing, but I knew I must be in a lot of trouble for the school to bring in someone from the outside to talk with me. Maybe, I thought, they had found out about the shoplifting incident.

The man asked me a lot of questions about where I was living and who my father was and what the conditions were like at our house. Of course I wasn't very happy about my conditions at Barbara's house and about being put to work there, so I was more than happy to tell him so. I was hoping that maybe he would find my father and have him come to get me out of there! Knowing that no one would be home, the man suggested that we go take a look at the house. Well, I was horrified that he would want to come to look at the house right now, knowing its current condition. But the man insisted, and he and the principal came over to the house. As I feared, it was really a mess because we hadn't cleaned it up for a while. I had to agree with them that the one little bathroom we all shared was certainly "filthy;" and our clothes and things were lying all over the floor and the cobwebs were so thick in the living room that they were enmeshed together with the little plastic horses on the window sill. I imagined they must be thinking that I surely wasn't holding up my part as a house cleaner very well. Nothing lasted very long in the refrigerator at that house, so it was no surprise that it was pretty much cleaned out when they looked in there. In the cabinets there was only one burlap bag partly full of flour, and on the counter some raw beans that we kept in a jar. We had been surviving on oatmeal that week and fortunately there was still plenty of it in a bag next to the refrigerator. I told them I was sure that Barbara was coming home soon with some groceries. (Though I knew she hadn't been home for days).

Much to my surprise, right then and there, while they stood and watched, they had me find and pack up my clothes and belongings and put them in a pillow case. Then they marched me right out of the house and into the man's car. And after dropping off the principal at the school, he drove me straight away to the other side of Tucson to what would be my new foster home. When we got there my foster mother, called Mamma Jo, was obviously expecting me when we arrived. It was as if the whole episode had been planned out in advance. I was told this was to be my new, if temporary, home.

I was very worried about what would happen to Dawn and Sharon and Brian. I would hear later from Mamma Jo that Barbara's children were taken away from her and put into foster homes as well. I prayed that they were able to stay together in one home and not be separated. I could only imagine what Barbara and the kids must have thought about me for blowing the whistle on their little house of cards. I felt that somehow I was responsible for the whole collapse and wished that I had not been so candid with the people at the school.

Later I was told that my father, who had since gone back to live with Valora, got into a lot of trouble with the authorities as well – and I didn't hear from Dad or Valora for months on end. Over the three-year period that I stayed at Mamma Jo's foster home I only received a couple of calls from them. And even though they lived in the same city, I would not see them or my little brother Curtis again for two years.

Mamma Jo

In retrospect, going into an official government-run Foster Care program at the age of thirteen was probably one of the best things that could have happened to me. Once in the State's care I had my first thorough physical and dental examinations. Although I was in good physical condition, I had not been taught very well how to maintain my teeth – other than to brush them daily, which I sometimes did. I had teeth growing over teeth and my mouth was pretty much a mess, so they took care of that right away and I had several tooth extractions. Dentists were not my favorite people after that.

Right in the first week of my arrival, Mamma Jo took me to a large County-owned warehouse full of clothing and with her supervision I was allowed to pick and choose almost anything I wanted. What a thrill! From there, I remember how terribly embarrassing it was to go into a department store to try on new bras with Mamma Jo standing there with me the whole time. I had been wearing one of Barbara's old bras, stuffing it with tissue paper as I had seen Valora do. My new foster mother figured that out right away, and quickly I went from an A-cup to a training bra in nothing *flat*! (No pun intended.)

The biggest challenge was the shoes. My big toes were already getting ingrown toenails from wearing shoes too small for me. I should have been wearing a size nine, but they didn't make stylish women's shoes in size nine in those days, so while living at Barbara's house I would wear her smaller more fashionable shoes. But Mamma Jo would have none of that. So there I was with all those pretty new clothes and I had to wear big clunky black and white Oxfords! At the time those cute little T-strap and slip-on Ballerina-style shoes were in style. I felt foolish and out of sync with the times – once again set apart as foreign to the tribe that I was trying to fit into.

Also, being taken so suddenly from Barbara's house was a bit overwhelming for me. I was in shock for days with everything happening so fast. I remember that first day I was introduced to Mamma Jo. The kids were all at school and her husband Hershel (a day sleeper) was fast asleep in the master bedroom with the door closed so I didn't meet him until later. After the social worker left, Mamma Jo toured me around what I thought was a *spacious* three bedroom, *two* bath house. (Although we couldn't go in to see the master bedroom.) I thought the Buckner House was so beautiful and well-kept, with everything in its place – even all the beds were made. The house was located in a nice suburban neighborhood surrounded by cleared, level fields where new houses were being built. She showed me my room, and pulled out two empty dresser drawers for me to store away all my worldly possessions. The room had a double bed plus a set of bunk beds. I was assigned to the top bunk. I would ultimately share that room with three other teenage girls – Judy, Mary and Sandi.

Mamma Jo, better known to the outside world as Kathy, reminded me of Harriet in the Ozzie and Harriet Show. She was a lovely, cheerful woman in her late thirties with shoulder-length brown hair and a kind smile. She glowed with energy and good health and appeared to be a woman who was used to being in-charge. In today's world she would probably best be described as a soccer mom. She was married to Hershel Buckner, who worked at night as a foreman for the Rosemont Copper Mining Company nearby. She had two children from a former marriage – a daughter Judy, who was twelve, almost my age, and a son Rick, who was six. She talked to me as if she was *so* excited to have me at their home, and seemed eager to tell me all about what life would be like at the Buckner house. She even had *me* excited about my prospects of living there – though I was still expecting that my father would come and get me pretty soon.

I was able to spend a little time settling in that first day and getting acquainted with Mamma Jo before Rick and Judy arrived home from school on the bus. Judy was a cute, petite blonde with horn-rimmed glasses, and Rick was a thin, active boy. They seemed a bit surprised to find me there, but were very nice to me. I wondered what it was going to be like living with them and how they would take to me. I was told that they were also expecting other foster children to come to live with them soon.

The house came alive around dinner time because by then Hershel was awake, showered and shaved, and no one had to think about being quiet around the house. Everyone was expected to pitch in and help serve dinner and then wash the dishes afterwards. Unlike Barbara's house, I could see that food at the Buckner house was plentiful. There were pork chops and piles of mashed potatoes and mountains of peas and corn and bread with real butter. I had to really check my manners so as not to put too much food on my plate or in my mouth all at once.

Judy and Rick were very respectful of me, and I was included in their conversation during dinner time. School was discussed and I could see their parents were genuinely interested in how the day had gone for them. They showed interest in me too, but were careful not to grill me with too many questions or get too deep into the details – I think they figured it was best to give it some time.

After dinner when the table was cleared and the dishes were done, the kids took out their homework and sat down at the dinner table and started working away. Hershel went off to work, but Mamma Jo was around to help them with their studies as needed. After homework was finished it was dessert and TV time, and we went to sit down in the living room to watch the latest shows of the day, such as "Car 54 Where Are You?" and "Bonanza." Over time as we became more familiar with each other, Judy and I would argue over who was the dreamiest TV doctor, Ben Casey or Dr. Kildare. I was all about the dark-haired doctor with the attitude, Ben Casey, while Judy favored the blonde-haired, smiley, do-gooder, Dr. Kildare. We also had our favorites on "Bonanza" – Judy favoring the good son "Little Joe," while I went for the older, moody brother, Adam Cartwright.

"Gunsmoke" was one of my all-time favorite shows and I instantly admired the rough and tough saloon keeper, Miss Kitty Russell, for her no-nonsense, don't-mess-with-me attitude. I think that was how I was feeling at the time – the "don't mess with me" part. Even if I was a good and loving person deep inside, I didn't feel like one; I was angry and hurt about my circumstances – with people always pushing me around and telling me what to do. By then I think my self-esteem was at an all-time low and I had developed a bit of an attitude problem.

Nevertheless, I have fond memories of the first school I attended after I arrived at the Buckner House.

Laguna Elementary – with grades Kindergarten to eighth, was a small school made up of old and new buildings. I started there during the fall of 1961, coming into the first half of the seventh grade. The school had big playing fields and a sports track and it backed up to the Union Pacific railroad tracks. Since I had always been athletic, I loved it that these fields provided plenty of room for me to run and lose myself.

For once I didn't feel that I had so much trouble fitting in at school. With Mamma Jo being so involved as a volunteer and PTA President, I think she helped pave the way for me. It also didn't hurt that Judy was a popular girl at the school and she took me under her wing to curb the teasing from the kids. She was cute, witty and smart – all the things I felt I was not. While I was always a bit jealous of her, she had a warm and compassionate heart; I liked her and felt that she was someone I could trust. She and Mamma Jo would even be there to help me with my homework so that I didn't lag behind the rest of the class, which had been typical for me in the past - given that I was always starting classes in the middle of the school year.

The other reason it seemed different from the other schools I had attended was because there were compassionate teachers who embraced their profession and their students with love and enthusiasm and who would engage us in animated class discussions, thus making the material interesting. I began to actually *like* school and looked forward to going every day – which was a real switch for me.

I also got along well with Judy's brother, Ricky, as he was called. He was a good kid and stayed clear of the teenagers. He had his friends in the neighborhood and at school, and was pretty much off on his own – separate from us girls. I think he liked it that way as he could always escape to his own private room when things got a little unruly, as they sometimes did.

The Barbie Doll

The first Christmas at Mamma Jo's house was an eye-opening experience. My soon-to-be foster sister, Mary, had not yet arrived, and the two boys that Mamma Jo had first taken into her foster care home before me had already gone before I arrived. So, as far as I can remember, I was the only foster kid living there with the Buckners during that Christmas of 1961 – when I was thirteen years old.

While I knew that Christmas was a religious holiday, I have to admit that at that point I had not lived in a family that was devotedly religious. I had been taught about Jesus Christ and considered him to be my savior. I prayed to him and God a lot – mostly to help me get through a bumpy passage, or to bring back someone I had lost along the way – like my mother. Christmas to me had always been a delightful and important season because it was a time when people and families were brought together for joyful occasions. There was food, presents, colorful glimmering lights, singing, school pageants and Christmas tree decorating.

Other than at the Bedford house I was not used to getting a lot of presents at Christmas – but then no one else had received much either, so the gift giving usually had seemed pretty fair and equitable. Now at the Buckner house, Mamma Jo was always painfully careful about treating everyone equally – with no obvious special attention or favors shown to her own children, Judy and Ricky. However, weeks prior to Christmas, presents started to arrive from out-of-area friends and from the large extended Buckner family. It seemed that the mailman would deliver boxes of presents on a daily basis. After a while the area in the living room under and around the tree was piled high with them. It is safe to say that I had *never* in my life seen so many presents all in one place!

I can only imagine Mamma Jo's dilemma, as most of these presents were directed to Judy and Ricky by family who were obviously unaware that she had recently started taking in foster children. It wouldn't have surprised me then or now to learn that Mamma Jo took it upon herself to go out and buy a few presents for me, or redirected some of the shipped presents to me so that I wouldn't feel slighted. So Christmas morning came and it was truly a magical time as we all gathered around the tree and opened our presents. I received some great new sweaters and other much-needed clothing. There was fun girlie stuff too, like a package of new curlers and an Elvis Presley record. By far, one of my favorite gifts was a Barbie doll. I was thrilled when I opened the package and saw her. She had on a black and white striped bathing suit, makeup on her eyes and cherry colored lips – and beautiful thick black hair pulled back into a ponytail.

Meanwhile the Buckner kids kept opening one present after the next, and though Mamma Jo tried to space out the giving of the presents, it finally got down to me sitting there for what felt like half the day waiting for Judy and Ricky to finish opening up all their presents. *I really feel guilty writing about how disappointed I felt when I know I should have been so very thankful for the presents I did get and the wonderful home and family I was blessed with at that time. I think, however, that it is equally important for me to address the honest feelings of a foster child given such a circumstance. I'm sure if you had asked me at the time if I was thankful I would have said yes . . . for being there, but somehow this gift-giving part didn't seem fair, needy as I was.*

But Judy was a generous girl and was always happy to share most of her things with me. That Christmas was no exception, so I eventually passed through the feelings of unfairness when we took our presents into the bedroom to sort them out and discuss them for a while before joining

Mamma Jo in the kitchen to help with dinner. She had been slaving away in the kitchen for days, maybe even *weeks,* and the dinner was really something special. I remember there was a big red platter full of spiced ham with cherries and cloves on top, candied sweet potatoes, piles of roasted potatoes and vegetables, and an assortment of pies and cakes. What a feast! We all sat down and ate until we were so stuffed we couldn't eat any more. Later, after dinner, Judy did her usual disappearing act and went to hide in the bathroom so she didn't have to help with dishes, but Mamma Jo found her and made her come back out to help.

I couldn't wait to find time alone to play with my new Barbie doll. You would think that girls our age would be too old to play with dolls, but Barbie was all the rage with the young teens in those days – and besides, Barbie was a beautiful *grown up* doll, not for babies. She had makeup on her face like *we* wanted to wear, and long, thick hair like we all wished *we* had. She also had the perfect body that we all dreamed of having . . . to start with she had *breasts*! Barbie also had a tiny little waist, with narrow hips and long thin legs. She even had tiny little feet! Oh, did I ever wish I had tiny little feet! Over time, with Judy's blessings there were occasions when I could steal away some private time and space in our bedroom alone and immerse myself in the secret fantasy world of Barbie. In that make-believe world I was beautiful and every boy and girl on earth liked me. I had all the latest fashions which, of course, looked great on my perfectly-shaped body. Everywhere I would go I would get my way and people would all flock to see me and want to be my friend. I was living the life of Barbie, totally lost in a world of love and total acceptance by all – a completely new and wonderful feeling for me.

I remember one day when I was deep into this fantasy world. I had to stop and run to use the bathroom.

Still deep in thought, I turned to wash my hands at the sink and made the mistake of looking at myself in the mirror. The smile left my face as I stood there and stared in surprise. At first I thought who *was* this girl? Then the mist of imagination started to clear and gradually my whole fantasy world evaporated before me – I began to recognize that the freckled girl in the mirror was me. I realized at that moment that my make-believe Barbie future would never come to pass. I covered my face and dropped to the floor. With my back against the tub, I sat sobbing into my hands, realizing that all those wonderful thoughts and dreams were made up for a pretend world and I was just stuck with me – *and I didn't like me.*

Looking back on that moment I can partly blame my awkward adolescent age and past experiences with my peers that left me crying in self-pity there in a heap on the floor. But I think that equally responsible for my feelings of devastation was the cruel judging eye and critical voice of society. I had bought into their negative perception of me and my imperfect body; they had me agreeing with them whole-heartedly about how unsightly I was and how I didn't conform to the norm – the norm being that perfect image of the Barbie doll. I figured at the time that the best I could hope for was to receive some meager sympathetic acceptance for this image of a sorry little red-headed Raggedy Ann doll.

That incident changed me somehow. The revelation that I had caught myself escaping into a complete fantasy world seemed to be a rite of passage for me. I swore that I would never let it happen again. I put away the Barbie doll, refusing to believe I could ever find hope or joy in creating a world that could never be.

Track and Field

With my long arms and legs it didn't take long for me to figure out that Track and Field was something that I could be good at. There were a couple of star girl athletes in the school, and after a while I found that with a little encouragement, training, and practice I could out-run them in races, out-jump them in the Broad Jump, and out-distance them in a soft-ball throw. *I finally found something I could do better than anyone else!* This gave me some self-confidence and had me feeling good about myself! After taking on the girls in the school, I started racing with the boys and found out that I could beat most of them too . . . all except for this one guy, Lee Thornton. No matter how hard I trained or tried, I could never seem to beat Lee Thornton. Among other awards, Lee was known to have the school record for running laps around the track. But I figured one day, since I couldn't beat him in a race, I would set out to challenge his lap record.

After I had been training – running for about a half-hour on the track – someone found out what I was doing and ran to tell Lee Thornton about it. Lee soon came out to the track and started running alongside me asking what I was doing, and I told him. Then much to my surprise he just took off running around the track as fast as he could and low and behold, he beat his own record, leaving me defeated in his dust. *Oh well, I decided that was okay, because at least I knew I was the fastest girl in the school.*

During the Track and Field season our school would regularly compete on a *regional* basis with other schools. I found that in these regional games I would still win occasionally, but there always seemed to be *some* girl from *some* other school that could beat me at *some* event. By the age of fourteen I was still lacking maturity and polish – and once when we were competing regionally at a track meet I almost got our team eliminated from the competition! The games were already over when I got into a heated argument with a girl in one of the neighboring teams and flipped her off as her school bus was driving away. In my defense, she and her friends were looking out the back window of the bus making faces at me. Well, *their* principal called *our* principal and I got a good talking-to by the Laguna School principal – *and* the coach, *and* Mamma Jo about the meaning of sportsmanship-like conduct. I learned a good lesson that day and it has paid off later in life.

While attending Laguna School, I was somehow given the privilege of becoming a school crossing guard and, while I might have been a little bossy at first, it made me feel so proud that they would trust me with that important position. I got to wear a white strap over my shoulder and across my chest – complete with a *badge*!

~

About six months after I arrived, another foster girl, Mary, showed up at the Buckner house. She was quiet and shy and at age fourteen, was just a couple of months older than me. She was thin and very pretty with her long straight brown hair, of which I was quite envious. Observing Mary and her difficulties over the next few weeks, I learned more about myself and how hard it truly was to be taken from your family and have to adjust to a whole new lifestyle. I realized that even if your own home environment is dysfunctional and unhealthy and the new transition is a good one for you, the change is still a huge psychological slap to the psyche and it takes time to adjust and get your bearings.

I have found that with every new family there is a whole new set of rules and boundaries and religions and beliefs and personalities that you have to figure out how to adjust to and get along with. As a foster kid I learned that it is best to lay low and take it easy for a while to find out who the "Good Guys" are – and who are the "Bad Guys." This is not as easy as you might think because sometimes the Bad Guys come off as the Good Guys in the beginning. They pretend to be your best friends and gain your trust and get you to tell them all sorts of things you should keep to yourself. Sometimes this information can be used against you and you can be shunned and teased in front of your peers about it. Even today as an older adult I still feel the need to be careful as to whom I can trust with the stories from my past.

Sisters

The 1960s were glory days at the Buckner house for music, friends and neighbors. We would often all meet in our backyard with our hula hoops and turn up the radio real loud – swiveling our hips to the songs of Elvis Presley and bellowing out hit tunes such as "The Lion Sleeps Tonight" – which was the number one song when I arrived at the Buckner House. The Beatles were just coming on the scene and were all the craze.

Mary, Judy, and I got along pretty well. We later teamed up with a couple of other girls and became cheerleaders for Laguna School. Mamma Jo got busy making uniforms for us. It was great fun practicing all the cheerleader songs and routines and going to the junior high practice games to cheer for our team. I discovered that the hardest part of that whole exercise was learning the rules of the sport and knowing *when* to cheer and when *not* to cheer!

About a year after I arrived, Sandi, showed up at the Buckner house – the third and newest teenage foster sister to arrive. And we were all staying in the same bedroom! (*One can only imagine.*) Sandi proved to be the wildest one yet, but when I first saw her she appeared to be just as shell-shocked and traumatized as Mary and I had been when we arrived. Perhaps the strangest thing about Sandi was that she had big clumps of black hair randomly jutting out on her head. She also seemed miserable. Mamma Jo later told us that Sandi had just had a big physical fight with her mother, who held her down and hacked off most of her hair with scissors! The first thing Mamma Jo had to do was to haul her off to the barber shop and have her head shaved, which helped with her appearance somewhat. And Mamma Jo gave her a couple of her scarves she could wear until her hair grew out again.

Sandi was sixteen years old – one or two years older than the rest of us girls. We could tell right off from the language she used that she had been around the block a few times . . . if you know what I mean. But unlike me, Sandi seemed to know *just* who she was and *what* she was all about. She exuded confidence and a maturity beyond her years and seemed much more experienced in the ways of the world. To me she was the epitome of Gunsmoke's Miss Kitty – so I secretly adored her. Sandi was smart too and could carry on a regular grown-up conversation with Mamma Jo and Hershel. In fact, they took to her right away which caused a little riff of tension in the air of the Buckner House. I'm sure you can guess our biggest problem – that's right! Time in the bathroom! It had been bad enough with *three* teenage girls, but with *four* I had to get up at the crack of dawn to have a moment alone in there. As for Mamma Jo and Hershel's master bathroom, it was off limits to us kids – even Judy – unless there was an absolute emergency. After all, I guess they had to find sanctuary somewhere in the house!

Maybe because of what my step-mother, Valora once referred to as my "pitiful" appearance, Sandi took an interest in me and seemed compelled to help me along and teach me a few things about life – in fact I became her new pet project. She befriended me right from the start and I have to admit I felt pretty special to be noticed by such a worldly, smart, older girl like Sandi. After a few months at the house, she somehow convinced Mamma Jo to let her spend the night at one of her old girlfriend's houses, and asked if she could take me along with her. Much to my surprise after talking with the girlfriend's mother, Mamma Jo consented to it! I was beyond excited at the prospect of going on a sleepover – even though at our house it was like having a sleepover every night!

It's amazing all the things you can learn by just lying there in the dark of night listening to teenage girls talk! Wow, I had no idea about some of that stuff, especially as it pertained to boys. Up until this point I hadn't had much experience with boys my age, but I got a real earful as Sandi and her girlfriend talked into the night about their intimate experiences with the opposite sex. It was a good thing it was so dark that they couldn't see my eyes bulging out of my head with surprise. I giggled along with them at the stories of their close encounters – but half the time I didn't even know what they were talking about and wasn't about to appear naïve by asking.

Later, in the wee hours of the morning there was serious talk about wanting to go out and steal a car and meet up with some boys that they knew. I figured they must have been messing with my sleepy head to see what I would do – and, sure enough, they got a good laugh at my reaction to that caper! I couldn't even *imagine* that they would do such a thing. Stealing food or cosmetics from Woolworth's was one thing, but it sounded like these girls were in the big league! Well, we never did venture out to steal a car, but they told me stories of times they had gone out at night and stolen signs right off the streets around town. In fact, one such trophy was hanging across from me on the bedroom wall; it read "Caution, Men Working Ahead."

Once we got back to Mamma Jo's I waited for an opportune time to take Mamma Jo aside to ask her if some of the sleepover things I had heard about were true. (In retrospect, I'm not sure if I was really looking for answers or if I just wanted to undermine Mamma Jo's view of Sandi.) To my chagrin Mamma Jo brought Sandi in and confronted her about it right in front of me! Of course Sandi denied it all, telling Mamma Jo that I had just made it all up. Needless to say, things were never the same between Sandi and me after that. We were always at each other's throats, with Sandi acting the part of the superior being, not to be caught dead in my *pathetic* shadow.

And so it went with *all* of us four girls. One day I would be the best friend of one of them, and then the next day she would be my arch enemy and best friends with one of the *other* girls. One day I was in, and the next day I was out. We all took turns, either being the best friend or the outcast to the others. Sometimes we would even form teams against each other. It was just a matter of which way the hormones ebbed and flowed and whose were raging more.

At the start of the Thanksgiving holiday 1962, Mamma Jo and Hershel packed up the whole group of us – Ricky, Judy, Mary, Sandi, and me – into the family car to go visit Hershel's family in a small suburb of Kansas City, Missouri. We were all looking forward to the drive from Tucson as an exciting adventure, but it proved to be a long and uneventful trip, with everyone all squished up together. Sandi and I were placed on opposite sides of the car from each other, but that didn't prevent us from throwing snide and sarcastic remarks back and forth whenever we got a chance. Despite trying to amuse ourselves by playing games, we were all bored to death and attempted to sleep whenever possible. Speaking of sleep . . . we managed to somehow live through the trauma of all seven of us staying in a motel room together, with us girls sleeping on a blanket on the floor, and all of us sharing one tiny bathroom. After a pretty rough night we were thrilled to reach our Kansas City destination the next afternoon, the Wednesday before Thanksgiving.

The grandparents met us at the door and were so happy and excited to see Judy and Ricky that they were even hugging and kissing the rest of us tired stragglers. After the formalities were over, it didn't take long for us girls to get antsy and bored, and we begged to take a walk over to the little group of stores that we had seen close-by. We were allowed to go out for only a short while and told to come right back, in time for dinner. The four of us strolled down the tree-lined street admiring the gardens and the fabulous Fall colors of the Maple trees. As we were *checking out* the stores, we noticed that the townsfolk were *checking out* us. We just stayed together, minding our manners and keeping to ourselves. After we looked around the stores for a while, we hurried back to the house so as not to be late for dinner. Mamma Jo was amused to tell us when we got back that an elderly neighbor had phoned to tell Hershel's parents that they should lock their doors and windows because there was a "gang of girls" roaming the streets! I guess they weren't used to seeing strangers in those parts.

On our first night there, we four girls were given the large master bedroom with its own bathroom at the back of the house, while Mamma Jo, Hershel, and Ricky were assigned the upstairs bedroom and the grandparents took the guest room downstairs in the front of the house. I remember as we started getting ready for bed, Sandi and I got into a blazing argument and Mamma Jo had to come in and tell us to quiet down and to stop using foul language. Then later when I went to use the bathroom, Sandi stood in the doorframe and wouldn't let me pass, taunting me by saying "make me" when I told her to move. Well, I knew that Sandi was an experienced fighter and I didn't want to engage her in an all-out battle there in Hershel's parent's home – (truth be told I was afraid of her) – so I just threw out some of my usual nasty verbal barbs and turned to go back to the bedroom. The next thing I knew Sandi had launched herself onto my back, grabbing my hair. I backed up and rammed her into the wall of the hallway with all my might . . . and so the fight began. This mobilized the entire house full of people, who all came running to stop us. Needless to say poor Mamma Jo and Hershel were mortified by our behavior.

It seems that we brought some real live action and adventure to the senior Buckner house. I guess, when it came down to it, the neighbors had been right – we *were* just a gang of girls. Feeling pretty ashamed of our behavior, we managed to keep ourselves under control during the rest of the short stay and during most of the long drive back home to Tucson. It was only a month or two later that Sandi left the foster home to return to her family . . . much to my relief.

We had several babies that came through the Buckner home. They would often have medical problems, like one little boy who didn't have any toes. Mamma Jo also took in a one-year-old baby named Jackie and we all thought she was the sweetest thing alive! She came to us with some health issues and at first *only* Mamma Jo could feed her because she had a tendency to choke on her food and turn blue in the face until you could dislodge the food from her throat. She had a cleft palate and had had surgery on it, but the roof of her mouth had not closed up all the way and the State wouldn't do anything more to fix it. One day I was left to take care of Jackie while Mamma Jo went next door to talk with the neighbor. She was over there for a while and she had given me some food to give the baby, along with the usual instructions on what to do if she choked – not expecting that she would. Well, *of course* she choked, and try as I might I couldn't get the food dislodged from her throat and she just kept getting bluer and bluer in the face. I finally grabbed her and ran her next door to the neighbor's house. Mamma Jo had to rescue her and get her to breathing again. I remember I felt like I wasn't cut out for taking care of others (especially babies). After baby Jackie left our foster home, Mamma Jo told me that she got a phone call from her new adoptive parents. They thanked her for taking care of Jackie, and told Mamma Jo that they were people of means and that Jackie would get the best medical care available and for Mamma Jo not to worry about her – and that she was welcome to come to visit anytime.

~

I turned fifteen that April of 1963 and my upcoming eighth-grade graduation was just over a month away. It had not been an easy journey through school and it seemed like a real miracle for me to finally be graduating from eighth grade – I had now finished the same grade level that my father had. However, now I had an escalating level of anxiety attributable to an even bigger miracle. I heard from Mamma Jo that she had located my father and invited him to the graduation ceremony and that he had promised to come! (In case I didn't mention it before, I simply *adored* my father.) This was the best news ever! Being with him always made me feel special.

Mamma Jo helped Judy and me pick out the dresses for our graduation. I selected a beautiful light, pink-colored lace dress with a satin ribbed collar and long sleeves. It was the most beautiful dress I had ever seen! Mary helped with my hair. She had already graduated from the eighth grade the year before and was attending high school, but when that much-anticipated graduation day for Judy and I finally came around, she got into the party spirit with the rest of us – in fact, the whole household was in a tizzy. We teased and put up each other's hair in lavish Grecian curls and applied shiny pink lipstick to our lips and mascara to our eyes. We were beautiful!

I was a bundle of nerves thinking about seeing my father again and on top of everything else I was supposed to sing "Over the Rainbow" at the ceremony with two other graduating classmates. From the time I arrived at the school late that afternoon I started looking for my dad. I must have asked Mamma Jo ten times if she was *sure* he had the directions.

The ceremony started and everyone was seated and *still* my father was nowhere in sight. I really wanted him to see me sing, but he *didn't appear* during my performance. The whole time I was up on stage I was scanning the crowd looking for his familiar face. I knew I was singing off-key as I was trying to contain my emotions and not burst into tears. The graduation ended without my father being there. I was devastated – it took the joy out of my miracle. In fact while everyone was running around laughing and hugging and congratulating each other, I was spitting mad, trying to hold back a total breakdown in front of my peers. Mamma Jo and Hershel came over to congratulate and comfort me, but I was inconsolable.

Then at the last possible moment – across the expansive room coming in the door, I saw my father's red hair looming over the mass of kids and parents. I squealed like a little girl and went running through the crowd. My father had come! Much to my surprise, Valora had come with him. They both looked very happy to see me, though I think they were a little embarrassed that I was putting on such a fuss! I was so excited to see them that I was jumping up and down and squealing and laughing and crying and hugging them all at the same time. It had been two years since I had seen them and I had grown a few inches. To add to that I also had on a pair of low pumps (my very first pair) and with my hair all done up and make up on, they couldn't believe their eyes – their little girl was all grown up!

They stayed on during part of the graduation dance and I took them around the room introducing them to all my friends and teachers. I was so proud of my dad. He and I danced the Twist together and I could swear that all the girls in the room were jealous of us. What a wonderful time I was having . . . and then they said *they had to go*. They explained that my brother Curtis was staying with a neighbor, so they had to get back and not be too late. It was *painfully* hard to pull myself away and I didn't understand why I couldn't just pack up and go back home with them *right then and there*. But they said no.

Riding back home with the Buckners I sat all scrunched down, arms folded, in the back seat of the car – talking to no one. I could still smell my father's Old Spice cologne lingering on my clothes, and I tried to hold back the tears. When we got home, I jumped out of the car and stomped into my bedroom and slammed the door. With my new glittery pumps and pretty pink dress still on I jumped right up onto the top bunk, covered myself with my blanket and cried until I couldn't cry anymore. Mamma Jo and the girls stayed out of the room and didn't even try to approach me. They knew I needed the space and time alone to work it out of my system. I promised myself that night that somehow I would find a way to go back to live with my father again.

First Kiss

It was 1963 and Mamma Jo had her hands full with three teenage girls in the house. Mary and I were fifteen and Judy was fourteen years old. Three girls in high school – I don't know how Mamma Jo did it, but you can imagine what it was like trying to rein in and corral us all, plus she had little Ricky at home too! So she was pretty strict about certain things. And one thing she would not let us girls do was get into a car alone with a boy. One of the other girls always had to be present and vigilant when there was a boy involved. That was the rule. Well, you can imagine how that went over! But, somehow we all managed to survive it, though there were times when this could be pretty frustrating.

I think one way Mamma Jo kept her sanity was getting lost in the "True Confessions" magazines that she would buy and hide from us girls. Well, we found out about them and would locate them and sneak into a corner of the house away from everyone else and consume them like candy – sometimes alone, sometimes together, giggling. Perhaps that was why I was all fired up and ready for my first kiss. There was a boy that everyone seemed attracted to at school named Dean Jackson. He was a big guy with a kind of sexy macho-cowboy style about him and he seemed to have a way with the girls. I think he was trying out for a John Wayne role or something. Dean would come around our house from time to time since all the girls hung out there. One day when I was left alone with him in the living room – feeling awkward – he asked me if I had ever been kissed. I thought I would *die* from the embarrassment of his question and I said nothing, but my face flashed red, revealing my immediate discomfort. Then he walked over and plopped himself right down next to me on the couch . . . way too close for comfort. I was poised to bolt any second when he reached over with his hand and gently took my chin, turning my face to his and softly kissed me square on the lips! He was so smooth about it that I wasn't even alarmed and thought, hmmm, this isn't so bad. Visualizing the scenes in my head from "True Confessions", I thought that this was the beginning of real romance – and it was finally happening to me! Unfortunately, I quickly brought us both back to reality, spoiling the moment as an uncontrolled giggle escaped my lips – brought out by my pure embarrassment. The magic moment had passed, and we got up and went outside to join the others. I wish I could tell you something more exciting happened, *but at least I had my first kiss!*

In those days it was the fad to wear your boyfriend's ring around your neck like a necklace, usually tied with a string or ribbon. It seems strange now, because I ask myself: Where did the boys get those rings . . . maybe from sports or fraternities? The other thing that the girls would do was to walk around school wearing their boyfriend's sweater or jacket, usually with a varsity letter on it. I think this was more for the older, especially popular girls as not all the boys had yet earned a letter for their sweater. I don't remember ever wearing a ring around my neck or wearing anyone's sweater, but there were a couple of boys I had crushes on. The boy I was madly in love with (as was every other girl on earth) was our next door neighbor, Tony Domingo. He was a year or so older than us and this made him more worldly and intriguing, not to mention his handsome Italian vibe – sparkling brown eyes, dark skin and gleaming black curly hair. It was like having a rock star living right next door to you! All of us girls swam in his wake.

What a temptation it was to connect with him, but I'm sad to say that he had no interest in me whatsoever. He was just the boy-next-door to us Buckner girls and we were all off-limits in his book – partly out of respect for Mamma Jo, who just happened to be his mother's best friend. They had an above-ground Doughboy Pool in their back yard and we would all go over there and swim and goof around together. Even though I had lived right near the water in Florida when I lived with my dad at the Driftwood Shack, I had not really learned to swim and had had a few bad experiences in the water.

One day when no one was around and Tony and his mother were not at home, I snuck into their back yard and got into the pool. I had seen other kids turning somersaults in the water and standing on their hands with their feet sticking out of the water. So, I tried this a few times, and scared myself silly. In an effort to challenge my fear, I tried it one last time, but this time when I tried to turn a somersault I got vertigo, losing my orientation between up and down. When I kicked at the bottom to bring myself up, there was no bottom and my feet just kicked water instead. I thrashed around trying to get my bearings and totally panicked as I searched for the surface. When I finally came up I was gasping for air, coughing and choking. I managed to climb out of the pool and promised myself never to try turning somersaults under water again. How tragic it would have been for the neighbors to find me drowned at the bottom of their pool! (And for me, of course.)

Another near disaster for me took place in the neighborhood. The Domingos had a scruffy medium-sized dog named Eisenhower. Tony and his parents had gone away on vacation, but one summer night around dusk when a group of us were out playing Kick The Can, I saw what I thought was Eisenhower up on Tony's fence. I went up to see the dog, but as I started to approach him he jumped down the other side of the fence so I didn't get a good look at him. Later as we kids were milling around, a big Tom Cat came up over the fence and was walking around close to where we were playing. The cat was so big I could see how in the dim light, I had mistaken it for Tony's dog. Always being the animal lover, I approached the strange animal and bent down to pick it up.

I must have startled the cat – all of a sudden it turned and jumped right onto my head! It grabbed me with all four paws – bit my face, and its claws dug into my scalp. I must have gone into shock because I just stood there until the kids finally started throwing rocks to get it off me. It all happened so fast. While I don't remember so much about the attack – which was later recounted to me by the kids – I do remember running into the house with my head and face all bloodied, screaming desperately for Mamma Jo. She came running to see what had happened and when she saw my bloodied face she rushed me into the bathroom and tried to clean me up, while I fought her off the whole time – screaming for her not to touch my face.

While I was inside with Mamma Jo getting cleaned up and trying to explain what had happened, the kids were outside trying to hunt down the big Tom Cat which had bolted out into the field. Fortunately I didn't know it at the time, but as the kids went from door to door in the neighborhood looking for the cat and telling the story – a rumor had started that I may have been infected with rabies from one of the feral cats across the field. I somehow made it through that miserable night and in the morning Hershel took me to the doctor. The doctor cleaned out the cat scratches on my face and scalp with some kind of sharp instrument that hurt like Hell during the process. Then, to add insult to injury he applied stinging Iodine onto the open wounds. In addition to the yellow medicine dripping down from the scratches on my face, my right eye had turned black and blue because I had hemorrhaged from a bite to the temple, and my hair was matted with blood. I looked like a horrid mess and was so afraid that someone would see me as Hershel drove me home in the car.

Once I got home I heard Hershel tell Mamma Jo that the doctor had talked about the possibility of my needing rabies shots since no one had been able to locate the cat. Fortunately, it was decided later that day by Hershel, Mamma Jo and the doctor that I would *not* have the shots. While I was happy about *that*, I read in the Encyclopedia about the rabies virus and became terrified that I might actually *have it* and die a horrible death. I began to go through a whole calendar count-down, waiting to see if I would start foaming at the mouth or have symptoms of delirium and mental dysfunction. None (beyond the ordinary) ever occurred, but I went through many days of high anxiety, waiting it out. Perhaps I was overreacting, but I remember it being very scary for me at the time. After the Tom Cat experience I have always been cautious about approaching animals that I don't know. Most of the scars have disappeared over time, but you can still see them on my face if you look up close.

~

We all know the 1960s were memorable times. I recall when I was still living with Mamma Jo and in my freshman year at Flowing Wells High School in Tucson, an announcement came over the intercom system while I sat in my history class. It was just a few days before Thanksgiving – on November 22, 1963 – President John F. Kennedy had been shot and killed! I had no real concept of politics at the time, but was very aware that this was our wonderful handsome president – the man who was married to the beautiful Jackie Kennedy – who I admired for her style and grace and tried to emulate in every way. Like the rest of the room I sat there stunned, looking at the teacher and wondering what she would say. I could hear sobbing coming from one of the girls at the back of the room, and I thought about how *I* felt about our president being shot dead and tried to get in touch with my feelings. I think I was more fearful of how this would affect all our lives in general. We kids had already been trained to duck for cover under our desks when the loud warning sirens would go off. Would this mean war? And what about "A-bombs." The teacher, also stunned and visibly shaken, tried to give us some comforting words and dismissed the class. I ventured out into the hallway where I saw students and teachers alike who were really disturbed by the news – some rushing out from their classes, some sitting along the curbs of the walkways, crying and being consoled by others. Still saddened, I walked on toward my next class, not quite sure what to think – looking for my friends – trying to hold in my emotions.

~

By February 9, 1964, the Buckner girls (as we had come to be known) were in full hormonal swing. We waited with great anticipation for the upcoming Ed Sullivan show when the Beatles band was going to play. I remember that day well because we all huddled with delight around the TV, glued to the set. Once the British boys started playing, we were there at home reacting just the same as the girls in the audience: all screaming, hugging each other, and jumping up and down with excitement. Little Ricky quickly retreated to his room, shaking his head with his hands over his ears. By the time they played "I Want to Hold Your Hand" at the end, we had practically lost our voices and were out of control! This had to be one of the greatest days of our teenage lives and I'm so glad we were all there to share it together! Unlike my usual attraction to the dark and moody TV stars, my favorite Beatle was Paul McCartney because of his sweet, young, innocent look. He reminded me a lot of Ricky Nelson, who I was also crazy about. I would later switch to also liking John and then George. I really didn't like Ringo at the time, but was crazy about the Beatles – and remain so to this day.

When I turned sixteen in April of 1964, we had a Sweet Sixteen Party for me at the house and invited our girlfriends over. Though boys had started to play a major part in our lives, according to Mamma Jo it was still a little too soon to invite them to a party. We set up a special table in the carport with plenty of chips and dip and popcorn and other munchies. Our friends were asked to all dress up and bring over their favorite seven inch 45 RPM records – with the little removable plastic center piece – so that we could all dance to our favorite songs. Everyone came and we had a great time, playing music, eating, gossiping and teaching each other all the latest dance steps like the Mashed Potato, the Watusi, and new versions of the Twist. We played on the Ouija Board and tested each other out with Chubby Checker's Limbo Rock to see how far down we could go! News flash: I wasn't the winner.

More excitement. I remember that we waited until Mamma Jo was occupied outside of the room and ran to the kitchen phone and called one of the boys we knew. When we got him on the phone, we asked him if his refrigerator was running. When he said yes, we told him he had better go out and catch it! We hung up on him and laughed and screamed with delight. Those were truly days of innocence and joy!

I'm so glad I lived those days at the Buckner house as I think it grounded me and helped me establish a much stronger sense of values and self-worth. It was a good thing that I experienced this stability as it would only be a few months until I would leave it all and go back to live with my father.

Back Home with Dad

When asked, Mamma Jo couldn't remember just how it had all come about so fast. It was summertime in 1964 she said, when she got the call from the County social worker. He told her that he would be coming by to pick me up the following Thursday, barely a week away. Mamma Jo was to have all my belongings packed and ready to go by then. At first Mamma Jo said she couldn't believe her ears since I had been there almost three years by then. "Are you sure?' she found herself asking. "Yes", he said, "she will be going back to live with her father – arrangements have been made. I will see you on Thursday." Mamma Jo told me that when she hung up the phone she just sat down and cried.

I'm sure it must have been a double whammy for Mamma Jo when she sat me down with a serious look on her face and told me what was about to happen, because rather than being sad or upset as she expected me to be, I jumped out of my chair with excitement and glee. Don't misunderstand. I adored Mamma Jo and the Buckner family home, but I think I felt like most foster children, who just want to go home to their parents no matter what the circumstances might be. Perhaps it is just in our DNA.

Also, I have to admit that at the age of sixteen and approaching my sophomore year in high school, I found the pressure of all the rules and regulations enforced at the Buckner house to be stifling and seemingly excessive. And I anticipated having a lot more freedom living at my father's house – as things had always been a little lax with him when it came to restrictions.

The day of my leaving came upon us all too soon. During that week I thought a lot about the value of the care that Mamma Jo and her family had bestowed on me over the years. There were moments when I wondered if I was making the right decision to go back to live with my dad, but then it wasn't my decision anyway. I would certainly be leaving with much more than that little pillowcase of belongings with which I had arrived. Not only did I have a real suitcase and several bags of belongings this time, I realized I was now more grounded and mature – blessed with a stronger set of family values and sense of self-worth.

As I sat in the car that day, the scene felt way too similar to the one in Virginia when I was six years old being driven away from my screaming mother . . . only this time, *minus* all the drama. I was apprehensive as the Buckner family gathered around the car and said their final good-byes. Mamma Jo and I both found it impossible to hold back our tears. She reminded me that I was only going across town and I could always call and come to visit them anytime I wanted. While I felt a ray of hope in her words, given my past experience with leaving people, I sensed that this might be the last time I would see her.

Today as I look back, I think how very different my life would have been if I had stayed on with the Buckner family until I was 18 years old. You will see what I mean as we go on . . .

The social worker, a nice enough middle-aged man, drove me across town while trying to engage me in conversation, but I didn't feel much like talking. My emotions were raw and conflicted; I was sad about leaving Mamma Jo's house and the family I had come to love. Three years was about the longest I had stayed *anywhere*. Then again, I was still excited about the prospect of going back to live with my own family again. Mamma Jo's words echoed in my head, and I asked the social worker, if it didn't work out with my father, could I go back to live with Mamma Jo. He said he wasn't sure. So it seemed the decision had been made, and I pondered the possibility that there may be no turning back. It was scary.

The social worker told me that my dad, step-mother and step-brother, Curtis (who was now ten years old) had been back together for almost two years now, living in a house that I had not yet seen in the South-East part of Tucson. He said it was within walking distance to Catalina High School where I would start in September, a couple of months away. As he drove down the little dead-end street with RVs, and pickup trucks parked in the driveways, I was once again reminded of my meager roots. We came up to a little one-story dark green adobe cottage with a flat roof and a tall lone phallic-looking cactus in the front yard. This would be my new home.

As we pulled up, my chic and lovely red-headed step-mother, Valora, came running out of the house with my brother trailing behind her. (The shocking part was that she was pregnant! The social worker had forgotten to tell me that part.) She was all hugs and laughter and introduced Curtis to the social worker and then again to me because after all it had been over three years since I had seen him and we both stood there awkwardly staring at each other. He had really grown and though he was about the same age as Ricky Buckner, he was much taller. I guess we both took after our father in the height department. It was good to see him.

I had to laugh when I entered into the house as the first thing I saw were three naked women standing in the living room. Valora explained that while my dad was still the Art Director of Old Tucson, *she* was in the middle of a store window mannequin design project and had just moved the mannequins into the house to start working on them.

The small cottage, thankfully, had three little bedrooms in it and I was told that I would have my very own room! Can you imagine? After living with three other teenage girls all in one room at the Buckner house, I was finally going to have a room *all to myself*! Well, that is once the room was cleared of all the art supplies and papers that were still piled up in there. Valora explained that with the new mannequin project, she hadn't had time to clean it out yet. I said that it was okay as I was just thrilled with the promise of my own room! While Curtis went out to play with his friends, Valora sat me down with a cup of tea and we had "the talk." She told me how much she and my dad had missed me over the years and was sorry about how things had turned out for me. She explained that everything was more stable for them now and they were so happy to be able to have me come back to live with them again and how it would be so much better than before. She even apologized for all those terrible things she had said about me before I left, almost four years ago – when she and my dad had split up. She said they had been under a lot of financial stress.

Valora said she was so looking forward to us being friends now and was excited at the prospect of having a teenage girl in the house, especially with a new baby coming. With her being a designer and artist, she said she would help me with a whole new make-over for my face and hair. I didn't know I needed a make-over, but it was so wonderful for me to hear all this coming from her – as I had the impression from before that she didn't like me very much. In return for all her kind words, I promised her that I would be good and help her around the house, and not give them any trouble. So a pact was formed and we were both excited to be starting out with a clean slate.

When my father came home later that night I was so excited to see him and ran to greet him when he came through the door. He was happy to see me too and called me' his "beautiful, long-legged baby." His appearance had really changed since I last saw him at my eighth-grade graduation. His thick sandy-red hair had grown almost to his shoulders, and he was wearing corduroy pants and a madras shirt – which was the latest fad with the boys at school. I was once again reminded of his cool, artsy vibe and his dashing smile and good looks. *I was so in love with my father.*

I remember later that night we all sat down to a delicious Chow Mein dinner that Valora had prepared in my honor, since she remembered that it had been my favorite dish. We had a lot of catching up to do and sat there for hours laughing and telling stories to each other. My dad was a regular comedian! It was so much fun and I was so happy to be back home with my *real* family.

Since my bedroom was not yet ready, when it was time for us to go to sleep Valora made up a bed for me on the couch in the living room. After all the excitement of the day I had a hard time falling asleep and, along with the tossing and the turning, I did a lot of thinking and cried at the thought of Mamma Jo and Judy back at the Buckner house.

Lying there in the quiet of the night with everyone asleep, sharing the living room with the three lofty nude mannequin ladies looking down at me, I felt like somehow I had been transported back in time to when I was that little girl at the Driftwood Shack, who had finally come home to her daddy. I was both happy and sad and wondered what lay ahead.

~

The artist's lifestyle of my father's family there in Tucson was quite different from that at Mamma Jo's house. My dad would play music on his guitar at night on the porch, while friends and neighbors would gather around. During the day there was usually no one home as both my dad and Valora would be off working, and my brother Curtis would be with them or off with friends. At the age of sixteen, it was nice that summer of 1964 to have the whole house to myself and the freedom to come and go with no one looking over my shoulder. My first concentrated effort would be clearing and packing up all of my parents' stuff from my newly acquired bedroom and getting my room personalized and put together the way I wanted.

My bedroom was just to the left of the front door where you entered into the living room from the outside. The main problem with my room was that it provided the primary access to the *only bathroom in the house!* Every now and then someone would claim urgency for the need of the bathroom and suddenly come barging into my room unannounced. It was especially annoying when Valora did this. I was getting paranoid that perhaps it was just her way of snooping on me.

My room had two windows, one looking out to the front porch, which faced east and the other overlooking the side yard which faced south. While it wasn't the most private room in the house, it was the best room for natural light exposure, which I liked. The walls were made of thick rough cinder blocks which were painted a dark forest green. The floor was a cool black linoleum over cement. The room was furnished with a twin bed that was positioned into the corner, and next to that was a really cool white and gold vanity table with a couple of little drawers, three paneled mirrors and a matching stool. Valora said she found it for me when one of the neighbors was moving out and getting ready to throw it away. I loved it! On the other side of the room was an old chest of drawers that was leaning off to one side and you had to struggle to get the drawers in and out – but I thought everything was just perfect because the room was *all mine*! To finish off the room decorating, I placed a couple of my plastic horses on the dresser and put up a big promotional poster of the Beatles that I brought from Mamma Jo's house.

It took Valora only about ten days to show her true colors. Since I had not experienced her rants for a number of years and had not seen that kind of behavior coming from an adult lately, it completely took me by surprise when she exploded into a rage one Saturday morning. Because it was directed straight at me as if it were coming out of a fire hose, it was hard for me not to take it personally. In looking back at the scene, it must have had something to do with housekeeping as I remember standing there in the bathroom with the toilet brush in my hand feeling very threatened as she was literally screaming and flailing her arms at me. I was devastated and felt demeaned by her behavior and hurtful accusations. At first I tried to defend my position, but finally acquiesced and promised to do better, do more, do it right, or do whatever it took to just stop her from yelling at me. We somehow got through that first blowout, and later that night she came into my room to apologize. I accepted her apology, but the damage had been done, and I realized that it was what I might expect from her at any time again. My rekindled trust in her had been extinguished and now I didn't feel safe around her. I felt like I was walking through a mine field, waiting for the next bomb to go off – never knowing what would trigger another emotional explosion.

Years later as an adult I observed her erratic behavior and could tell that Valora was an extremely sensitive and insecure person who most likely had some kind of bipolar condition.

About a week after getting my room all put together

and trying to rekindle the bond again with my brother, I ventured out into the neighborhood looking for friends. The neighbor to our left was a single mother with two boys about seven and nine. Her name was Margie and she was a good friend of Valora. Curtis would often spend time over there with her boys when they were home. The big bonus there was that Margie had a *telephone* and we did not. She and I would eventually become great friends.

Our neighbors to the right were three college-aged girls and although I tended to be drawn to them as they were a lot of fun and there was always something going on at their house, Valora had warned me to stay away from them as they were too old for me to pal around with. I could see that my father was also drawn to them, as I would occasionally find him in their house, flirting with the girls. Of course this would infuriate Valora, especially since she was pregnant, and the rants would start again and we would hear all about it at night after my brother and I had *supposedly* gone to sleep. It was almost like old times again, trying to sleep with the pillow over my head.

During that first summer my father carved out the most beautiful wooden cradle for the new baby-to-be, due in September. I think during that time in my life I was so self-absorbed – getting acclimated to being back home with dad, missing everyone at Mamma Jo's, and anticipating the start of yet another new school – that I didn't pay much attention to the changes that Valora must have been going through with the pregnancy, both physically and emotionally. I'm sure that it could have also had something to do with her unpredictable behavior.

I did finally find a friend across the street, or so I thought. She was a girl about my age and would talk with me sometimes when she came home after summer school. It seemed quite apparent, however, that her parents did not approve of our friendship as they would always cut our talks short and would make her go inside. At one point she had to come to tell me that her parents didn't want me over at her house anymore as they disapproved of me and my family and didn't think I would be a good influence on her. We were both very sad and frustrated by this and I was angry at her parents about it.

Valora had a dirty old black Desoto that looked like a Mafia car. It was so full of junk that you couldn't even put your feet on the floor without stepping on stuff . . . not to mention finding a place to sit on the cluttered seats. I decided to clean it up for her one day, except that it took two days by the time I completed the task. She had stuff under the seats, on top of the seats, piled on the dash – piled up so high you couldn't even see out the back window. Heaven forbid if the police ever looked in the trunk! There were body parts from the mannequins everywhere! I had to separate old food and garbage from anything of possible value. When I finished up by washing the car for her, I felt a real sense of accomplishment and Valora was thrilled. She discovered things in the packed boxes that she thought were long gone.

One day when it seemed that everyone from the neighborhood was gone, and my dad and brother were away and Valora was off with a friend . . . I had a great idea! Valora had left her car at home and since she always left her keys in the car, I thought that maybe I would just sneak out there and try to drive it. No one would ever know. I remember I got in the car and turned it on and sat there with a devilish smile on my face. When I stepped on the gas and shifted like I had seen Valora do, the car just jerked forward down the street a short distance and stalled. There I sat with the car in the middle of the street; I was clueless as to what to do next. I didn't know how to drive it forward or put it in reverse or how I was going to get the car back home. What had I been thinking? Finally I went to a nearby house I knew belonged to an older retired couple who were always at home. I knocked on their door and was shaking by the time the old man came to the door. I shamefully told him about what I had done and asked if he could help me out. He smiled and calmly walked out to the car with me, started it up and drove the car back to the front curb of our house where it had been. I was so thankful to him and he said not to worry, that he wouldn't tell my parents. No one would ever be the wiser – it remained our little secret.

Valora was not known to be a great housekeeper, but she herself was always meticulously dressed. She had an artistic flare about her that people seemed to admire. I know I did. She had that knack of mixing and matching her outfits and color schemes to blend beautifully with her tan skin and gorgeous thick red hair. The Southwestern colors looked great on her. Whenever my dad and Valora would dress up to go out they always looked like a glamorous Hollywood couple right out of the movies.

My father's employment at Old Tucson had its advantages. We occasionally got to meet some very interesting and famous people. Bob Shelton was now my father's boss at the Old Tucson Studios and he was also a Hollywood producer. I was at his house one Sunday with my family – it was a big sprawling hacienda, probably the most beautiful house I had ever seen. And I remember there were several of the latest models of cars parked out front. The part of the house that impressed me the most was the den – which had wall-to-wall framed photographs of Bob with every imaginable Hollywood star, past and present. I was so impressed.

One time my father and Valora got all dressed up and went to a big party at Bob Shelton's house. Unfortunately on this particular night I wasn't allowed to go to the party along with them. I remember Valora was so excited because she heard that Sean Connery was going to be there. He had just played Agent 007 in the movie "Goldfinger" earlier that year. Other Hollywood stars were supposed to be there as well. When they returned home late that night Valora was all giddy, tipsy and excited because she said not only had she *seen* Sean Connery, but he had actually *kissed* her on the cheek! She talked about it for weeks and wouldn't wash that part of her face for the longest time. She told everyone she knew, right down to the mailman at the front door about her glamorous night out on the town with Sean Connery.

Another famous person that we got to meet was Nino Cochise, the disputed grandson of the great Indian chief, Cochise, and a nephew of Geronimo. Nino, who was by then in his late 80s, had a house in Tucson and our family went there to visit him. He was still very active and was involved in many things at that time, including acting in Western movies. In fact, a few years later in 1967 at the age of 92, he would perform in the pilot episode of "The High Chaparral." He had visited Old Tucson from time to time on some business there and that's how he and my father had met. He was an interesting character and looked just like the Indians in the movies with his long hair and headband. He had a fascinating place with lots of old artifacts and unusual plants and we all walked around his gardens looking at everything. It was like a museum. I recall we were in his garden when he challenged me to a gun fight. He gave me an old western pistol and a holster (which always seemed to be handy in Tucson) and told me to walk over to the other side of the garden and, at the count of three, I was to draw my gun. I walked over and turned to face him with my feet firmly planted and my hand over my gun ready to draw. He stood likewise with his gun ready and we stared each other down as he started counting slowly while my parents and brother looked on from the sidelines: *one . . . two . . .* and then with a loud animated voice he said: *two-and-a-half!* Well, of course I drew my gun and pulled the trigger at *two-and-a-half*, not *three*. We all had a good laugh at that one. Thank goodness there weren't any bullets involved! Before we left his house, Nino gave Valora and me each a beautiful necklace of black and white beads. I wish I still had those today, but the necklace was not something a sixteen-year-old would usually wear and I gave mine to Valora to put away for safe keeping. With all the moves over the years, somehow both necklaces were lost. What a shame.

Catalina High

Once my sophomore year started I settled down to more serious matters. I remember my father driving me to school that first day. I made him park his old red pick-up truck down the street so no one would see me coming to school with my father. I don't know why he even bothered to take me since the school was only a few blocks away from our house. I think it was more for moral support, as here I was again starting another new school – *the tenth one I had attended at that point.*

Fitting in was always a problem for me and this school wasn't any different. I remember laboring for hours in the mornings in front of the mirror trying to make my hair look right. It would often make me late for school. And then gym class was usually the first class of the day and that sure didn't help my hairdo. I was good at sports, but I didn't like early morning cold weather and I hated having to go outside in those skimpy little one-size-fits-all, one-piece uniforms they made us wear.

One of the classes I took at Catalina High that year was Driver's Education. I remember the teacher telling us that at least three of us in the room would encounter some form of serious car accident in our lifetime. He then showed us classroom slides of really bad accident scenes. They would go something like this: "See that white mass there on the road? Well, that is his brain!" Stuff like that. It made me glad I never got the old Desoto off the cul-de-sac!

I remember there were certain girls in school that compelled you to stare at them because they were just so perfect and beautiful. This was the case with Jane Ward. She was blonde, tanned, beautiful, and popular and always dressed in the latest fashions. Throughout most of the school year I would stare at her and wish I could look like that. I started trying to imitate her with my walk and talk and dress and even ironed my hair to try to get her look. Well, true to our Driver's Ed teacher's forecast, wouldn't you know that it was beautiful Jane who would be the one who never came back to school: She was decapitated when the car in which she was riding slammed into a telephone pole and she went through the windshield. The kids had been drinking that night, and two people in the car were killed and one seriously injured. Miraculously the driver survived, but had to live with this horror for the rest of his life – and was never the same after that. I can't imagine what kept him going. It was truly a sobering lesson for us all at Catalina High.

At home there was always something exciting going on – especially since my baby sister Star arrived on the scene. Even as a tiny baby, she was extraordinarily beautiful with ivory skin and thick red hair. People made a real fuss over her and she became a complete obsession for Valora. I tried to help Valora with her, but she made me feel like I was just in the way, and so I was happy to be somewhere else. Unfortunately, Star and I never really bonded then and we spent very little time together.

People liked to come over to our house and hang out on the front porch (just outside of my bedroom window) – sometimes with much talking, smoking and playing music into the wee hours of the night. And there was no one around like Mamma Jo and Judy to focus and stabilize me – to help with homework and hold me accountable for getting it done. So I was beginning to fall behind again. I just wasn't into academics anyway. Since my current grade level was higher than that reached by my Dad or Valora, they didn't understand my homework well enough to answer my questions. And it didn't help that I received such little encouragement. In fact, my father once said to me, "Why are you going to school anyway – you're just going to get pregnant and stay at home with the babies." As I continued falling further and further behind, I began to wonder if he might be right.

The Trouble with Boys . . .

My dad and Valora were quite popular. Older guys who were friends of my parents would often come over to the house to play music or cards, or just to have a drink. My father loved to show me off to his buddies, and the guys would flirt and give me a lot of attention. Of course I loved it. One of my dad's friends had a son a little older than me named Brian, and his dad brought him over to the house one night to meet me. I was embarrassed by it all and thought Brian seemed like a real dork although he was taller than me – which was rare to find a boy around my age that tall. My dad said it would be okay if we went out to the movies together sometime, though Valora objected because she said I was too young. Even though I wasn't interested in Brian, who nonetheless seemed smitten with me, I agreed to go out with him. After all, it was a *date* and at the age of sixteen I hadn't yet gone out alone with a boy – thanks to Mamma Jo's rule.

A few nights later Brian picked me up in his father's car, and off I went on my first date. I remember we went to a drive-in movie together, although I couldn't tell you what the movie was about. Fortunately, Brian was a perfect gentleman and kept his *hands* off of me, but he couldn't take his big puppy dog *eyes* off of me and kept telling me how beautiful I was. I found this to be unsettling to say the least. I didn't *feel* very beautiful and considered him a bit of a creep for staring at me. I couldn't wait to get home and get away from him. A few weeks later he came by the house to show me the fancy new car he got for his birthday. It was such a beautiful car that I almost reconsidered our relationship, but after we talked a while I sent him on his way . . . and that was the last I saw of Brian.

I always liked the bad boys. Something about them intrigued me and I seemed naturally drawn to them. One of the guys I still remember after all these years is Kevin. He drove a black Harley motorcycle and reminded me of James Dean. He was a little older and didn't go to high school anymore – I'm not sure if he graduated or dropped out. But I would see him hanging around the parking lot after school with some of my friends. He must have been interested in me too as he started stopping by my house once in a while in the afternoon when my parents weren't home. While he seemed to thrive on my attention, he was a bit shy and aloof, keeping a distance between us. I remember him telling me that I shouldn't get involved with him because he was "bad news." (Actually, that was *good news* for me because I liked "bad news.") We had a strange relationship – him often coming by, but yet keeping his distance. There was great sexual tension between us and I was dying for him to kiss me. But in those days it wasn't appropriate for the girls to make the first move – and he didn't take the initiative.

Then late one night after everyone was in bed asleep, I was awakened by a knock on my bedroom side window. When I opened it, there was Kevin on the other side of the screen – drunk as a skunk. He blurted out that he was in love with me and held out a beautiful ring for me to see. He pleaded with me to come away with him and get married *right then*! Wow, was I impressed – my first marriage proposal! While he stood there – outside the window – leaning to and fro and going on about how he really loved me and wanted us to go off and start a new life together . . . my father walked into my room. I'm not sure if he had overheard the conversation or was just awakened by all the commotion. Whatever it was, he told Kevin in no uncertain terms to "get lost" – that was strong language coming from my easy-going dad. My father's presence and behavior so startled Kevin that he stumbled off into the dark with my beautiful diamond engagement ring back in his pocket. I could hear his motorcycle start up like thunder in the night and – much to my surprise – that was the last I ever saw of Kevin. When I asked around school about him, one of his buddies said he had mysteriously moved out of town. Maybe it was for the best – but that wasn't how I felt at the time and I was really mad at my dad for barging in on the proposal. It's possible sometime later that Kevin came back for me after I had moved away. But if he did, I never heard about it.

As time progressed and I turned seventeen, I began to get more unruly. I became more independent of my parents who were busy caring for their two younger kids. So I became more occupied with my newly acquired friends. One of them – a girl named Lisa Travis, was a year younger than me, but in the same sophomore class. Lisa was a smart, cute brunette with big brown eyes. I looked up to her as a mentor as well as a friend and she was good for me because she seemed grounded. She took the time to sit and listen to me as I talked about my home life and sometimes she helped me with my homework. We soon became best friends. Lisa had a brother at home who was handicapped, so she didn't have much time to hang out with me after school because she needed to go home and help out her single, working mother. I'm not sure what had happened to her father, but he was never around. Her mother was very religious and strict and kept Lisa on a short leash. Still, Lisa was fun-loving and mischievous, and we always had a good time together. The boys liked Lisa too, and sometimes I would play second fiddle to her latest boyfriend. There were occasions when we would double-date, and a few times we ditched school together. It wasn't a regular practice – we would just take a class off occasionally and go to the park down the street from the school and sit and talk about the latest gossip or scandal going on at school. We would also talk about our latest boyfriends, and sometimes we would meet up with our friends and go to someone's house or out to the desert to drink beer, smoke cigarettes and make out – though I don't remember that happening very often. I do remember a couple of times we were caught by the truant officer and had to go to detention.

Whenever I had a date or if friends were coming over to the house, it was a *big* deal for me. First, I was extremely sensitive about the chaotic condition of our house and our old ratty, torn-up couch. Dad and Valora's art supplies were everywhere and papers were likely piled high and scattered on the dining room table. The mess didn't seem to bother them when *their* friends were coming over, but I would spend hours just straightening and cleaning the house in preparation for a visit from my friends. Valora would love it of course – that is as long as she could still find everything I had put away. If my friends ever came over unannounced, I would be *horrified* and quickly slip out of the house to meet with them on the front porch.

Then there was my dad. He was such a cool character that I sometimes had to compete with him for my friends' attention! He would engage them in the latest talk of art and music and movie stars, and I would have to practically *force* them to leave the house! Sometimes I think they would rather have stayed and hung out with my dad than have gone out with me.

Dating at that time in Tucson consisted mostly of

cruising down Speedway Boulevard to see who *else* was cruising down Speedway Boulevard. Or, we would go to the local drive-in diner where the waitress would come out to the car to take your order and then would place a tray at your car window with your food and drinks on it. (No they weren't on roller skates.) I also loved it when my friends and I were all together in someone's car riding down the street singing loudly to songs on the radio like "Do Wah Diddy Diddy" by Manfred Mann or The Righteous Brother's song "You've Lost That Loving Feeling," or Petula Clark's song "Downtown." Ah yes, those were the days.

Around this time, one of my parent's friends, Kirby, was one of the guys who would occasionally come around to our house for jam sessions at night. He was an attractive, gregarious and likable man always clowning around and getting everyone into the party spirit. Even though he was married, he was a big flirt and would relentlessly tease Valora and me when his wife wasn't around. Of course we were flattered and I think Valora may even have had a crush on him. I would sometimes babysit for Kirby and his wife who lived just a few miles away. They had two children aged two and six and I always enjoyed spending time with them. One night when Kirby was driving me to his house to babysit, he took a wrong turn. This startled me, but he told me to calm down and explained to me that he wanted to show me something really beautiful. We drove on through a residential area and then started up a hill and drove for what I thought was quite a while . . . all the time him talking away, engaging me in conversation probably so I wouldn't panic. We reached the top of the hill, and he drove out to a barren turnoff on the road, where he stopped the car. I was getting extremely nervous, but then, there below, *was* "something really beautiful" – *the* glittering lights of the city. We got out of the car and walked around and he pointed out some of the landmarks of the city beneath us.

Since it was a little cold he took off his jacket and put it over my shoulders, and in doing so he put his hand onto the small of my back and drew me to him and gave me a gentle kiss. Well, that was *embarrassing*! Well, at first anyway. I wasn't used to someone who knew how to kiss like *that* . . . and so it went from there. At the age of seventeen I hadn't "gone all the way" yet. The only experience I had so far was just making out – which involved only kissing and limited personal intimacy.

As Kirby helped me back into the car, I didn't quite know what to expect next – beyond the usual making out, so I let Kirby take the lead. This wasn't something I had expected that night – it was just that the timing was right. As things progressed my inexperienced response to his loving-making, and my naïve comments seemed to take Kirby by surprise. My dad had been parading me around like a sex kitten or something, and I think Kirby, understandably, got the wrong impression about me. When he realized I had not had sex with a man before, he acted really upset with himself – obviously shamed by his actions. He started to apologize to me over and over again. I remember I was embarrassed by him going on and on about it, and didn't want to make a big deal out of my lack of experience. He soon turned the subject to that of my parents, and his wife, *and the need for absolute secrecy*. He then drove me back down the hill and stopped to pick up a couple of cokes at the local convenience store where we sat outside in the dark car, discussing everything once more before he dropped me off at home.

I went straight into my room, feigning exhaustion from the bogus babysitting job. Once safe inside my room, I tried to make sense of all the mixed-up thoughts spinning around in my head. It had actually been adventurous, exciting, and pleasurable – a whole new experience. It seemed like everyone else in school was "doing it." But despite that, I soon started feeling ashamed of myself and angry with Kirby for taking advantage of me. I didn't know how I was going to keep this from my parents. My first time with a man and it had to be my *father's married friend*! The possibility of pregnancy didn't even enter my mind at the time – though I wondered if I might have been headed in the direction of my father's prophesy.

After that night Kirby stopped coming around our house – claiming work, family obligations and responsibilities. Given time to think about it, I was more confused than ever as to how I felt about the whole thing. Since he was the only person I could trust with my sexual experience and was no longer available, I wasn't sure what to do with all the pent-up feelings of sexual anxiety I was having. I eventually became more interested in the pursuit of finding the "right boy" – which began distracting me even more from my studies. Since I was already a borderline student, that wasn't a good thing – though I did somehow manage to graduate from tenth grade.

~

After the school year was over, I got a part-time summer job at the local library, thanks to President Johnson's "Head Start" program – which was a vocational training program for disadvantaged youth. My job was putting away books and alphabetizing library subject cards. While it seemed simple enough, I learned a lot about books and language at that job. The library people were surprisingly patient and nice to me, and the work kept me out of trouble. Having a job was empowering – a great confidence builder. I felt proud of myself to be holding down a job for the first time in my life (other than babysitting, that is). I remember standing in my living room looking down at that first paycheck with the U.S. Government seal, and . . . *my* name on it. I was also happy to have some money to buy clothes and a new pair of shoes for the fall semester.

Shoes! Yes, shoes were still a big problem for me –
I had refused to wear my old saddle shoes anymore and my
feet were really a mess. I still had a terrible time with
infected ingrown toenails. And my feet were growing so
fast that the flats I had been wearing were too small for me,
so the condition continued to get worse. I was in constant
pain that followed me through the day and made me
irritable. But my parents didn't have insurance of any kind
and couldn't afford to take me to a doctor.

I expressed the problem with my feet a couple of
times to our next door neighbor, Margie, when I would go
over there to use her phone or to babysit for her boys. Her
latest boyfriend was a doctor, so she said she would talk
with him about my foot problem. Weeks later he called
and told Margie to bring me into his office at the end of the
day, after his staff had gone home, and he would take a
look at it. My parents consented and Margie and I arrived
at the doctor's office around seven o'clock in the evening.
He looked at my feet and thought that the big toenails
should be taken off altogether. For some reason, perhaps
by law or something, he couldn't give me a shot of
anything to deaden the pain. Instead, he went with the old-
fashioned route and gave me a couple of shots of whiskey
that he kept in his office. I managed to get that down, but
while it made me exceedingly drunk, it didn't kill the pain
enough for him to proceed to tear off my toenail – though
he attempted to a couple of times! Margie finally
convinced the doctor to abort the procedure, and he
bandaged up my toes which now were more swollen and
painful than ever.

Margie then tried to distract me from the pain of the
botched-up procedure by suggesting that she and I take a
cruise down Speedway Boulevard to get a coke. This was
enough to get me up off the doctor's table, and she helped
me hobble into the bathroom where I promptly *passed out
in her arms*. When I woke up I was on a cot in one of the

doctor's offices and he was leaning over me, looking into my face. My feet were throbbing and Margie was nowhere in sight. As far as I know, nothing unusual happened between the doctor and me – I just remember drifting back out of consciousness. Later when I woke up again alone in the room, I managed to hobble around, holding onto the walls until I could find the bathroom. Both my toes and my head were throbbing. I saw that Margie was asleep on the reception couch, covered with a blanket. I'm not sure where the doctor was. I just found my way back to the cot and eventually went back to sleep.

Later, in the wee hours of the morning, Margie woke me up and took me home – still very drunk and half asleep, and with very sore toes. I might add that to this day the toenails never grew back again looking normal. *I am still too sensitive about the appearance of my feet to wear open-toed shoes, even in the summer.*

Calamity Jane

In the summer of 1965, my dad got our whole family involved in performing with a local theater group in a Western melodrama called "Deadwood Dick." It was a real blast for all of us and it had a bonding effect on our family. In the play my father performed the part of the evil villain. He wore a dark wig over his red hair and had a black handlebar mustache and a cape. The audience got great pleasure out of booing him when he came out on stage. One of his lines was "Curses, foiled again!" Valora played the part of the virtuous damsel in distress. My brother Curtis was dressed up as a Chinese servant with a little cap covering his red hair and a long black braid hanging down his back. And me? Well, I got to play the role of (drum roll here) . . . Calamity Jane! This suited me quite well – I could channel my favorite character, Miss Kitty from the "Gunsmoke" series, along with a little dash of the John Wayne vibe to get it just right. Since it was a melodrama, I had to really exaggerate my actions to play the animated character of the rough and tough Calamity Jane. I still recall my favorite line was "I've got a feeling of foreboding . . . ."

On the weekends we would sometimes take our little theater group of about ten people out on the road. We would all pile into our cars and caravan to our destination, sometimes even staying overnight at a hotel. We performed at country clubs and theaters in small towns near Tucson – like Bixby, Arizona. With all the audience participation – booing the villain and cheering on the hero – it was great fun. I remember a few stories to tell of our adventures – like the time the actor to whom I was playing ad-libbed one of his parts and spit out a mouthful of his "whiskey" when I wasn't expecting it. I had to fight to contain myself from laughing out loud and breaking character. We really did have a lot of fun. I enjoyed it so much that once the school year started, I enrolled in the Drama class which proved very beneficial to me during that time of my life.

The drama department for Catalina High had a wonderful teacher, Miss Karen Kincaid – who was young and pretty and so enthusiastic about her job. She liked me, probably because she could sense the artist in me, and introduced me to the other students in her classes. I found that there were some fun, talented and creative students involved in the school theater program. Miss Kincaid also encouraged me to bring up my grades and do well in school so I could participate in the plays. She was a real inspiration. During the 1965-1966 school year I performed in a couple of the school plays and my picture even made the year book.

While I was doing better in school, overall I don't think I was a particularly good student. I had a short attention span for academics and went around most of the time with a bit of a chip on my shoulder. Like most teenagers I was trying to find my way as to who I was and what I stood for. I think this was particularly hard for me given my unstable upbringing. And things weren't the best at home either with what seemed like constant arguments with Valora. She was extremely jealous of the relationship between my father and me, and we could hardly be in the same room with each other without Valora starting an argument. I felt trapped at home and took refuge by going out drinking with my friends.

I even had a run-in with the law: One night a few of us – all underage – went to a party where alcohol was being served. But then there is more to the story: The party house was owned by one of our friend's parents and was on the market for sale. It was vacant except for a few pieces of furniture to stage it for showing. A group of about eight of us showed up late one night and were having a grand party there –drinking, dancing and making out – you know . . . the usual. Well, the neighbors must have called the police, because about an hour into our mischief-making there was a loud knock at the front door. Someone yelled "POLICE," and we all scattered and ran for the back door. But the police were swarming in from the back door too! We were busted. They lined us up and made us sit on the living room floor in our various stages of soberness and disarray. I have to admit it must have been quite a sight for the police officers – since it was a great challenge for some of us to just sit *up*, sit *still* and be attentive for the serious interrogation. After documenting our identities the officers piled us into police cars and to our surprise – took us home to our parents.

It was no fun riding home in the back seat of the police car that night. I got the nervous giggles – which got me a reprimand from the police officer driving the car, making matters worse and thoroughly upsetting the two others from the party who were riding in the back with me.

My dad and Valora were pretty shocked when they came to the front door and saw me standing there looking all disheveled, with a police officer at my side. I was humiliated – ashamed and angry with myself for the whole situation. I braced myself for the wrath of Valora while the policeman explained to her and my dad about some kind of court hearing that we had to show up for, and how we would be notified as to the date and time.

After he left, Valora started yelling something about me being a "bad seed" – saying "I told you so" – reminding my dad that she had said so long ago. Well, that didn't make me feel any better. I could see in my father's face that he was also upset. He wasn't one to rant and rave, but he told me that he was very disappointed in me – which was enough said, coming from him.

It was a month or so before my parents and I went to the hearing. The word had already gotten around to other kids at school that I had been busted, so that was really embarrassing. I was even more shocked and appalled when the judge told me that I would be on *probation* for a year! Worse yet, he said that I had to *stay overnight* at the Juvenile Hall – just to get a taste of what I was in for if I was brought into his court again. I couldn't believe my ears!

At "Juvie" I was first taken to meet with a youth counselor who talked to me about probation and what that meant. He told me that during the year of probation I couldn't see or talk to anyone I had been with at the party. This included my new boyfriend Michael, who I had been with at the party. That news didn't have a significant impact on me since I was already mad at him for taking me there in the first place. So, after meeting with the counselor I was taken into the Juvenile Hall and locked up – and I blamed it all on Michael.

That one night at Juvenile Hall made a big impression on me. I was pretty much an innocent in some ways, and had been forewarned by the counselor that some of the kids there had done some really bad things – like beat up their parents and things like that. He said to stay clear of them. I'm not sure if he was just trying to scare me . . . but it worked. Fortunately I had a room to myself. I recall that my room had a bed, a small sink and a little window in the door that I could see out of and into a community room where other kids like myself were sitting around long tables. I remember feeling really afraid that night, like a certified criminal of some sort. While I sat there on the bed and cried, I took a paperclip that I found and carved my initials into the thigh of my right leg – perhaps to punish myself. I was sure that everyone would find out about the juvenile hall incident and I would be further stigmatized. I thought that maybe my destiny in the world was to be seen as a tough girl. Maybe I was a true life Calamity Jane.

~

One late afternoon – several months following the Juvie episode – after Lisa and I had ditched school again together and I had gone home, I received an urgent phone call at our neighbor Margie's house. It was Lisa and she was in a panic. She said that she and her mother had a big argument about her ditching and her mother had called the police on her! Though she pleaded with me not to come, I told her I would be right over and took off down the road – to support my friend. Sure enough by the time I got there, the police car was parked in front of the house and Lisa was in the back seat! I walked up to the car and started talking with the policeman and ended up saying something really stupid like, "if you are going to take Lisa you might as well take me too." "Well," he said, "that could be arranged." Fortunately for me, instead of taking me to jail or Juvenile Hall, he took me back home. This was the second time I had arrived at our quiet little cul-de-sac in a police car –

only this time it was in broad daylight with all the neighbors around . . . another embarrassing moment for me and my parents – who were both home by then. They couldn't believe their eyes that there I was again at the front door with a policeman. You would think I was a real criminal or something.

The policeman talked with my parents about me ditching school and then proceeded to give me a lecture – in front of my parents – about getting in trouble while still being on probation and what that could mean, like me going back for an extended stay at the Juvenile Hall. After that he drove off in the car with Lisa still in the back seat. I imagine that he didn't arrest me because I was just a few weeks away from my eighteenth birthday – nearly an adult. Now I was really in trouble . . . again – and my parents had been openly shamed right in front of the neighbors. The consensus was that maybe I really *was* the "bad seed" that Valora had prophesized, and this "bad seed" was grounded indefinitely.

But my main concern after that was what was going to happen to my friend Lisa. After a lot of persistence I was able to extract from her mother that Lisa had ended up in some State juvenile detention center – and that I was *not* to try to contact her. This was devastating to me. I couldn't imagine why they would do that, since Lisa wasn't a bad person and didn't do anything really wrong . . . other than drink, smoke, hang out with boys and occasionally ditch school – *you know, the usual teenage stuff.* It was a sobering experience and I didn't want that to happen to me, so I tried to focus on my school work and my drama classes. Miss Kincaid was a big help. But there wasn't a day that would go by that I didn't think about Lisa. She was my best friend and had been a stabilizer for me. She was the one I told my hopes and dreams to, along with my intimate boyfriend experiences. Little did I know then that this police incident with Lisa would shortly lead to a great adventure and change both our lives forever.

In the meantime, Valora and I were just not getting along at all. Her jealously of me around my father just got worse, and as I neared adulthood there were times she would completely lose control and smack me. One day there was one too many of these occurrences. She had me on the bed hitting me and I rose forcefully up off the bed and pushed her back off me. Well, that struck fear into her heart – and became a defining moment in our relationship. When I stood up for myself and said *"Enough! I'm not taking this anymore,"* Valora realized that she no longer had control over me – which I think terrified her. When my dad came home later that night, he heard Valora's hysterical rendition of our "fight" – with her saying something like: "She hit me! I'm afraid of her and she can't live here anymore." My father was obviously at a loss as to what to do. So, ironically with me now age seventeen, he laid me over his knee and gave me a *spanking*! Well, that was it for me. I ran to my room, grabbed my purse and jacket, and took off out the front door. Once out the door and down the street I didn't know what I was going to do. Normally I would have called Lisa. It had become nighttime by then . . . I had no idea where to go or who to call . . . finally I called Kirby. After all he was an adult and he knew my parents – and I knew I could trust him not to say anything to anybody about me. He met me and drove me to a restaurant at the edge of town and we talked it all out. Kirby's adult voice of logic and reason said that I would soon be eighteen and needed to calm down and stay put to complete high school, so I could get a good job and support myself. I listened but didn't know how that was going to be possible given that I hadn't even finished my Junior year yet! How could I live with my parents through summer and another whole school year? But for the time being I just assented to Kirby's advice and kept quiet.

Kirby dropped me off close to home and I crept in

and went into my room. I didn't know until the next day at school that my father had found an old address book of mine and had called all of my friends trying to find me. That was particularly embarrassing because my friends were coming up to me and asking what had happened and where I had been the night before. What was I going to do, tell them I left home because my father had *spanked* me?!

Needless to say, from then on things were excruciatingly tense between Valora and me and we spent our days tiptoeing around one another – occasionally slamming doors, and mostly not speaking. With the combination of my history with the police and our little "fight," I felt truly viewed as a criminal element. My involvement with the drama department and Miss Kincaid's encouragement was the glue that held me together during those trying times. Summer was just around the corner and I knew that I would need to find a job to get me out of the house. But things continued to be tense. Even my sweet little brother Curtis and I had our run-ins and I can remember laying into him a few times. I knew I had overstayed my welcome at my dad's house and it was time once again for me to move on as soon as possible.

My "out" came a few months later when, late one afternoon in May of 1966, Margie came running over to say that I had an urgent phone call. I dashed over to her house and on the phone was one of my school friends, Cindy. She said that Lisa couldn't reach me so had called her to say that she and another girl had *escaped* from the State girl's home and were hiding out. Cindy said she would be right over to pick me up and drive me to Lisa. When Cindy got to my house I took off in her car with her without even waiting to get permission from Valora. Cindy and I rode over to Mark's apartment, one of Lisa's college boyfriends. After sneaking in the front door, I was almost knocked over by Lisa who gave me big hugs and kisses and told me how much she had missed being with me. Then she stopped and introduced me to her runaway inmate and co-conspirator, Susan McKendry. Susan, an adorable little sixteen-year-old curly-haired, blonde girl with big brown eyes was standing there looking terrified. I guess she thought when I first came in the door that the police had shown up. I remember wondering why anyone who looked so innocent would be in a State girl's home.

The five of us – Lisa, Susan, Cindy, Mark and I all sat down around the big, messy living room coffee table, drank some beer and worked out a plan for the next step. We concluded that Lisa and Susan were fugitives now and we had to figure out where we were going to hide them. Doubtless from the viewpoint of an accomplice harboring fugitives in his house, Mark suggested that there would be less of a chance of them being caught by the local police if they were to *leave town.* Then from there, the next thing we discussed was Lisa and Susan *leaving the state of Arizona altogether!* Of course we decided it made *perfect* sense that, because I was older and had more travel experience, I should go along with them. Besides, I sure didn't want to be left behind to stay around Tucson and Valora anymore anyway – even though I was only a few weeks away from completing my Junior year at Catalina.

So it was decided – and with a rather *generous* loan from Mark, the trust fund kid – that Lisa, Susan and I take a bus to California, and escape the law!

Later that night all giddy with excitement mixed with a tinge of fear, Cindy drove me back to my house to get my things. Upon arriving we were relieved to find that no one was at home. It occurred to me that the family was at a play rehearsal that night. So while Cindy waited outside in the car, I threw all my possessions into an old suitcase that I found in the back of my parent's closet. These valuables consisted of my clothes, both clean and dirty, my college friend's furry zip-out lining from his trench coat that I had promised to return to him, a plastic Palomino horse from my collection, and of course . . . all my toiletries and makeup. I quickly scribbled a note to my parents that said: *"I am leaving and never coming back"* . . . with a P.S. at the bottom that said: *"Don't try to find me!"* I taped this onto the TV set so that it wouldn't get lost in the chaos of the cluttered house.

Lisa, Susan and I all stayed at Mark's place that night. Between the anticipation of the next day's journey and the fear of being caught by the police at any second, we barely got any sleep. The first thing in the morning, thanks to Mark's (never reimbursed) loan, the three of us girls boarded a Greyhound bus which took us out of Tucson, through Phoenix and west on Highway 10 as far as Indio, California, a small town near Palm Springs – far from the Arizona border.

Part 3

California Dreaming

Escape

Lisa, Susan and I were so excited about running off to California together – it was a real live adventure. Everyone was listening to songs such as "California Dreamin" by the Mamas and Papas and "California Girls" by the Beach Boys; we knew that California was *the* place to be! After boarding the Greyhound bus and getting under way, we discussed what we would do in California. Maybe we would become movie stars or join a band or become surfer girls. Lisa especially wanted to go to Hollywood. We knew that whatever we did we had to head for the ocean first – that was where all the real action was, and Lisa and Susan had never seen an ocean. Having lived in the Navy town of Newport News, and also in St. Petersburg just down the street from the Gulf of Mexico, I had seen and loved beaches and the ocean and I was excited to share the experience with Lisa and Susan.

As we approached Indio, we started seeing palm trees everywhere – but no ocean. We saw fruit stands advertising dates and date shakes all along the highway. We didn't know what they were so thought we should try one while we were there – just to say we did. As soon as we got off the bus in Indio, we walked over to the fruit stand/restaurant next to the bus station for food – and a date shake. Mark had been generous with his loan and had given us enough money to last for a couple of weeks – until we could get ourselves situated and find jobs. In retrospect, I think he wanted to get us out of his hair . . . fast! But we knew we had to be careful with our spending and we made a pact not to buy anything but the essentials – like date shakes. As we slurped away and ate our lunch, we checked out the surroundings and decided that we really didn't want to end up there in Indio. All we could see was a glorified fruit stand/tourist trap with a shabby looking motel and a gas station – no place for three adventuresome teenage girls headed for the ocean.

In the 1960s it wasn't unusual to hitch-hike to get where you were going. We had seen hitch-hikers all along the highway on our way there and decided that this was the way to go to save money. After we stood out on the highway with our bags and suitcase, it didn't take long for people to pull up and offer to give us a ride. But we had decided at the beginning to be picky and only go with whom we felt safe. We also agreed that it would be fun to ride in a *cool fancy car.* At first we turned down a couple of drivers because they weren't going far enough for us – after all, we were headed for the ocean!

As it got later in the day, we thought maybe we shouldn't be so picky – but fortunately our plan finally paid off. The older man who we allowed to pick us up that day acted as if he couldn't believe his good luck when the three of us girls piled into his brand new red Ford Mustang. "Bob Johnson is my name and car sales is my game" he said merrily. Sure enough he was driving what he called "a brand new beauty" back to his car lot in Compton, a town that he said was somewhere near Los Angeles. That sounded pretty good to us – so at last we were off on the road again. We had a grand time joking around and singing along with the songs on the radio and teasing our new best friend Bob – because after all we felt that he had to have *some* fun for taking us all the way to Los Angeles. Bob, a heavyset, balding thirty-something, was a good sport about our noise, and after driving for a couple of hours we finally arrived at a residential college neighborhood in Compton. We were sure glad to get off of the packed, crazy freeway. The highways we knew around Tucson were nothing like what we had just experienced!

We pulled up to a hamburger stand and Bob was particularly generous – treating us all to a nice hot dinner. When we were through eating our burgers and fries, Bob took out his map and spread it out across the table to show us where we were and that if we continued South we would come to a town called Long Beach – there we would find the ocean. Wow, that was *just* what we were looking for . . . . a *long* beach! The excitement of the adventurous travel day had taken its toll and we were all very tired. We were happy to hear Bob suggest that we get a motel room and that he would pay for it. Lisa and I exchanged knowing glances and said *sure* that sounded great. Lisa and I were no dummies and we had out-foxed the foxes before, so we figured that this would be no different.

It was dark by the time we arrived at the motel. As Bob suggested, we girls laid down low on the floor of the car while Bob got out and went into the office to register for a room. We continued to huddle down as he got back in the car and drove up to the front door of the room. Bob then jumped out of the car and unlocked the motel room door and waited until everyone outside was gone and it was safe for us to go inside. He stood guard while the three of us quickly piled out of the car – one-by-one – bags and suitcase included and ran into the room. Lisa was the last one out and she rushed from the car. Then, much to Bob's surprise she quickly grabbed the keys out of the motel door and closed and locked it behind her – leaving Bob outside on the sidewalk in front of the room and us three girls inside. Up to that point Bob's luck had been going so well, I'm sure he couldn't understand what had just happened. He must have thought it was a mistake that the door was locked. He quietly tapped on the door (trying to be discreet of anyone who might pass by) and half-whispered "Hey girls! The door is locked, let me in." We were all on the other side of the room crouched down between the far wall and the bed wondering what would happen next. Being the smooth car salesman that he was, Bob made several attempts to talk himself into the room and even offered to drive us to the beach first thing in the morning. Time passed and more people started to check into the motel and it started to get busy outside. So Bob finally gave up and we heard him drive off.

We felt bad for Bob since he had been so generous to us, but then since he *was* a stranger, we didn't know what he might do to us if we let him inside. After he left the doorway, we became anxious that he might say something to the motel clerk or call the police. Considering the circumstances of hiding us, I guess he must have decided that it was best to just go away and leave us alone. On the one hand we were so happy to have a bed to sleep in that night, but then we were worried about the possibility of getting caught and turned over to the police. So, even though we were exhausted, we sat up most of the night talking. Lisa and Susan told me stories about the State Girl's Home. I learned that Susan and her friends were caught having stolen a car and got mixed up in an ugly scene at a liquor store. Wow, I thought, she sure had a lot of experience for a sixteen-year-old girl.

Since we were awake anyway we thought we would devise a strategy for going forward. The first thing we thought we needed to do was to change our names. After discussing this for a while, I settled on my new name: Kitty Martin. The name "Kitty" came from my adored heroine Miss Kitty from "Gunsmoke," and "Martin" because it was easy to remember – being the name of my college boyfriend from whom I had *borrowed* the trench coat zip-out lining. Lisa's new name was Ruth Summer, while Susan decided to stay with "Susan", but changed her last name to Miller which was simple to remember because it was the name of her favorite beer.

After selecting our aliases we agreed that from then on we would only call each other by our new California names. The only other plan detail that we decided was to head toward the ocean first thing in the morning, because we knew staying on at the motel was not an option. We figured that once we got to the ocean we could meet some cute surfer boys who would help us get jobs as house cleaners or waitresses or something until we got our bearings and could settle down together in some adorable little beach house somewhere. For three teenage girls from Tucson, that seemed like a logical, reasonable and well thought-out plan.

After sneaking out of our motel room in Compton the next morning – no sign of Bob – we were confronted with the challenge of getting to the LA freeways. We weren't very familiar with freeways, or for that matter, with the high density of the buildings that lined the streets leading to the freeway. We walked along carrying our bags and suitcase in hand and managed to find our way to the highway heading south toward Long Beach, just like Bob had shown us on the map. I'm sure there were signs posted everywhere that pedestrians were not allowed on the freeway – but I have to admit that we were probably *denser* than the local housing in the area.

We walked up the side of the on-ramp and stood there by the freeway with the cars whizzing by, thinking that we might die anytime soon – just from the noise alone. We weren't out there very long when a VW bus pulled up and slipped open its doors and we quickly hopped inside. It was an African American man with his two children. We were so grateful to him for getting us off the freeway – but he was spitting mad at us for being what he called "stupid white girls" and was saying things like "you don't have a brain in your head for walking on the freeway." We were taken aback as we were not particularly familiar with outspoken Black people in Tucson. As he drove on he eventually calmed down a bit, but only took us a short distance down the freeway before turning off and dropping us in a residential area. He showed us another route on the map to get to where we were going so that we could stay off the freeway.

Long Beach

With me carrying my suitcase and Lisa and Susan looking like little disheveled bag ladies with their meager sacks of belongings, we made our way through the residential streets of Compton – hoping to find the way to the ocean. We became very aware that people were watching us as we passed by and we were afraid that someone would report us to the police. There seemed to be nowhere we could hide or sit to rest, without people seemingly becoming curious and suspicious of us. I remember at times how we would just pick up and start running like a frightened pack of wild dogs, spooked by some phantom ghost. With my track training, I would often get way ahead of Lisa and Susan and would have to double back and find them again. Then we started to worry that we would get separated and lose one another, so we made an agreement that we would always stay within sight of one another.

When we finally got to the busy road recommended by our *freeway savior*, we once again took the risk of hitch-hiking, hoping to find a ride to what we referred to as the Long Beach Ocean. Things were different back then in 1966 – it was a more innocent time and people were not afraid to hitch-hike or to pick up hitch-hikers in those days.

Sure enough, shortly after we started waiting, a couple of college boys stopped to give us a ride. They seemed like nice, wholesome guys and the three of us piled into the back seat with all our stuff. At last, traveling with a couple of fun-loving guys who knew their way around, we left our fears behind us and felt like we were once again back on track for some carefree fun and adventure. After talking with Chris and Mike for a while and getting to know them better – we felt comfortable enough to tell them what we were all about. They seemed impressed that we had come so far and were happy to give us a lift to Long

Beach and the ocean shore, which they said wasn't very far away.

Once in the Long Beach city limits, they drove toward the ocean strip and we could see right away that this was where it was at! So many shops and surfers and cute guys and gals – *this was the California Dreamin' we had come to see!*

When we laid eyes on the ocean for the first time, all of us girls started screaming and squealing with delight, bouncing up and down in the back seat hugging and kissing one another. We had arrived in paradise! The guys must have thought we were crazy, but they got in on the fun and laughed and yelled right along with us. Before letting us off at the beach, the boys said they wanted to show us something – and somehow convinced us all to contain ourselves long enough to experience what was in those days, a cutting-edge, high-tech, drive-through hamburger stand. There was a giant clown kiosk that we drove up to and by some miracle the clown talked and took our order from a remote intercom system! We were amazed and thought that it was truly hilarious. We had never seen anything like it in Tucson. It was called "Jack in the Box." We sat there in the parking lot and ate in the car with the guys, thanking them for their generosity for driving us there and buying hamburgers. I'm not sure if it was because we were so hungry or because we were so happy and blissful to have arrived at our California destination, but we all agreed that those "Jack in the Box" hamburgers were the best we had *ever* eaten!

It was midafternoon when we arrived at the beachfront. We jumped out of the car and ran screaming down the beach toward the ocean, dropping our bags and suitcase as we went . . . laughing hysterically all the way. The few people still left on the beach looked at us as though we were either drunk or crazy. Off came the shoes and we ran for the water – which surprisingly turned out to be extremely cold! While it didn't seem to affect Lisa and Susan so much – they jumped around splashing themselves, screaming and laughing, their clothes and hair all wet – it was *way* too cold for my sensitive skin, so I stopped in my tracks and only entered up to my knees and danced around like a puppet on a string – sharing in the joy and the thrill of the moment. *It had to be one of the best days of my life!*

Chris and Mike stayed on the beach watching us for a while, laughing and cheering us on. They eventually waved, and bid us farewell. As they drove off with places to go and people to see, I waved back in earnest – but I remember as I lowered my arm and looked around I was overcome with the fear of not knowing anyone and being totally unfamiliar with where we were. What would happen to us next?

After spending some time being one with the Pacific Ocean and hanging out on the beach, we picked up our stuff and walked along the busy ocean-side streets, looking through the touristy gift shops. While we stood outside one of the stores admiring some bathing suits (which we hadn't brought on our trip), a well-dressed man about my father's age approached us and said that he would like to buy us all a bathing suit! Wow, that seemed very generous of him and, for about a second, we were excited about it . . . until he told us that the only payment he would require would be for us to *try on* the bathing suits . . . *in front of him.* Well, *eeewwww* . . . we knew there had to be a catch. No way!

We went on our way, blending in with all the beach people and the tourists. After more window shopping and exploring our immediate surroundings, we saw the sky starting to turn such amazing colors. We had to pause and watch the sun set over the Pacific Ocean. The sky became pink and yellow and then finally turned to a flaming array of red and orange. It looked as if it were on fire. We had seen outrageous sunsets in Arizona, but not over the ocean like this. It was a wondrous sight! We sat there on the steps of the boardwalk, leaning against each other – Lisa, Susan and I counting our blessings and thinking just how lucky we were to be there in California. We were truly living for the moment . . . no plans . . . no one to tell us what to do or when to do it . . . just experiencing life and all it had to offer, which at that moment felt pretty damn good.

The Pike

We were not oblivious to the huge roller coaster in the near distance, silhouetted against the glow of the setting sun. There were also lights coming on at what looked from where we sat, like a big amusement park up the beach. We started to make our way in that direction, meanwhile wandering into shops and flirting with the cute guys who seemed to be everywhere. We thought we had discovered a new America – the land of the free, the young, and the gorgeous! We weaved through the tourists and street vendors who shouted at us to come play their games – past the tattoo parlors and the fortune tellers and the bars and the restaurants. The closer we came to what we found out was called the Pike amusement zone – where the roller coaster lay waiting – the more we found handsome young sailors in uniform. It was almost like a parting of a White Sea, as we three flirty girls walked along, grinning – marveling at the attention, and flattered by the cat calls, compliments, and offers we received from the playful sailors. We surely were in Heaven.

We learned that "Cyclone Racer" was the name of the massive 85-foot high roller coaster, built in the 1930s. We had never seen anything like it. It was ominous and eerie, like a giant looming dragon made from twisted wood and iron – hovering over the dark Oceanside. There was certainly nothing like *that* in Tucson! We could hear screams coming from it and were drawn to it more out of curiosity than anything else.

At some point the three of us were encouraged to ride the Cyclone with a group of three sailors we had befriended. The only time I had ridden on a roller coaster was when I was five years old – at a kiddie park. I was leery about getting on this one, but Lisa and Susan wanted to go and I was being called a chicken – which convinced me that I had to suck it up and go. As my sailor friend and I got into the roller coaster car at the front of the train, I could see Lisa and her sailor getting in behind us way at the back of the train, several cars away. Susan was standing at the front of the line waiting with her new sailor friend for the next train to load.

There are no words to describe the fear I encountered on that ride. I must have been as white as the sailor's uniform beside me as we both screamed our heads off along the way. If I had had any idea that it would be so scary, I never would have gone. Part of the fear came from the deafening noise, but even more from the concern for structural failure of the rickety old wooden pilings and piers holding up the beast. The train went up the first steep incline and then dropped out of the sky, going what was advertised as 50 miles per hour . . . plummeting down, down, down. As we rocketed back up and rounded the towering curves jutting up into the night sky and then down and out over the ocean below – I was sure we were all going to run off the track *and die*!

After what seemed like a lifetime, we *finally* came to a grinding halt. As I got out on my shaking jelly legs, I could see one girl throwing up and people were even *crying* around me. It was quite a harrowing experience. While I tried to gather my wits, my sailor friend was hugging me, or more likely holding onto me, trying to regain his own equilibrium (and here he had seemed like such a big tough guy). Through the crowd I could see Lisa squatting down on the ground next to her sailor friend – way at the back alongside the last train car. So my sailor and I began making our way through the tight crowd to reach her.

Lisa and I and the two guys all huddled together – still laughing, and shaking from the ride while we waited for the next train to arrive with Susan. But when it got there, *she wasn't in it!* Lisa and I started to panic and searched the area shouting her name over the noise of the crowd. Then we thought that maybe she got on the next train, or had cold feet and decided not to go on the Cyclone after all and went on another ride. We waited for the next train and when there was still no Susan, we checked the bathrooms. She was nowhere to be found. We didn't know what else to do but to hang around and wait for her to find us.

Well, we waited there for what seemed like hours, thinking that she must have gone off someplace with her new sailor friend – who was also missing . . . although Lisa and I didn't think she would go off like that with a stranger. *We didn't know what to do.* We didn't want to report her disappearance to the police because we feared we would get ourselves arrested. So we ditched the sailors – who were no help – and stood at the entrance to the roller coaster where we had last seen her. But after several hours passed, the park started to close down and we noticed more and more police showing up. We thought it was best to leave before they focused any attention on us and why we were there so late.

We left the park in very gloomy spirits. Lisa especially felt responsible because she had promised Susan to take care of her when they escaped from the girl's home in Arizona. I felt responsible because I was the oldest and should have known better than to leave her alone with a complete stranger in the first place.

Now it was close to midnight. We headed back to the beach where we had been earlier, hoping that Susan would come there looking for us since the park had been closed. After a while, given that we were homeless, tired and hungry, we once again went against our better judgment and agreed to be taken to breakfast at a little all-night restaurant there close to the beach. The two sailors were tall, blonde, handsome Norwegians with thick accents and a shy, polite innocence about them which attracted us to them – much less threatening than the bold, loud and cocky Americans. After breakfast and being around these polite and good-natured guys for a while, we relaxed and felt a little better – though we were still worried sick about Susan. Now it was after midnight – we had waited a couple of hours around the beach where we thought Susan may look for us, but it didn't seem like she was coming back. We couldn't get back into the amusement park and it seemed she wasn't *anywhere* around the area. While we waited there with the Norwegians, during the course of conversation, one of them asked if we had ever been on a Navy ship. Lisa piped up and said she had never even *seen an ocean* before much less been on a Navy ship! Well, that caused some guffaws and next thing you know the guys were inviting us to tour their ship! We didn't think that was possible – that they would let girls come aboard a Navy ship, but the guys assured us that it *could* be done. Since they didn't seem to present a threat to us, we agreed to give it a try. After all, what options did we have anyway? Better to stay aboard a Navy ship protected by big strong guys than to walk the streets and likely get arrested . . . or worse. So Lisa and I got into a taxi with the sailors and headed to their ship.

When the taxi drove up onto the dock and we saw the massive ship, we couldn't *believe* that we could actually get to go aboard! Fortunately, it was in the middle of the night and no one was around. Still it took some doing – the sailors went aboard first, while we stayed in the taxi with the meter running. We were hoping they wouldn't just leave us there because we would have had trouble paying the taxi driver. The guys finally came back and paid the fare, and as the taxi drove off, we quietly boarded the ship. We were awed and afraid as they led us through the narrow metal corridors to a small cabin with two sets of bunk beds. Once we got into the room the guys were polite and nice to us. At first we sat on the beds and talked for a while – though we knew why they had taken the risk of bringing us there . . . so we kept talking.

We weren't in the room ten minutes when a naval officer came busting through the door and demanded that we *leave the ship immediately* before he called the police. We were then abruptly escorted off the ship and left standing alone out on the cold vacant docks. We seemed to be in the middle of nowhere. It was dark and foggy and not a person was in sight – not even a place to call a taxi! What on earth had we been thinking!

The Mob

We started walking along the docks until we finally came upon a night watchman station. The lights were on and there was a mean grumpy old guy inside. He couldn't believe his eyes when he saw us – and said he had absolutely no tolerance for a couple of "stupid" teenage girls in the middle of the night . . . *on his watch!* Not knowing what else to do – after his rejection of help – we just hung out sitting close to his station next to some smelly wooden crates, waiting for the light of day. At least we felt safer there close to him than roaming around the docks. After about an hour of seeing that we weren't going away, the watchman made a phone call. We figured it had to do with us because he kept looking over at us. We couldn't hear him and didn't know who he called. But we had pleaded with him not to call the police, so I guess he assumed that we were in some kind of trouble.

It was about 4 AM when a man in an old black car

drove right up to us. As he got out, he glanced over at the night watchman and nodded. Without even introducing himself, he just opened up the back door of the car, and told us to "get in." We looked over at the guard for reassurance and he motioned with a wave of his arm for us to go with him, so we did. I think we were so tired and cold by then that we had taken leave of our senses. We were speechless and just followed orders. The mystery man drove us to a dark little house in a suburban area of Long Beach, about 20 minutes from the docks. He shuffled us in with our bags and turned on the lights. No one was home. The house smelled like cigar smoke and was a bit of a mess. Once we were all inside, the man turned to leave. But before he left he said: "don't touch anything." This man of few words then added that we were only there to sleep and that the owner would be home later in the morning to "figure things out." We were such trusting souls, thinking it so nice that a perfect stranger would come to rescue us from the docks of Long Beach. As he walked out the door we thanked him for his kindness . . . though he didn't look very kind.

Lisa and I snuggled up on the couch together and fell asleep. We woke up several hours later to a bright and sunny new day. We felt more rested and positive about our chances. We thought perhaps the owner of the house would take us back to the Pike – in case Susan would come back looking for us. Meanwhile we made ourselves some toast and found fresh milk in the refrigerator. While eating breakfast and waiting for the owner to show up, we thought of ways that we could thank him. (We found out it was a "him" by the looks of the place and the clothes in the closet.) We decided in appreciation for him letting us stay there we would clean up his house. *Yes, this was after we were told not to touch anything.* We really got into it and scrubbed down the disgusting bathroom and cleaned the kitchen and everything.

As we were finishing up in the kitchen, we were

startled by two men who walked in the front door. They looked tired and dirty and rough – probably after working the graveyard shift all night. Lisa and I introduced ourselves, and were told that the older one, Rico, was the owner of the house. We thanked him profusely for his generosity, and told him that we had happily taken on the housecleaning chores. At first this seemed to infuriate him and his face got all red, but then his expression softened somewhat. Perhaps it could be that he was simply amused at how really stupid and naïve we really were. Well, it was true – we were so dense that the two men's sudden lunge toward us took us completely by surprise.

As I write this I find myself with pen shaking in hand and wondering how to proceed. I think it is best not to elaborate as to the terrible details of what followed next – but will pick up the story further into the day.

After that nightmare was over, Lisa and I eventually found each other in the quiet house. The men had gone. We hugged each other and huddled together – trembling, weeping and naked on the dirty orange carpet. I saw that Lisa had been beaten in the face and had a swollen eye and a bleeding busted lip. Her black mascara was running down her cheeks. My face was all puffy and red and my body was so sore I could hardly move. But between us we could count our blessings that we were still alive with no broken bones – *most of the damage done could not be seen.* We helped each other up, and limped and hobbled to the bathroom. We would need to find our clothes and escape, but we were still too shell-shocked and weak to move very fast.

While we were cleaning ourselves up in the bathroom the doorbell rang. Lisa and I gasped and looked at each other as if to say "Now what?" While we tried to ignore it, we wondered if it could be a neighbor or a delivery man – someone who could help us. Then the doorbell ringing stopped . . . and there was *pounding* on the door. I grabbed a robe hanging from the back of the bathroom door and made my way over to the vibrating door. I cracked it open to take a look who was there. I was instantly knocked aside as the door burst open and a wiry Hispanic man came barging into the house.

"Quick!" "Get dressed!" he said, "We have to go!" Lisa and I froze in place taking it all in – staring at him like he was crazy. Then he yelled "NOW! Your life is in danger!" We jumped and scrambled and got dressed as quickly as we could – trying to find our clothes scattered around the house. We rushed out the front door, not caring to look back at the house of horrors, and followed the man to his waiting unmarked white van. He had to actually assist us into the back of the empty vehicle as our legs did not have the strength to lift our bodies up and over the high door frame. Once we were inside, the man jumped into the driver's seat and sped off at top speed. Lisa and I laid down in the back seat holding hands and whispering to each other – asking ourselves why we should trust ourselves with *this* man, given what we had just gone through. After weaving in and out of traffic down the city streets, we merged into the middle of the slow crawling mass of cars on the freeway. There our driver finally seemed to calm down and relax a little. He then introduced himself to us as James. James Nunez. He told us that we had gotten ourselves mixed up with a rough group of mobsters – and that word had gotten out about us at the docks – and more dangerous men would be on their way to the house where we had stayed. As the story went on, we discovered that James had put himself in grave danger to rescue us from further harm. I guess he was our Knight in a white van.

Riding along in stunned silence for a while, taking it all in, we reached James' house. His wife stood waiting at the front door while we got out of the van. She must have known we were coming as she welcomed us warmly and sprang into action – running a hot bath and turning on a tea kettle on the stove. We could see that she had even made little cheese sandwiches for us. She told us her name was Teresa, and she even stayed in the little bathroom and held us as we shivered and cried – the hot bath finally washing away our emotional defenses. After the bath Teresa gave us some T-shirts and robes to wear while she set our clothes aside to wash them. They made up their own bed for us to lie down in, and closed the blinds to darken the room. Lisa and I were exhausted, and feeling safe with James and Teresa, we quickly fell asleep.

We stayed there at the Nunez house for two more days. We were quiet and somber – still grieving from our traumatic experience, and spent most of the time sleeping. James and Teresa had two children in grade school, and when we weren't sleeping on the couch, we ended up sleeping in the twin beds in their room after they went off to school. The modest little house was on a hillside overlooking the shipyards below and it was flooded with soothing natural light. We gladly embraced Teresa's warm hospitality and home as our healing, rehabilitation center.

While we felt like we could stay there forever, James and Teresa asked us after dinner the third night, where we would like to be dropped off the next morning. After a group discussion of our options and considering some of their suggestions (such as calling our parents to send us money to go back home), Lisa and I still chose to go back to the beach close to the Pike – in hopes of finding Susan. We didn't want to give up on her, even though it had now been three days since we had last seen her.

The next morning we had breakfast with the Nunez family and packed up our meager belongings. Lisa and I still looked like we had come from a battlefield – with scratches and bruises on our faces and bodies. But now we were strong enough to get back into the van without any help. While James waited in the driver's seat, we said our good-byes to Teresa and thanked her for all her wonderful support and generous hospitality. We felt that we owed our lives to the Nunez family and promised to keep in touch. James drove us back to the beach by the Pike, and dropped us off there by the Jack in the Box. After our good-byes with James we started to search the area to see if by any chance we might run into Susan.

In our rush to leave the "mobster house," we were now left with only the clothes on our backs. My suitcase with my palomino horse and all my other prized teenage possessions had been left behind in an alley in Compton – too heavy and conspicuous to carry around. We had at least managed to salvage our bulging purses – which carried what remained of our necessities for survival – makeup, tooth brushes, a few small souvenir items and what little money we had left. Somehow we expected that our Long Beach adventure could soon take us on a whole new, more promising path. And this time, we pledged, we would be making better decisions and watching our backs.

Night Out at the Movies

Lisa and I never found Susan. We searched the streets, and asked shopkeepers and vendors, but no one had remembered seeing her sweet face. We got the feeling that we were all just a blur of tourists with open wallets. Later that day, Lisa and I sat down on the soft sand of the beach and tried to figure out just what we should be doing – beyond looking for Susan, that is. We would soon run out of money and we had no idea where we were going to stay that night. Of course, we no longer felt like the happy-go-lucky, freedom girls we had been a few days before. In fact we were pretty depressed – given that we had lost Susan and we continued to worry about what had happened to her. Our bodies were still stiff and sore from the attack by the mob characters, and we were angry at ourselves for our foolishness, terrible choices and lack of experience that had been instrumental in creating this dismal moment. Reality had set in.

We thought maybe we could apply for a job as a waitress or shopkeeper, but then after we took out an application we found that we had no address or phone number for people to reach us. Besides, neither of us had our social security cards with us and we hadn't memorized our numbers. It was hopeless. We knew that we could always pick up guys to help us through this, but needless to say we didn't want *anything* to do with guys . . . and besides, if we were going to be independent of others, we had to figure this out for ourselves.

It was getting late and after sunset the streets started filling up with sailors and tourists out looking for a good time. But we were not in the mood for the games that came with a good time. While we may have been flirty and fun-loving a few nights before, now we had *had* it and just wanted to get away from the noise, crowds of people, and obnoxious men. Lisa noticed a line forming for a movie theater up the street, and we decided that we could buy tickets and sleep in the theater – it would be cheaper than a motel room. I can't remember the name of the movie that was playing that night – we were so tired and sore that we really didn't care. We just wanted a dark, quiet, and safe place with a soft seat so we could rest.

Lisa and I stood in line, paid for our tickets and streamed in with everyone else – finding a couple of seats near the back, as far away from other people as we could get. We sat down and found that the film was some boring war movie which was great to sleep to, so we settled in and eventually nodded off. It must have been about eleven o'clock when we woke up and the movie was still playing. I had to take a trip to the bathroom and we decided to go together – we weren't taking any chances leaving each other's side. As we got up from our seats, collected our things and walked out to the lobby, we took note of the two men sitting in the back row who also got up and started to follow us out. Lisa and I hurried into the ladies room so we wouldn't have to talk to them. We spent quite a bit of time in there washing up, changing clothes and repacking our vagabond purses. When we finally came out, the guys were still there. They were obviously waiting around for us because they came right up and greeted us – all smiley and flirty, wanting to know if they could take us somewhere for a drink. What was it with guys anyway? We just put our heads down and tried to ignore them, walking away and back to the theater seats. That's when they got serious and showed us their badges – *they were undercover police officers.*

The pleasantries were abruptly over and now they were down to business – demanding to see our IDs. Given that they had shown us evidence that they were police officers, we reluctantly groped around in our fully packed purses looking for them. When we presented our doctored and crumpled up identification cards, they took one look at them and said they would not accept them – that they would have to take us to police headquarters. This really upset us and we demanded what grounds they had to arrest us. They said that they were booking us on vagrancy charges and for being out after curfew. Curfew?! We didn't know anything about a curfew. I recall that it had something to do with age – if you were under the age of eighteen and not in the company of an adult, you couldn't be out in that area after a certain time. While I had just turned eighteen a couple of months earlier, Lisa was only seventeen. We figured we were lucky that we hadn't been arrested a few nights before – and wondered if maybe that was what had happened to Susan. If so, in some ways she had been luckier than we had been so far.

In retrospect I have to believe that this arrest was probably one of the best things that could have happened to us, though that's not what we thought at the time . . . and that's not the end of the story. . .

Who knows what the protocol was back in 1966 for undercover police officers to escort their prisoners around, but they did not cuff us. Instead they just took us firmly by the arm and walked us out into the busy, crowded street. We walked right alongside all the tourists and fun-seekers until we came to a busy intersection and waited there for the light to change. Then a bazaar combination of things happened. A loud group of sailors with probably too much to drink, came up behind us. They saw that these two guys were handling us rather roughly and started to make snide comments to the plain-clothed police officers. Of course Lisa and I played our part as the poor innocent victims – grimaces and angry faces – aiding the escalating situation that came next. There were verbal exchanges back and forth – the officers never telling the sailors who they were. Instead they said things like "Get lost Buddy" and "Mind your own business." Well, you can imagine what happened next . . . we ended up right in the middle of a street brawl!

While at first Lisa and I were knocked around in the scuffle, we eventually found ourselves tucked away in the crowds standing on the sidelines. We quickly ducked into a darkened storefront while the fight was underway. We crouched down whispering to ourselves, trying to figure out what to do next. Lisa said we should run away, but all I could picture from watching TV Westerns and detective stories, was being gunned down during our escape attempt – lying there bleeding and dying on the pavement in front of everyone. The other scenario I imagined was becoming a fugitive . . . then being arrested later with charges against us for resisting arrest – *in addition to starting a street brawl and getting the officers beat up!* Lisa was against staying put, but she stayed there with me anyway.

We hid in the storefront and watched as the back-up police cars arrived with their lights flashing and sirens blaring – cops jumping out of their cars with their billy clubs in hand, chasing down the sailors. We remained there observing the police arrest the sailors one-by-one and put them into the back of their cars. *Lisa and I had been completely forgotten! It would have been easy for us to escape through the crowds that gathered around to watch the free-for-all. Who knows how our lives would have unfolded if we had run like Lisa wanted us to do.*

Our undercover policemen friends, who now looked pretty messed up and pissed off, finally saw us standing there – *waiting to be arrested.* It looked like they were ready to punch us – but they seemed relieved to find us. This time we had the honor of getting handcuffed right then and there in front of all the tourist and onlookers, and then hauled away in the back of a police car headed for the Long Beach jail. *And what had we done wrong?*

No Going Back Home

Lisa and I rode to the police station together, but upon arrival we were separated right away. This gave me great anxiety. I was worried if I would ever see her again. I expected to see the sailors there – but they must have been admitted in a different area or were further into processing. I was just there alone with a no-nonsense, female police officer who asked me questions, finger-printed me, and did a strip-search – not necessarily in that order. After I was duly processed, she walked me down the hallway to a cell block. It was about three o'clock in the morning and as I walked between the cells holding my newly issued blanket and pillow and escorted by my armed female guard, I couldn't see or hear anyone else – though I knew Lisa and the sailors must be there somewhere. Good thing I didn't have to march past the sailors! I bet they were pissed. I learned early on in my childhood to disguise my stress and fear with humor, and I made snippy little joking comments to my jail keeper – like "I never pictured that when I marched down the aisle it would be with a woman carrying a gun!" While she ignored my comments and kept a stern, bull-dog face, I thought I detected a slight smile when I asked her for the breakfast menu as she was settling me into the cell . . . perhaps it was just my imagination.

Surely I must have been given the Queen's luxury chamber – I had my own toilet and small sink right there in the cell. Once the guard closed and locked the door and left, it took me about a minute to get my bearings, accept my fate – and *want out*! Even though it was well into the early morning hours, there was no way I could just lie down and fall asleep. I called out for Lisa just in case she happened to be in one of the cells nearby, but I didn't get an answer. *I must have been in the cell block alone.*

It was rather embarrassing to use the toilet knowing that someone could just walk up and see me at any time. I took my chances and when I was done, flushed the toilet. Right after that I could hear another toilet flush somewhere behind the cell wall. *So I guess I wasn't alone after all.* Giving it some more thought, I flushed the toilet again and heard the other toilet flush behind the wall. Ah, ha! Communication. I imagined it must be Lisa. For the third time I flushed the toilet to test if my theory was right. Sure enough the other toilet flushed again. Not surprisingly, this was about the time the guard came down the hall and reprimanded me and told me to get some sleep because *I would need it*. I wasn't sure why I would need it, but settled in with my scratchy grey wool blanket and tried – but was too fidgety to sleep. The bed squeaked every time I tossed and turned and the lights were still on, although dimly lit. Lying there I finally took to unraveling my blanket one strand at a time – my way of getting back at authority. This stitch therapy must have worked because I finally fell asleep.

The next morning I was awakened by the noise of my cell door opening. I was presented with a breakfast tray complete with eggs Benedict and a hot frothy latte – just what I ordered. (Well, actually it was cold sticky oatmeal with a banana and a carton of milk.)   At least I got breakfast in bed (where else was I going to eat it) . . . and what *service*, a uniformed waiter and everything! Who says life isn't good in jail? Just as I was getting ready to start flushing the toilet again to test out my communication system, the guard arrived with my clothing and told me to get dressed because I was going to go for a ride. Go for a ride to where? Were they taking me back to Tucson? She didn't answer.

After I dressed and left my cell and before saying goodbye to my newest home at the Long Beach jail, I was once again patted down and searched. Perhaps they were afraid I might take off with their designer silverware or their precious silk threads from that blanket I shredded last night. The good news was that as I was released into the hallway, there was Lisa standing under the illuminated EXIT sign. We weren't allowed to hug or anything – just in case. Just in case of what, I never quite understood. But we gave each other sympathetic nods. Lisa and I then got the first-class-platinum handcuff treatment and were shuffled out from our concrete walled prison and into the back of a large waiting station wagon-type vehicle. Once settled in, we asked the two officers in the front seat behind the thick wire screen where they were taking us. They said we were going to the Los Angeles County Juvenile Hall. We didn't know why they had to take us all the way up to Los Angeles, but we were happy to know that we would finally arrive in the city of our dreams – only under slightly different circumstances than we had envisioned.

We were at least allowed to sit next to each other on the ride up so we were able to speculate on the prospects of our future – despite the fact that the handcuffs irritated my boney wrists and the more I squirmed the tighter they got. When I complained, one of the policemen said that they were designed that way – and wouldn't do anything about it. As Lisa and I discussed our fate, we thought that most likely they would send us back to Tucson and we would have to serve time there. I would likely be charged with aiding and abetting a fugitive (that would be Lisa) and Lisa would probably have to go back to the State girls' home and serve out extended time there until she was at least eighteen, which was in about six months.

The Los Angeles County Juvenile Hall was nothing like Lisa and I could have ever imagined, even in our wildest dreams . . . or should I say nightmares. We both had had some tough times navigating our way through our troubled family lives and through the shifting sands of instability, but Lisa and I were really innocents compared to the people we saw there. Upon arrival the officers turned us over to the impersonal staff who blandly ushered us into a holding room with some of the meanest, roughest women I had ever seen on the planet. They were only what could be described as hardened street people – prostitutes, addicts, and some nasty people I didn't even want to get near – some of whom were obviously mentally unbalanced. And there we sat, two runaway girls from Tucson – once again *completely* out of our element. I had a bit of a fighting record, something I forgot to disclose earlier; plus I was a pretty big girl and most people wouldn't want to mess with me when I got *really* mad – however, I realized I was now *way* out of my league. I was more afraid for Lisa, who was 5'2" when she stood up tall, and worried what she might encounter in that tough environment. It is possible that the staff had similar thoughts because Lisa was called in first, after only a short wait amongst the "Thunder Dome" people. We squeezed hands and exchanged glances of love and support before she disappeared into the hallway behind the thick-windowed door. Meanwhile, I was left sitting there watching the Crazies and trying not to draw attention to myself.

152

It was one of the longest hours of my life, but I managed to stay out of serious trouble and the staff finally recued me only to bring me into a small room that looked like a doctor's office. Then they promptly put me down on a cold hard metal table to do a full cavity search – right in front of the three other people in the room. There was a brief questioning and health assessment that went along with that. They discovered during the exam that I had been raped and questioned me about it and wrote everything down in their file – so that now the whole world would know about it. After that horrifying exam I was ushered into another containment area where I showered, using some nasty smelling soap (I was told it was used to kill lice) and then dressed in their inmate clothing, which was too small for me – with the pants stopping two inches above my ankles. The whole experience so far was definitely an exercise in humility.

I waited for what seemed like centuries in yet another holding area, only this time it was in a more civilized environment. Then I was taken into a clerk's office and seated in front of her desk. She asked me questions about my family and what I was doing in Long Beach and a few more questions about my history – questions I had already been asked and answered a dozen times. After I gave her Margie's phone number in Tucson, she actually made the call to our neighbor who eventually got Valora on the line – the most humiliation for me now, almost worse than the cavity search. From the one-sided conversation I could see where this was headed . . . no money to send me home . . . verification that I was indeed eighteen. Valora got to be right about me – I was a criminal, at least to her. *So, now what?*

After hanging up the phone, and making some more notes to my file, the clerk, who really needed a nap, or lunch, or something by that time, looked up at me and told me that they would be releasing me from the Juvenile Hall.

What?! Releasing me to where? The clerk saw the shocked look on my face and could probably sense that I was about to completely freak out, so she sighed, rolled her eyes and added in a slow, mechanical voice that the County system would support me with room and board for a week, until I could find work and a place to stay. I sat in shock, contemplating that for a while as she made more calls to arrange for my release and transportation. When she was free and looked up at me, I asked her if I could say good-bye to my best friend, Lisa. She said "no, she is being processed." Well, it wasn't as if Lisa and I didn't know that this would happen at some point, but this was too soon and so abrupt and I really got upset. I could see that the clerk had seen and heard it all – and that my hissy-fit meant nothing to her. I was escorted out of her office by an officer and put in a hallway waiting area. All I could do was sit there and cry. I couldn't believe that I would not be able to see Lisa – who was in fact later sent back to the girl's home in Arizona.

I was picked up by a social worker who drove me in a van to a County building of some sort. We entered a large room with a mass of people walking about and sitting on fold-out chairs – sort of like the DMV. After waiting in line she handed the clerk some paperwork and checked us in. We both waited there for what seemed like hours until my name was called. I was given some paperwork and instructions and found out I was going to go stay at the Salvation Army shelter in downtown Los Angeles. The social worker and I headed there next.

Downtown Los Angeles . . . I had made it to the Big Time. Though it wasn't the same without Lisa . . . at least I was free!

Summer of '66 – Downtown Los Angeles

The County social worker dropped me off at the front door of the Salvation Army shelter on Sixth Street. It was an old building that had been dedicated in 1924 as "a safe and affordable place to shelter women." After I gave the pleasant, motherly-looking lady at the front desk my paperwork and was checked in, she had someone take over her desk and walked me up to my room on the third floor – also showing me the bathroom down the hall that I would share with other guests on that floor. While my room was small and old-fashioned, I remember that it had a familiar smell of old wood, like my nana's attic from long ago. This was comforting to me, given that this would be the first time I ever lived alone in a place of my own. I was relieved to find that it was clean and light. I had my very own dresser and a neatly made-up little twin bed with crisp white linens. To add to the ambiance of the space – through the flowing white curtains of the open window – I could hear the din of the city life from the street below, beckoning me to come and explore it at my first opportunity. Even though I felt comfortable and safe there in my room, I had to remind myself that my new home wouldn't last long and I would quickly need to look for more permanent housing elsewhere.

After the desk clerk handed me the room key and left, the first thing I did was to pour everything from my overstuffed purse, out onto the bed. After going through my few possessions piece-by-piece, I started putting things away in the dresser – because I could. While I didn't have much, it was my way of claiming the space as mine. I remember that the essentials were still there – brush, comb, lipstick, mascara and miscellaneous teenage girl's stuff like mementoes from the trip. I had also hung onto a folded-up newspaper article from Tucson showing a picture of Lisa and me at a "Sam the Sham and the Pharaohs" concert!

Now that I was alone in my room, I had time to think and tried to make some sense of all the events that had taken place during the last few days since I left Tucson. What a whirlwind it had been! Now here I was in the middle of downtown Los Angeles all by myself – not knowing a soul. It was crystal clear when the clerk at the Juvenile Hall talked with Valora that all bridges to my parents had been burned. *There was no going back.* It was now up to me to make it on my own here in California – there was no place else for me to go. This prospect got to be a little too scary and upsetting to think about. And after a while of agonizing about what the future might hold for me, I decided to go downstairs to the lobby and look around for someone I could talk to. After an hour or so of sitting on the overstuffed couch in the old vintage parlor – watching people come and go, I finally started up a conversation with a chatty young girl about my age. She told me her name was Diana and she had come to LA to see if she could be "discovered" as a movie star. She didn't look like my idea of a movie star, with her limp brown hair – although she resembled Twiggy, a popular, skinny British model I had seen on TV. Being around her made me a little nervous because she was very hyper and talked a lot with her hands, which made me want to duck for cover. She said she had been staying there at the hotel for a couple of weeks. We talked about the hotel and some of the people in it and about the immediate neighborhood places to go.

After going back to my room later that night, I thought that even though Diana wasn't a nurturing soul like Lisa, she was the only person I knew in LA, and it might be fun to get together with her again to take a tour of the neighborhood. The next morning however, after I took a shower in the hall bathroom, and came out a few minutes later to go back to my room, I saw Diana walking briskly down the hall, away from the direction of my room. I hurried to my room to see if she had been in there – cursing myself for not locking the door (we never locked our doors back home). When I checked my purse to see if anything was missing, I saw that all my cash was gone, as well as my favorite tube of hot-pink lipstick. I quickly got dressed and went downstairs to hunt her down. I caught up with Diana as she was leaving the lobby for the street and stopped her in her tracks and confronted her. She acted insulted and started a big scene, swearing up and down that it wasn't her and she didn't know what I was talking about. I insisted that she empty out her purse right then and there, on the spot in front of me. People were stopping to stare as I raised my voice, but I persisted and she finally emptied her purse – and there was my lipstick. I took my lipstick, and grabbed her wallet and took back my money as well. She knew not to mess with me again after that, and it was the end of any preconceived friendship we might have had. I could tell already that I would have to start watching out who I trusted in the big city.

Over the next few days I ventured out of the shelter during the day to explore my immediate neighborhood surroundings. On the first night that I went out on the streets by myself to see where the movie theater was, I was followed in a black car by a couple of men. It was about nine o'clock, and I was on a busy street with stores and lights and people all around so I couldn't understand why they would be following me so blatantly – I just kept on walking and ignored them. Then they yelled out from the car at me "Hey Honey, where ya going? Come over here." I just walked faster and closer to the store fronts. Finally they stopped their car alongside the street in front of me, got out and showed me their fricking badges! Geez, couldn't these people just leave me alone? They escorted me to the back seat of their car and started asking me questions. I realized after a moment or two that they thought I was a prostitute. Once I told them my story they finally let me go, but this was only after I spent 30 minutes in the back seat of their car, expecting them to arrest me. I was so shaken up by the experience that I just went straight back home to the Salvation Army shelter, and swore to never venture out alone at night again.

From my first morning of neighborhood exploration I had discovered a restaurant that I really liked just down the street from the shelter. While I can't remember its name, it was inside a big hotel called the Grand Hotel. I was able to get a pretty good-sized breakfast there with my daily food stipend. The people were friendly too and the décor was interesting. It had red vinyl booths, a black and white tiled floor, and big picture windows. I could sit there at the end of the counter and eat while watching all the interesting people walking by outside. There were interesting people inside as well and I immediately hit it off with one of the waitresses named Sherry and her crazy, cook husband, Hank – who was a big tease and would lean out from his kitchen every now and then and kid around with people at the counter. It seemed they had a regular customer following because I saw some of the same people there every day for breakfast.

After my third day of eating there, I mentioned to Sherry that I was going to need a job real soon and asked them if they knew of any jobs available within close proximity of the hotel. They said the Grand Hotel was getting ready to have a big NAACP convention and that they were looking for people to hire to help them out during that time. They suggested I talk with the restaurant manager when he got in later that day.

When the manager, Pete, arrived, Hank and Sherry introduced us and put in a good word for me. Pete and I had a good talk and I was honest with him about my situation – laying out for him the whole recount of the last week of my adventurous trip from Tucson. I couldn't help but get emotional when I told him that I didn't know a soul in town, had no clothes or money and could only stay at the

Salvation Army for a few more days before I would be out on the street. He was sympathetic and sincere and said that what they could do was to set me up with a room in the Grand Hotel and give me an advance on my pay – enough to buy a good pair of shoes, a black skirt and two white blouses for a work uniform. He said that Hank and Sherry could train me as a server. And of course, I would have to repay the advance out of my paychecks over time. I was thrilled, surprised and somewhat suspicious that he would trust me with a big advance like that – he didn't even know me and that was a big commitment to someone with police problems, like me. I had never had anyone do anything like that for me before. *Was there more to the story?* It turned out that his offer was in fact sincere and generous, with nothing requested in return. I saw it was just Pete's general nature to help out people who were down on their luck.

After making arrangements through Pete and procuring a room at the Grand Hotel, I quickly went back and checked out from the Salvation Army and then came right back and checked into my new room. It was even nicer than the room at the Salvation Army. It was on the fourth floor overlooking Grand Avenue. There was a double bed, a dresser, a desk and chair, and a sink in the room. There was no toilet – that was down at the end of the hall with the showers. I even had a fire escape right next to my room, which I thought was pretty cool. This was officially *the very first home of my own.* I was so excited that I even decided to call Valora to tell her about it and my new job. I was able to reach her and she said she was very happy for me, although she seemed surprised that I had found stable footing so soon.

Hank and Sherry who were about ten years older than me (in their late twenties) seemed very well-versed on the LA scene. They instantly became my new mentors, friends, and role models. Sherry took on the protective role of an older sister and showed me how to wait on tables and treat customers in a friendly and efficient way so that I was more likely to get a bigger tip. Hank, who I soon found out had a serious anger management problem, tried his best not to explode when I screwed up some of the food orders. My training started at the bare basics. For instance there was an elderly lady customer who called me over to tell me that there was a hair in her eggs. I looked down and sure enough there was a hair there (though not mine). I just reached down and picked it up and said "There, how's that?" When she complained, I took her plate to Hank in the kitchen and instead of being spitting mad at me like I thought he would be, he immediately stopped what he was doing and made her a new breakfast plate – explaining to me that I should *never* question a customer's complaint and never *ever* touch the food of a customer. He walked out the new plate of food to the customer and apologized to her himself. Eventually Hank and I and the other restaurant employees learned to work pretty well together – despite my blunders during those first couple of weeks while I was in training for the big, up-and-coming convention.

I would go out after work sometimes with Hank and Sherry and they would show me new places to go in the neighborhood – like the movie theater down the street and their favorite bar and restaurant hangouts. They also lived at the Grand Hotel, and I would go up to their room sometimes to play cards or board games and drink beer. As I got to know him better, I found Hank to be pretty "hard-core" and most people could probably tell by looking at him that he must have been on drugs. But I didn't know enough to question that sort of thing or to identify what it was he was on. Once when I was in their room I saw him take out a needle and stick it into the thigh of his leg. When I freaked out about it, Sherry told me not to worry, that he was a diabetic. I found out later from one of his friends that he was a heroin addict.

Hank and Sherry introduced me to one of their friends, Steven, who brought over a little bag of marijuana one night. Though I had never really gotten into it, I knew about marijuana because the college kids back in Tucson were into it. It was highly illegal at the time, but I remember trying to smoke a shared, rolled-up joint there at the hotel with Steven, Hank and Sherry. The smoke seemed to burn the inside of my ears when I inhaled, and didn't have much of an effect on me for all the trouble and threat it presented. (The guys would get down on the floor and go through every inch of the carpeting to make sure that not a single tiny leaf or stem had dropped onto the floor.) I remember having some pretty good times with that group – my LA friends – they were fun-loving, yet protective of me, respecting my youth and innocence and didn't try to force anything on me.

I guess because people of color were coming to the hotel for the big NAACP convention, management decided to hire a few African-Americans onto the hotel and restaurant staff. One of the people they hired was a large-boned Black woman named Mike. Now that was very confusing to me . . . it was a *woman* and yet her name was Mike! I had never heard of a woman named Mike before – she even had Mike tattooed onto her arm! She was a real tough mamma – wouldn't take anything from anybody, but she seemed to have an immediate liking for me. I looked up to her because at only thirty-five she seemed to really be a woman of the world – and sure knew her way around a restaurant. She had that "Miss Kitty" tough-gal vibe going on, which I admired. I paid attention and learned a lot about being an efficient waitress around her.

One day, as was normal after our shift was over, Mike and I took our trays into the back room and sat there alone, eating our lunch together. I really liked her – she was funny and made me laugh. We were sitting there talking about hotel gossip or something and I started telling her about my new boyfriend, Steven – who I had started seeing lately. Out of the blue she says, "Have you ever tried "it" with a woman?" Well, I had no clue what she meant exactly by "it", but I didn't think I wanted to know. Then she explained that she had done some jail time and that women in jail who don't have men, learn to "do it" to each other. Well, I'm sure my face was as white as a sheet and my eyes as big as saucers. I told her that I would never like *that* sort of thing, and that *I preferred men.* She said "Well, how would you know if you haven't tried it?" She then said "Someday there will be a knock on your door and I'll be there . . . then I will show you how it's done." I was terrified.

Insulted and indignant at Mike's threat I gathered my lunch, picked up my tray and stood up to go. I looked down at her looking up at me with that big smirk on her face and I said, "I would scream!" She laughed at that and said in a seductive voice, "Honey, once I got hold of *you,* you'd never want to scream . . . unless it was screams of joy!" This terrified me even more – *to think that I might like it!* From then on I saw Mike as a big threat to me and started keeping my distance from her. She thought that was real funny and would get a kick out of teasing me at the restaurant when I took special efforts to stay out of her way.

Reverend Brown

When the NAACP meetings got underway at the hotel, one of our frequent customers in the restaurant was a minister named Reverend Brown. He was tall, dark (very) and handsome – a sophisticated Black man of about forty, with a kind, pearly-white smile. When he came in for his breakfast each morning we would talk a little. I had never had a casual conversation with a minister before. He was nice and respectful; sometimes he would even read me phrases from his sermon and ask for my opinion, which made me feel honored and also a bit perplexed – that my opinion would mean anything to him. He said he was going to be preaching his sermons at the chapel in the hotel for the next couple of weeks. I said I didn't know that the hotel had a chapel. He was surprised and said that the hotel was owned by a religious group called "The Wings of Healing." That was news to me, but as I thought about it, it began to make sense. The Reverend went on to say that their mission was primarily to assist those affected by substance abuse and addictive behavior by encouraging "holistic intervention" and treatment. In fact, he said the Ministry was designed to impact the whole person spiritually, socially, psychologically and economically while bringing about healing and deliverance through Christ. (I wondered if the Wings of Healing knew that the cook in their kitchen was a heroin addict.)

After about three consecutive days of restaurant visits, the Reverend told me that he was getting behind in his work and needed to hire someone part-time to assist him with taking notes and organizing his paperwork and business while he was in town. I replied that I didn't know of anyone and that I sure didn't have those skills, although I had worked at a library last summer – a year ago. Well, upon hearing that, he convinced me that I was just perfect and *definitely* qualified for the job. He said it would be a great experience for me and provide me with some extra spending money – the hourly wage being more than I was making at the restaurant. I certainly could use the extra money so we scheduled a late afternoon meeting at one of the small hotel conference rooms upstairs.

When I arrived at the room the next day, Reverend Brown had a whole box full of papers emptied out on the conference table and was in the process of separating them into piles. He explained what was needed and we worked together sorting out the paperwork and making files. After

163

we were done with that, he had me make notes of some ideas he had for a future sermon. I was pretty embarrassed that my spelling wasn't very good, but he assured me that he just needed to conceptualize his thoughts and get them down in writing and that spelling really didn't matter – he would have his secretary type them out when he got back home in Oakland. After about three hours of work, the Reverend said that he had to take some of the files we had made to a man in another part of the city and would I like to drive over there with him – and then get some dinner. I was thrilled to be able to get into a car again and get away from the congested downtown area . . . so of course I agreed.

As we walked out of the conference room, down the hotel stairs and out through the lobby together, I saw some of the regular staff and residents staring at us. I could see from the expression on their faces that they did not approve that I was with a Black man – even if he was dignified and obviously a minister, given his dress and collar. I figured I would have to explain myself to them later.

Reverend Brown and I retrieved his car from the underground parking structure and took off for parts unknown. Once in the car and away from the hotel, he seemed to shed all pretenses and became very talkative and relaxed, turning his interest on me. I too felt happy and carefree just to get away and back into the real world again – another little adventure. On the way we listened to the radio and talked a lot about music, my favorite topic. He laughed when I told him that my new favorite song was Lovin' Spoonful's "Summer in the City," because I had recently started using the nickname Kitty at work and part of the lyrics to the song went: "cool town evening in the city, dressing so fine and looking so pretty, cool cat looking for a *kitty*, gonna look in every corner of the city." I explained that it seemed like the song had been written for me – living there in the summertime in downtown Los Angeles.

After we drove for a while I could tell that we were entering a neighborhood that was really run down and as I looked around I could see mostly Black people milling about – the district was called Watts. I was starting to feel really uncomfortable in my surroundings and slumped down lower in the seat, hoping they wouldn't notice me. Reverend Brown told me not to worry, that we would just stop in for a quick chat with his friend and be on our way to dinner elsewhere.

When we arrived at his friend's house, the man's reaction upon seeing me was one of alarm – he seemed very uneasy with me there at his house. Once inside I soon realized that Reverend Brown had not come to drop off files, but instead to pick up a bag of marijuana! Before we left, he and his friend tested the merchandise. I was offered some, but declined and was given a Coke instead. The conversation turned to me and what I was doing there, and the Reverend explained that I was his "new assistant" – (although I had only worked for him for three hours)! It was obvious from his friend's behavior and conversation with the Reverend, that he didn't want me there or to be *seen* there. So we promptly left after the Reverend finished his joint and completed the exchange.

Once back in the car, Reverend Brown was feeling pretty good and looking forward to a big meal. I, on the other hand, felt sort of disillusioned that I had just been part of a drug deal, in the middle of Watts . . . *with a preacher*. I realized I could have even been hurt, given the violent riots that had taken place just a year ago. Mike, the waitress, had told me all about that. Even though I was hungry and had been looking forward to a nice dinner and conversation, I told him now that I just wanted to get back home where I felt safe and sound. So instead of dinner, he ended up dropping me off down the street from my hotel and driving off to his restaurant in the sky. The thought that a holy man would be smoking pot was enough to blow my mind – without any assistance of drugs! At that point I didn't think I wanted his job anymore. He wasn't what I expected. Now, I just needed to figure out how I was going to get paid.

The next morning there was Reverend Brown in our restaurant ordering his breakfast. He appeared all prim and proper and acted like nothing had happened the night before. After I delivered his food, he mentioned to me that he would be preaching a sermon that night at the hotel chapel and wanted me to come to hear it. I have to admit I was curious. I wasn't a very religious person, though I did pray a lot and believed in God and Jesus. By the age of eighteen I had been to all kinds of churches – Baptist, Methodist, Unity. I was never settled in a place long enough to attend one church or to practice any one particular religion for very long. Nevertheless I had heard enough over time to be concerned that I might be a sinner and I would probably burn in Hell. But my curiosity got the better of me. I did want to hear Reverend Brown preach and I was intrigued about the chapel in the hotel. And perhaps I could use some inspiration from time to time. I assured him that I didn't *need saving*, but because I didn't have anything else to do, I would go along to check out the chapel and to hear him preach.

So, that night I met Reverend Brown at the chapel and he suggested I make my way down near the front. The room didn't really look much like a church, but there was some evidence that people came there to worship. There was a raised platform set up like a stage, with a podium surrounded by pots of flowers. There were bible-scene paintings hanging on the dark paneled walls, and a big picture of Christ the Lord bleeding in agony on the cross at the front of the room. *I was already uncomfortable.* I sat down next to a pale, white-haired elderly woman who seemed very nice, but who made me more uneasy by whispering questions in my ear: who was I, where did I live, where was I from, and who were my parents . . . it was enough to drive me crazy because these were not easy questions for me to answer right on the spot.

As the room started filling up mostly with older folks and people of color, it shouldn't have surprised me that the preacher who came up to start the services also was a Black man. Like Reverend Brown, who was seated by the side of the stage, he was tall and impressive – a powerful man with a big, powerful voice that made me jump when he started talking. I must have seemed scared because the lady next to me took my hand and held it tight in her gloved fingers. After the first prayer, the preacher asked if there was anyone new to the congregation and turned his gaze directly on me. People started looking at me, and the old lady who was holding my hand lifted my arm up to indicate a new guest. The preacher welcomed me, as he did a couple of other people in the back of the room.

My friend Reverend Brown was eventually introduced. He got up and started to preach his sermon. It began quietly at a slow pace, but then gradually increased in volume until he became wildly animated – crying out to the Lord. As his voice grew louder, people in the audience started chiming in – yelling out "Yes Lord!" and "Praise Jesus!" The old lady next to me was really getting into it and the next thing I knew she stood up and started talking in some foreign language (*I found out later that this was called speaking in tongues*). I just sat there looking up at her, not knowing what was happening – she seemed possessed, in a trance. The whole scene was freaking me out. Then the music started.

I had never seen such behavior in a church before. People were clapping, dancing, singing and calling out – the room was in complete chaos! But that wasn't the end of the story.   After Reverend Brown had warmed up the room, the first preacher took over again. He talked about sinners and people taking Christ as their savior. The more he talked the closer he got to me and his big voice got louder and louder. I was hoping he wouldn't notice me sitting there and I kept looking down, trying not to make eye contact. Pretty soon he was standing right over me and the next thing I knew he leaned over and pulled me up right off the chair! I was stunned! He was going on about Christ and sinners and sheep or something. I was too petrified to know just what he was saying – but I realized that I was being made into some kind of "sinner example" for the congregation.

Everyone's attention turned to me standing there and I looked over to Reverend Brown for help, but he had his eyes closed, his arms raised high, palms up – obviously communicating with Heaven on my behalf. Then with one strong arm around me and his big bear paw on my head, the preacher said a prayer for my salvation from the delivery of my sins. *He made it quite clear that I was a black sheep who had lost her way, possessed with evil and headed to the fires of Hell if everyone didn't fully participate in calling forth Jesus Christ to heal me from my "sinful ways."* I had begun to cry, and became quite hysterical; I wanted to run out of the room, but that wasn't an option! After it was finally over I remember dropping down into my seat, and the old lady next to me wrapped her arms around me and rocked me in her arms. I guess I had been exorcized. The show was over.

I remember barely making my way through the crowded room of people – everyone wanting to tell me how happy they were for me. Still on the verge of hysteria, I was a total wreck – now *really* looking the part of a Jezebel with my hair a mess and my makeup smeared all over my face. Even while making my way to the elevator to go up to my room, I couldn't escape attention from the people who crowded around me. I completely avoided Reverend Brown.

Finally alone in my room, I was able to let go of all my emotions and lay on my bed and cried. The whole ordeal had been totally traumatizing. I was angry with Reverend Brown for not helping me, and worst of all, I felt like a sinner and a bad person. At least I knew that was the way these people had seen me . . . *as a truly bad person*! But I knew I had not done anything bad – stupid perhaps, and maybe I had made some poor decisions, but I was not a *bad person*. I guess if you consider adultery a sin, then I suppose I *had* sinned with Kirby, a married man . . . *so maybe I would burn in Hell after all.*

This experience had a lasting, lifetime effect on me. To this day, even when I make a conscious effort to emotionally prepare myself, I have a difficult time entering a church – even for weddings and funerals. When I do go in, I make sure to sit in an aisle seat so I can quickly leave if I become emotionally overwhelmed. I especially get anxious when people sing in church and will often cry – or have to leave.

One time I embarrassed myself with a business client who invited me to their church. Even though I arrived before the service had started, I couldn't get myself through the church door and into the sanctuary where my client was waiting. I walked around the church and talked myself into it being okay for me to go inside, but every time I entered the doors and started to walk down the aisle I would experience such high anxiety that I would have to turn around and leave. At last I was finally determined to go in and to join him, sit it out and try to take control of my emotions. But in doing so, I silently wept throughout the entire service. Afterwards, instead of going out to brunch with my client as planned, I had to go home and curl up in bed!

~

After my experience in the hotel chapel I called in sick the next day. I surely didn't want to run into Reverend Brown and have to serve him his breakfast. I knew I would have to talk to him at some point if I wanted to get paid for my three hours of file work. I cursed myself for needing the money . . . and now I had to call in sick – he should pay me for the lost wages too, given that it was all his fault. Later that day in my room as I lay still partly hysterical in my bed, I got a call. Sure enough it was Reverend Brown. He said he missed me at the restaurant that morning and asked me how I was feeling. I told him I felt like crap and that he was to blame – that the whole church thing was probably just a big set-up conspired by him and the other preacher. His reply was that "it had all just happened in God's way." This infuriated me and I slammed down the phone. I continued to spend the rest of the day in my room feeling sorry for my big-sinner self.

The next morning when I went back to work, Reverend Brown was not there for breakfast. I was glad I didn't have to confront him, but was worried he would leave town without paying me the whopping $20 he had promised. That was a lot of money to me! Then, to make matters worse, Mike, my annoying waitress buddy, announced that she had just moved into the Grand Hotel and had a room *just up the hall from me*! She seemed to find the shocked look on my face amusing and took every opportunity during our shift to tease me . . . "You better watch out . . . there's gonna be a knock on your door. . ." Just what I needed.

A couple of days later I ran into Reverend Brown in the lobby of the hotel. He was kind, given that I had slammed the phone down on him. He mentioned that he still owed me the $20. I was relieved that he remembered. He said he would have the money for me later that day and would be in touch. Well, I didn't hear from the Reverend all day – that is until about nine o'clock that night when he called my room. It was a rare occasion that I would even be home at night and not out partying with Steven or Hank and Sherry – but I was still recuperating from the church experience.

Reverend Brown said he would be leaving for Oakland in the morning and would I please come up and get the money from his room. Warning bells went off with that and I told him he could just leave it in an envelope with Howard at the front desk in the morning. He said he would like me to come up so he could talk to me . . . and say goodbye. Well, it was against my better judgment, but I agreed. What could go wrong? After all he was a minister. I arrived at his door and gently knocked, not wanting anyone else to know I was there. He called for me to enter and once inside I saw that he was sitting up in the bed, underneath the covers - wearing a T-shirt. I thought that this was an inappropriate manner in which to receive a guest and I just stood by the closed door and didn't approach him – ready to bolt out of the room if necessary.

He was very calm and quiet and remained sitting there in bed with a book in his lap. He started in by saying that he just wanted to thank me – that it had been a pleasure to meet me during his stay, and he hoped I would stay in touch with him. He went on to say that our meeting there at the hotel restaurant was God's way of helping to put me back on track. He wanted me to promise him that I would look into further developing my secretarial skills which I could later transfer somewhere else, allowing me to get out of my current environment. He said that otherwise he feared that, under the influence of my local friends and associates, I could be hurt or eventually led down a dark path of evil – one of prostitution, drugs and crime. I appreciated his concern and told him so, but I still stood close to the door, concerned that he may have other intentions. After his precautionary lecture, he saw that I wasn't going to approach him and the Reverend motioned to an envelope on the bed stand. I felt a bit leery getting any closer and hesitated. He looked over at me as I stood there and we locked eyes in silence for a while. Perhaps it was just my imagination, but I thought he had just passed on the baton to me to decide what direction this meeting was going.

As I slowly approached the bed table, I could see that he realized that all I wanted was the money. This forced him to have to come right out and ask me if I would like to stay. I froze in my tracks, wondering if he was expecting me to have sex with him before he would give me the money. I was still mad at him and this made me even more furious. I quickly lunged forward, grabbed the envelope and retreated back to my position by the door. With that he sighed, took off his glasses, put his book on the side table and scooted himself down deeper into the covers – reaching over to turn off the light. As the lights went off I heard him say: "Well, I guess this is goodnight and goodbye then." Standing in the darkness by the door I said: "Goodnight. Goodbye . . . and thank you." I thought it was a sad conclusion to our brief acquaintance. I opened the door, peeking out both ways before quietly sneaking out of the room and down the hall.

Returning to my room, the first thing I did was check the envelope for the $20 – there it was. I was still feeling rather gloomy and was tempted to call Steven and have him come over to spend the night with me, or maybe go up to visit Hank and Sherry in their room and tell them what happened at the chapel and then with Reverend Brown. Rather than getting all worked up again, I talked myself into retiring for a good night's sleep before my early breakfast shift.

After changing into my robe and slippers, I collected my toiletries and made my way down to the end of the hall to go to the bathroom. As I stepped from the dimly lit hallway into the bright lights of the community bathroom, there stood Mike at the sink, washing her hands. "Well, looky what we have here. " she said. Not only did I dread seeing her there, I wondered why she just didn't use the Men's Room, after all. She started teasing me with her snide lesbian comments as I slowly made my way to one of the private toilet stalls. I was tired and grumpy by then and told her, in no uncertain terms, to fuck off. That got a good laugh out of her and after commenting that that was what she would like to do, to my relief, I heard her leave the room. I then felt safe enough to come out into the common area.

After washing up and brushing my teeth, I left the bright, stark bathroom and made my way back down the dim hallway headed for my room. Mike must have been waiting for me, because as I passed the door to her room, it swung open and there she was, standing there in a ratty maroon robe and a shower cap. She startled me and looked so menacing that I must have jumped a mile, finding myself plastered up against the wallpaper on the opposite side of the hall. "*Did you knock?*" she demanded. "No, I didn't knock." I said. Then she walked right up to me and confronted me head-on, hands on hips, staring me in the eyes and said, "Are you SURE you didn't knock?" I could see that she didn't have anything under her robe and there was a big red heart tattoo visible on her chest. By then I was getting really scared. She was a big woman and I had already experienced her mean side while on the job. I braced myself for the worst and I could feel my chin tremble and tears started forming in my eyes . . . "I didn't knock" I half whispered again. She stood there solidly assessing the situation. She could see I was terrified and would likely start squealing like a pig if she touched me – causing a big scene and waking up the place. She dropped her arms and took a step back. "Well if you're SURE you didn't knock." "I didn't knock" I said again, and with that quickly made my escape down the hall, back to my room – where I locked the door behind me.

OK, now I had *really* had it! I'd had it with *everything* – with Mike, with the Reverend, with the hotel, and with the Wings of Healing. It was time to move!

Moving on in La La Land

Unsettling moves seemed to be a recurring theme in my life. But being by nature a creature of habit, I really never liked the idea of moving too far away from familiar ground. So after I decided to move from the hotel, the next day I hit the streets in my waitress uniform in search of a new job. It was just as simple as that – after visiting several restaurants and talking with a few managers, I found an upbeat restaurant on the corner of Flower and 8th, just a few blocks from the Grand Hotel. They were hiring for the graveyard shift.

I hit it off right away with the manager and was hired on the spot to start work the following week. The only problem was that the job started at nine o'clock at night and ended in the wee hours of the morning. That meant that I would have to walk home alone in the middle of the night. But desperate for a change and confident that I could eventually prove myself and obtain an earlier shift – I took the job. Now I just needed to find a new place to live.

I was pretty pleased with myself that I had been able to pay off my debt for the advance for my uniform and hotel room to the Wings of Healing. I had made the restaurant manager, Pete, proud of me too. When I told him the news and explained to him why I felt I had to leave, he said he was sorry to see me go. He added that if I thought that I must move, I should check out the Figueroa Hotel because it was fairly close to my new job. Also he knew some people there and would put in a good word for me. So, within a week's time I had moved and started a new job. Of course, I didn't have much to move, but Steve, Hank and Sherry helped me with my things and threw a little house-warming party for me in my new room – presenting me with a Monopoly game as a gift – a reason for them to come visit.

The Figueroa Hotel, while only a little more expensive, was magnificent in many ways. It was an old Spanish-style hotel with a grand archway entrance, an elegant lobby with high ceilings, hanging Western chandeliers and Mexican tile floors and pillars. Best of all, it had a wonderful garden and pool in the back – it was then rare to find gardens and trees in downtown Los Angeles. I remember that I wished Valora could see me now . . . I was really living the high life in California.

Actually my room on the seventh floor wasn't anything too special, *except* that it had its own *bathroom – complete with a bathtub!* It was in this room that I experienced my first earthquake. I was lying in bed one night reading and the overhead ceiling light started swinging – which really freaked me out. I thought the place was haunted or something. I heard voices in the hallway, and when I jumped up and ran to see what was happening, I felt a swaying sensation. The people who had gathered in the hallway were talking about an "earthquake." It was a scary experience for me, but no one else seemed especially panicked. One of the male guests nonchalantly shrugged and told me that earthquakes happen in California all the time. With that I figured it must not be too threatening and so went back to my room. *But I'll never forget it!*

My new job was okay, but having to walk home alone in the middle of the night was really starting to worry me. Living in downtown LA in the 60s with its wild, drugged-out street characters was scary enough in the daytime, but venturing out in the wee hours of the morning was something else. The stores were all closed and homeless people gathered together mostly in storefronts and on the sidewalks, sleeping on rolled out cardboard beds with their shopping carts and wagons of worldly possessions close-by. I was relieved that by the time I got off work they were mostly all asleep because I had to step over and around them on my four-block trek home. One night, right across the street from where I was walking, I saw an elderly street woman get knocked down and robbed of her purse by some dark-clothed man. After that I would always bring a steak knife with me on those walks – not that I would know how to use it, but I did feel safer carrying it.

Life at the Figueroa Hotel wasn't too easy either. The people there weren't very friendly and there were a lot of rules – (like you weren't supposed to bring people up to your room – though I did anyway). It never really felt like home to me. But there was a swimming pool, so the first thing I did when I moved in was to go out and buy a bathing suit. Not just *any* old bathing suit, but a white-fringed bikini! I remembered a dancer on TV dancing the twist in a fringed dress and how cool I thought that was. I guess I was ready for action too . . . and action I got. The first time I ventured out to the pool, and not long after I had settled into a chaise lounge with my book, the pool attendant came over and told me that I had a phone call. I couldn't imagine who would be calling me, especially down at the pool. I went to the phone and it was some man calling from his hotel room overlooking the pool – he wanted me to come up to see him! When I said no, he even offered me money! Ironically, shortly after I hung up the phone, I thought I would do something a little daring for me (considering I was afraid of the water) so I jumped off the diving board into the water. Wouldn't you know, when I hit the water I lost the bottom half of my bathing suit! Fortunately, I was able to quickly retrieve it underwater and put it back on before anyone could tell . . . I think. Well, after that first outing to the pool, I didn't go out there much.

I thought one of my dreams had come true one day when I met a surfer boy who was temporarily staying at the hotel. We got into a lengthy conversation and he described his life of living on the beach. I got so excited that I suggested he take me to the beach with him sometime. He warned me that it wasn't all glamorous like the Beach Boys had described it in their songs. But he said, he loved to surf and had some really good friends that he liked to hang out with which made it all worthwhile. So, one day when I was off work, he granted me my wish and took me along with him to Santa Monica.

I was miserable. In fact, I would say that it was probably one of the worst days of my life! Imagine me there, standing out like a blazing beacon with my pale white skin and freckles, in my white fringed bikini. It was a tough crowd of tanned and hardened bodies – surfers, both men and women alike, all familiar with each other and they spent most of the day out in the water together. I certainly didn't fit into *that* crowd. The weather started out cold and I had to wrap up in a blanket. Then it got hot and windy and the gritty sand on my lotion-lathered skin was irritating. I sat around mostly by myself people-watching, annoyed and bored out of my mind. Even though I covered myself up with a hat and blanket, eventually I was cooked like a red lobster. It was obvious that being a *surfer girl* was not my calling. I could check that off my list of aspirations. It took me *days* to recover from that experience.

I was lonely in LA, so a few weeks later I managed to get involved with a smooth-talking new guy named Bobby Marshal, who was staying at the hotel with a couple of his friends. He somehow reminded me of Johnny Cash – a big tall man with a Tennessee accent. One night one of his friends, Ralph, came knocking at the door of my room.

When I opened the door and saw him standing there, I was immediately suspicious. But then Ralph said that Bobby was downstairs just outside the balcony fire escape across the hall and wanted to talk to me about going to a movie. I stepped out of my room and walked with Ralph onto the balcony and looked down. Sure enough there was Bobby standing down there on the lawn waving and yelling way up at me on the seventh floor. We yelled back and forth at the top of our lungs for a few minutes about getting together later to see a movie. Then when I turned around, Ralph was gone. I hurried back to my room and the door was ajar like I had left it, but Ralph was nowhere in sight. I looked in my purse and the few dollars I had were still there. Then, as I stood there feeling *something* was wrong, I thought to look under my mattress where I stashed all my cash savings. *Sure enough it was all gone! This was a disaster!* I had just been paid for the week and that money was to go to pay my rent. I rushed down to report it to the hotel clerk, and told him who the guys were and that they were staying right there at the hotel. The clerk told me that those guys had *checked out earlier that day.* He had the security guy look around for them, but they were nowhere in sight. Nothing ever came of it and to my knowledge the guys were never seen again. I didn't file a police report, given my record. I was able to get a loan from Hank and Sherry to hold me over until my next paycheck. Thank God for good friends. But this was still so unsettling and I felt more scared and lonely than ever.

However, I was now starting to really like my new workplace – it was a happening restaurant, although I never did get very close to the staff there. Fortunately for me though, as I'd hoped, I quickly worked myself into an afternoon shift, and no longer had to walk home alone at odd hours of the night. The café drew a lot of tourists, and one day a guy from my old high school in Tucson came in. I was so excited to see someone I knew!

And there were a few regular customers I was getting to know. One was a polite, attractive, dark-skinned man in his twenties, with a strong foreign accent. His name was Nasser and he said he was from "Persia." I had never met anyone from Persia nor did I know anything about Persia. He usually wore a suit and tie and seemed different from the other guys I had met. He lived, and worked as a desk clerk, at the YMCA just up the street. He said that he was only working there during the summer months because he was attending a junior college in a small town up north called Santa Maria. Although he was quiet and reserved around me, I grew to look forward to seeing him come in – partly because I could tell that he was happy to see me and would always come and sit in my station. Perhaps it had to do with my fair complexion – they say that opposites attract – I had always been attracted to dark-skinned men as well.

Opposites Attract

I'll never forget when Nasser and I went out for the first time. It was so different than anything I was used to. Even though he wasn't that much older than me, he came across as very strong, formal, worldly and mature – well beyond his 22 years. I'm sure his behavior ignited my desperate longing for a father figure – protection, security for my scary new life alone in the big city. He met me for that first date in the lobby of my hotel. I had never seen him outside of the café before this. When I stepped out of the elevator into the hotel lobby, I must have beamed from ear to ear. He looked so tall and handsome standing there in his nice suit. I wish I could remember what I was wearing that night, though at the time I'm sure I would not have considered it sophisticated enough for a date with this fine man. As we walked along the sidewalk to a nice restaurant close-by, I felt so secure. I could see that Nasser was used to being in charge and I was happy to fall under his control and watched in awe at how graciously he handled the maître d', the selection of our food, and our servers. He even knew how to pick out a good wine (even though I wasn't 21 yet). How long I had waited for someone like this . . . a real gentleman, to come into my life. He was like a prince in a fairy tale.

Although we may have been a little like characters in "My Fair Lady," Nasser and I found that we were quite compatible in many ways and started seeing more of each other after that evening together. In fact we became quickly attached, to the exclusion of everyone else – wanting nothing more than to be alone, together. After a few weeks, I was really happy and secure in the relationship and was anxious to introduce Nasser to my good friends, Hank and Sherry. (I had stopped seeing Stephen.) I finally arranged for all of us to go out to dinner one night after I got off work. We met at one of Hank and Sherry's favorite restaurants not too far from the Grand Hotel.

Well, I guess I don't have to tell you that it was a real disaster. As I sat there and observed the dynamics at the table, I could see that I had made a mistake bringing them together. There was such a difference between them. Hank came off as very crude and obnoxious in the presence of Nasser who was reserved and poised. It was awkward for all of us. Nasser just kept quiet and to himself most of the time, while the rest of us chatted nervously and caught up on the latest gossip of the Grand Hotel – talking over the silent noise of discomfort. After dinner, as Nasser walked me home, he seemed angry and started lecturing me. He said he couldn't believe that I would hang out with "people like that." He had somehow caught on right away that Hank may have been under the influence of drugs. This caused a big conflict for me as Hank and Sherry had been my saviors through tough times and they were my only real friends in the city. I argued that point with him, but didn't get very far as he explained to me where a relationship like that would end up – my becoming more like them – addicted to drugs.

Later that night in my room when things had calmed down a bit, the conversation was resumed. Nasser said that he was worried about what would become of me living in the city. I told him I had already heard that lecture before from Reverend Brown, but that I didn't feel I had a choice in the matter – *here I was*. We talked about where else I could and couldn't go (like home) and what I could do if I were to leave the city. One thing led to the next and soon he was talking about my going back with him to Santa Maria. He said it was just a little "cow town," but it would be a safer, friendlier environment for me to grow and prosper in; and that there was the college there where I could take night classes and finish my high school degree. No argument from me there. So as we talked on through the night we started developing a plan. Then during the next few weeks we both began preparing for our move to Santa Maria, and winding up our business in LA. It was so exciting - I just couldn't wait!

That last summer day in LA, I went around saying good-bye to everyone I thought was important to me there. Nasser's Persian friend, Reza, picked us up at my hotel and drove us to Santa Maria – where we stayed with him in his apartment for a couple of days until we could find a place of our own. Eventually we were able to rent a nice little one-bedroom, furnished apartment right across the street from Hancock College. After we had a chance to settle in, Nasser went back to college and I started working as a waitress at Denny's just a few blocks up the street. We didn't even need a car.

I found out that there was a large Persian community there in Santa Maria, and we would frequently have visitors come to our place for dinner. I was introduced to Persian food, which was so much different from the food

I was used to. I'm embarrassed to say that Nasser discovered the hard way that I didn't know how to cook. Cooking to me was basically frying or roasting a piece of meat or poultry, whipping up some potatoes and opening up a few cans of peas and corn. Nasser himself, along with a few of his friends, started teaching me some of the Persian recipes like *Baba Ganoush*, *Kebabs* and *Baghali Polo*. I started using saffron, turmeric, curry and dill – spices I was unacquainted with before. Over time I began to catch on.

~

After living together for a while it was obvious that Nasser and I were a good couple. We loved each other, and I wasn't about to go off anywhere on my own. I went back to school and got my high school certificate of completion – I was so proud. Money wasn't a big problem as we lived a simple life; I was working at Denny's, and Nasser received money from his parents. But at one point he felt that he should get a job, and started driving a taxi when he wasn't in school. This was great because not only did he make good tips, he was able to provide us with a set of wheels if we really needed them (though we had to pay a reduced fare). Eventually, between the two of us we were able to save up and purchase a used, red Volkswagen Bug. That was fortuitous because Nasser's job as a taxi driver soon came to an end when he led a taxi strike against the company for unfair business practices!

Still, life in Santa Maria with Nasser was good. We had fun together. We would go to a lake up north and go fishing – sometimes even renting a boat for the day. We also liked to go to a little place nearby called Oso Flaco where there were sand dunes and a small lake where we would fish for bass. One day Nasser surprised me and brought home a puppy. Our little dog "Buddy" was like a child to us and provided me with company when Nasser was away. Nasser's next job after the taxi fiasco was as a part-time appliance salesman at Montgomery Ward. He was so successful that he *quit school* and began working full-time. We moved to another larger and nicer apartment in Santa Maria – and on March 10, 1967 we were married. I wasn't even nineteen yet. We had talked on and off about getting married, but then one day Nasser just had it in his head that we were going to *do it*. We had our blood tests done and later that week went to the court house and were married right then and there in front of strangers. I remember during the ceremony I locked eyes with an older woman who stood in as a witness. I thought she looked down on us disapprovingly. I'm sure that, while it may have been prejudice, it could have also been because we hadn't dressed up for the ceremony. We had thought there was more paperwork involved, but once we got to the courthouse the clerk told us we could marry right then – so we just did it! We would joke for years how Nasser had been married in his *fishing jacket!*

It wasn't long after that when we received word that Nasser's parents had arrived in New York from Iran and were on their way to the West Coast. Nasser went into a panic – that was when I found out that he had not told them we were married.

I will never forget the night his parents arrived. His father was a head-strong, ruling figure; while his mother, who spoke very little English, seemed kind and gentle (she and I smiled a lot at each other). We all sat there in our living room until the wee hours of the morning. Every word spoken between them and Nasser was spoken in *Farsi,* except that occasionally they would look at me and briefly resume speaking English when they wanted me to speak. I could tell that they were talking about me . . . and I could see from his father's expression that it wasn't all good. It seemed that his parents must not have approved of Nasser marrying me and I'm sure they were really upset that Nasser had quit school. As the oldest son, they had counted on him to come back to Abadan, Iran to run the family shipping business. I started wondering if Nasser wanted to get married so suddenly because he knew they couldn't have a say if it was already done.

While I never knew what was being discussed between him and his parents, whatever it was didn't seem to ultimately change anything between Nasser and me. After several days the parents left – though not before trying to get me to come home to Iran with them. Suddenly Nasser's father had begun being nice to me. They made it sound so exciting and wonderful – we would be traveling through Spain, and they had a nice big home in Persia with servants to take care of me, etc. But Nasser would not have it. He later explained that they just wanted to get me there as bait to make him come home, and once I was there I might never be able to come back! I couldn't believe that those nice people would do that to me. But I trusted Nasser.

~

About a year after his parents left and things were returning to a normal routine, the unbelievable happened – I got the call from my father, who then put my long-lost mother on the line – after fourteen years of silence. It turned out that the reason my dad had found my mother after all those years was that he, Valora and Curtis had just moved from Tucson to Phoebus, Virginia – a small community close to where my father's family lived in Newport News. My mother also just happened to still live in Newport News and they met up again. Following that phone call with my mother (AKA Katharine Hepburn), Nasser and I didn't talk about anything else for days. And the decision was made that I should go to meet my mother and visit my family in Virginia.

The last two years of living on my own away from my dad and Valora seemed like decades. Now I had a secure life, was married to a good man who loved and took care of me, and I had even graduated from high school.

There was a new confidence and maturity about me. I was a new woman, and I was excited to let everyone "back home" see the new *me*.

While I may have felt like "a new woman," I had never been on a plane before and the flight to Virginia was weighing on my mind, especially since I was going there all by myself. Not only was I worried about the plane trip – this was to be a real homecoming! I was going to meet my mother and even see my beloved Nana, Aunt Elsie and Uncle Herbert. Of course my father and his family, and Valora and Curtis would be there as well. I was a nervous wreck. As far as I remember the long plane ride across country to Virginia was uneventful. However, I then had to hop onto a small commuter plane to fly to some dinky airport in the middle of nowhere – now *that* was pretty nerve-wracking. The airport was just outside Charlottesville, which was near Kent's Store, Virginia – close to my Aunt Elsie's farm where my Nana lived. That was my first destination. When I got off the plane with my big over-packed suitcases, I was surprised not to see more people waiting. More importantly, there didn't seem to be anyone waiting for me, and it flashed through my head that after flying clear across country, I might have landed at the wrong airport!

Then I heard the screaming . . . and a group of people were running my way. I didn't recognize any of them. "My Baby!" I heard someone scream and I could see this red-headed woman frantically running toward me, arms outstretched. It was quite a sight – she in her red patent leather high heels, hair flying – followed up behind by the saints and apostles and her weeping entourage. I was so overwhelmed by the sight that all I could do was stand there frozen to the spot until I was engulfed by the crowd.

Here was my mother! After all those years of wondering and longing and praying, I was staring right into the watery blue eyes of my mother.

As everyone froze in place looking on as she and I stood there wrapped around each other, hugging and crying, I heard a cry out from the lady next to us: *"But, I'm your Nana!"* she said. Oh my beloved Nana! It was almost too much to believe. After much more hugging, kissing and crying, I was introduced to my mother's new husband, Richard. He was there with camera in hand, although he seemed so overwhelmed by the emotional reunion *he hadn't taken a single picture!*

The first thing we did was to find a restaurant in the airport to go sit down. I especially remember this because before I found myself sitting at the table, everything was such a blur that I think I must have been ready to pass out. We were all so nervous and excited to see each other. The tension was broken and we all laughed hysterically when I dropped the tea bag in my cup of water – *with the paper wrapping still on it!*

And although I thought my mother, Helen, was beautiful, she really didn't look much like Katharine Hepburn.

Richard drove us out to Aunt Elsie's farm where Nana was living at the back of the property in a large trailer they had put up there for her and her second husband, John, who was confined to a wheelchair. Later that evening my mother, overwhelmed by the stress of our meeting, developed a debilitating migraine headache and had to be put to bed in a darkened bedroom of the trailer. I barely got to see her for the next two days which was really distressing. I had waited fourteen years and traveled so far and now she couldn't even talk with me. I had imagined a complete mother and daughter reunion, with long talks over tea. I did, however, get plenty of time to visit with my Nana and John, and Aunt Elsie and Uncle Herbert. I also had several conversations with my mother's husband, Richard. He was only *eight years older than me*, and a "career" military man stationed at Fort Monroe in Newport

News. He was kind and funny, always teasing everyone as we sat out on Nana's big screened-in porch, or out in the yard in a circle of chairs under the big oak tree. You could tell he was crazy about my mother as he would often excuse himself from the group to attend to her. I was so glad she had found such a nice man, who was good to her.

After about three days, when my mother was up to traveling, we said good-bye to Nana and the folks. Mom, Richard and I headed East toward Newport News – my birth place. It was a day-long car trip and finally my mom started filling me in on all the years we had been apart. She said she and Charlie Coleman got a divorce about five years after I left Virginia. I'll never forget when she told me her son Cliff was eight and her daughter Fran was six at the time of the divorce and that they were *taken away* by social services and put into a foster home *where they still remained!* She said that this was partly because she ended up in a mental hospital – after she had tried to commit suicide during the breakup from Charlie!

Overall the Virginia visit went well, although it was quite emotional and stressful. I met up with my father and some of his family and they seemed happy to see me – some of them meeting me for the first time. I also was taken by Richard and my mom to meet my half-brother and sister at the foster home. I remember this being very awkward. My mother was not allowed to come near the house and had to wait in the car – which was really hard on her. The foster mother let me go in to meet them for just a few minutes, but I don't think Cliff and Fran really knew who I was – and their foster mother seemed angry, like she had been forced to accommodate our meeting. The whole visit seemed destined to failure and it saddened me that they had to live with that woman when there were people like Mamma Jo out there. Several days later I returned home to Santa Maria – exhausted, but happy for the reunion with my mother and family. But being home was a welcome relief from all the family drama.

~

About a year after returning from my Virginia trip, Nasser had become so successful in sales at Montgomery Ward that they offered him a job in their big Sacramento store. I wasn't sure we should go. I had already signed up at Hancock College and was in the second month of classes. (*By-the-way, one of my classes was a computer class – with a computer the size of a school room!*) Nevertheless, at his insistence I left school and we packed up our stuff and moved to Sacramento. I never got very excited about that big city. I remember how hot it would get. But we rented a very nice two-story condominium in a complex with a pool on the south side of town, not far from the newly built Montgomery Ward store. Nasser was gone most of the time, and so I eventually made a few new friends there in the complex. One lady, who was old enough to be my mother, was a retired seamstress and she taught me how to sew and make my own clothes. Polyester pant suits were in style at the time and I was finally able to make pants and tunics long enough to fit me, with my 5'10" height and a 34" inseam!

It was close to Thanksgiving when Nasser and I made our move to Sacramento and one of the older salesmen at Montgomery Ward, whom Nasser had befriended, invited us to his house for dinner. He and his wife and kids (who were my age) – along with their large circle of friends eventually became our social circle. As the new kids on the block, they took us under their wings, and soon we bought a house in a neighborhood close-by.

Having such a home was surely a dream come true for me. It was a three bedroom, two-bath house with a two-car garage in a lovely neighborhood close to the American River. It had belonged to a pastor and was truly amazing in every way. We were told that the parishioners in the church had their hand in the detail of its design –from the exquisite well-tended professional landscaping and rose gardens to the custom design features within the house. Everything was new and updated to the latest 1970s fashion. When Nasser first walked me through it, I couldn't believe that *we* would be buying that house – surely I didn't feel worthy of such a prize. And another thing . . . I didn't know anything about taking care of roses.

After settling into the new house and taking on the full-time job of housewife, I soon became totally bored and started looking for something else to do. Now that Nasser had come up in the world, he didn't want me to work. He had taken up playing golf on his days off, so to be able to go out on the course with him, I took golf lessons and joined a couple of women's groups. I became a passionate golfer and for a number of years I filled up my lonely days on the golf course. Nasser and I had given some thought to having children and discussed it from time to time. But with Nasser's long hours at work, it seemed like a big commitment, so we just decided to put it off for a while. I started taking classes at Sacramento City College and eventually gave up the golf and became a full-time student with a focus on Business studies. I really enjoyed this, but still felt very much alone as Nasser worked such long hours, nights and weekends.

To put a social spin on things, I joined a sorority group of young women that one of my neighbors belonged to. I thought that this would finally allow me and Nasser to be around people my own age, since most of our friends were old enough to be our parents. However, Nasser never did feel at ease with the younger group. And when we would occasionally include husbands at social events, Nasser made no attempt at bonding with them and would sit off alone watching the group like some royal king holding court. It was frustrating and so I quit the sorority after the first year. And so it went. Life was good in

Sacramento and I had every reason to be happy. I was taken care of financially, I had all the creature comforts of a nice life-style, and I had the freedom during the day to come and go as I pleased. What more could a person want? As long as the house was clean and supper was on the table when Nasser got home, things went smoothly.

Then, out of the blue I got a rare call from my mother. She said she had a big surprise for me. First of all, her husband, Richard had adopted her two teenaged children, Cliff and Fran – who were now living with them. Wow! I wondered how that was working out. Then, an even *bigger* surprise . . . (drum roll here) . . . *they were all going to come to Sacramento to live, to be close to me, while Richard was stationed in Vietnam for two years!* Well, at first blush I thought that this was great news – my "family" would be moving to Sacramento. Nasser on the other hand did not think that this was great news. Why, he asked, would they move all the way from Virginia, where they knew everyone, out to California, where they didn't know anyone – just to be with me? They didn't even really know me for that matter. I had to agree, it didn't make much sense. Richard explained that the move would bring my mother and all her children together at last. He was doing it for my mother, Helen. And Mom seemed very excited and weepy about it as we talked on the phone.

Well, this was the beginning of the end for Nasser and me. My mother and the two kids moved out to California, and Richard took off to Vietnam. At first it was great having them around – only about ten minutes from our house. But Nasser didn't like my mother, or her teenage kids either for that matter. He thought she was a bad influence on me. I guess it was true, we acted more like mischievous girlfriends than mother and daughter. My mom was a party girl, always looking for a good time. She never really was a mothering type and had no clue what to do with two teenagers – it was a total disaster. She would beg me to come over and straighten things out with them at her house . . . as if I were the parent. If I said anything to the kids they would be furious – after all, who was I to be telling them what to do. Then to make matters worse, there would be times when Richard would not send money and Nasser would have to bail them out and pay the rent so they wouldn't be evicted. *Like I said, it was a continuing disaster!* Nasser and I began to argue over it all the time, and the relationship I had with my siblings was strained to say the least.

After my little sister Fran quit high school and ran away, Richard took leave from Vietnam and came home to help search for her. He found her at some bar in San Francisco. (How he knew to look for her there is still a mystery.) He straightened things out a bit with her, and bought my brother a car and helped teach him to drive so he could get a job and be more of a help to my mom. (Before that they didn't have a car, since my mother had never learned how to drive.) Then, after a couple of weeks, Richard went back to Vietnam again. But things still did not work out well for my mother. My brother ended up joining the Air Force and my sister permanently dropped out of school, got pregnant and lived on welfare with her Hispanic, soon-to-be first husband. Richard eventually came home from Vietnam. Then he and my mother moved down to Pacific Grove on the Monterey Bay, to be close to Fort Ord where he was stationed.

Meanwhile things were not working out well for Nasser and me either. He was fully engaged with his work and I felt abandoned and alone, especially now that my mother was gone. Finally at one point, about eight years into our marriage, we separated and I rented an apartment. But that didn't last more than a few weeks. Nasser convinced me that I was making a big mistake and should come back home – he promised he would start taking more time to be with me and we could start a family – things would be different.

I went off birth control – which was very strong in those days and took months to flush through the body. We tried to get pregnant and start a new way of life. Nasser's parents and little sister came to stay with us for about a month. They brought wonderful gifts from Iran – a beautiful Persian carpet, which they brought into the country as a "prayer rug" and a beautiful turquoise and gold ring for me as well as some Persian food items like spices, candy and pistachios. It was fun showing his mother and sister the California sights and getting to know them better. His sister Mia was adorable and we got along so well. She was about fourteen at the time. Our favorite trip was down to Southern California to go to Disneyland and the San Diego Zoo. Nasser and his father did not come along on such trips.

After I graduated from Sacramento City College with a degree in General Business, I was eager to start working. I convinced Nasser that I needed to get out of the house and went to work as an Office Manager for a place called the Fitness Institute. It was a new concept financed by a couple of real estate developers who had an office adjacent to the Institute. The facility was over 6,000 square feet and consisted of a lobby, gym, pool, spa, training rooms, offices and a snack bar. There was a nutritionist on staff and doctors were involved in the initial evaluation process.

Once a new member joined the Institute, they would go through a physical and nutritional evaluation. Then a physical fitness instructor (with a degree in the field) would meet with the doctor and nutritionist and plan an exercise program for them. We had state-of-the-art ergometers and equipment, and often had doctors in the classes monitoring the members. There was a class for cardiac patients, who were sent there by their personal doctors as well as expectant mother's classes – again, only allowed with their doctor's permission. It was a great concept, very well run and was written up favorably in local papers and journals. Many well-known community leaders attended. I loved working there and made a few new friends – it was fun and stimulating. But Nasser didn't like it – there were obviously too many temptations like young, healthy, fun-loving people who would want me to go out with them for lunch or to after-work events.

So to keep him happy I quit the Fitness Institute and instead went to work as an office manager at another new innovative start-up. This one Nasser approved of – it was working with seniors at a senior day care center. This was a pilot program put on by the State of California Department of Aging. We would bus seniors (many of them isolated and poor) in from their homes and provide them with medical evaluations, sometimes physical therapy if needed, lunch and snacks, arts and crafts and other programs – most importantly, socialization. It was indeed one of the most rewarding jobs I ever had. I would watch the participants blossom and change over time – with a whole new sense of self again. The staff was great and I made lasting friendships with them. *One of my oldest friends Naomi and I met there and we are still in touch with each other 38 years later.*

I recall that in 1977 the movie *Saturday Night Fever* had just come out and there was a place in Old Sacramento that had the colored-light dance floor and mirrored disco ball, as in the movie. What a blast! I always loved to dance – to let the music possess me to the point where I could forget about my worries and inhibitions and release that authentic primal self within me. (Maybe that was why Nasser didn't take me out much!) One night several of us from the Senior Center took one of the fun-loving participants, George Howerton, to a disco lounge for his 100th birthday party. (He was in a wheel chair and spoke through a mechanical voice box.) It was a great night for everyone. We rolled George out to the middle of the dance floor, and we all danced around him. He grinned from ear-to-ear and really got into it – "dancing" in his wheelchair with us by raising his arms and swaying to the music as the DJ yelled out encouragement. Everyone there at the disco got into the celebration and sang him Happy Birthday. Back at the Day Care Center, George couldn't stop talking about his "big night on the town!" (I heard from one of the staff members that kept in touch with him, that he lived to be 103 years old.) Unfortunately the State program lost its funding and the Senior Health Day Care Center was closed after a couple of years.

By then with me still not pregnant and between jobs, I was not sure what to do. I can remember in 1975, at the age of twenty-seven, sitting around at night in my La-Z-Boy rocker watching TV with Nasser and thinking there must be more to life than this. I decided to go back to school, and took a Women's Studies class at Sacramento City College. I'm sure that the 1970s "women's lib" movement must have shaken many a marriage – and mine was no exception. The class dissuaded me from ever allowing myself to be dominated by a man, and Nasser was a very dominating man. It wasn't long after that I decided I wanted a divorce.

I thought that Nasser was worried that if I ever left him I would want alimony and community property, but I came in with nothing and left with nothing – well almost. I did take my clothes, one of our two cars, a few pieces of our furniture and a small cash settlement. Nasser kept the house, the Persian carpet and everything else we had accumulated over the nine years we had been together. He hired an attorney to help with the divorce, and to make sure I wouldn't have any legal claim on the house. Despite this protection, Nasser was obviously devastated by the divorce and I admit that even though we were parting our ways, there were still strong feelings between us.

I will never forget the last time I saw Nasser. He had rented a truck to help me move the furniture from the house and into my new apartment. As we sat together in the raised cab of the truck on the way to the new apartment, we were quietly crying – the tears streaming down both of our faces. It was a pitiful sight and painfully sad. There were a couple of times after that when I tried to call Nasser to talk to him about something important, but he would just hang up the phone. One time when I called and he heard it was me, he stiffly said "Yes, young lady, how can I help you?" *It was really sad.* I have never talked to him again, although I understand from a mutual friend that he still lives in the same house in Sacramento, and has never remarried.

My Brilliant Career

Now that I was once again completely on my own, I had to quickly find a job. And I did find one I knew Nasser would surely never approve – working as an artist's model. I had met the artist Jerald Silva and his wife Susan in the Women's History class we all took together at Sacramento City College. When I first started the class I was still married to Nasser and angry a lot of the time because I was in the beginning stages of the painful divorce. Jerry and Susan, who were about ten years older than I was, were always warm and friendly and fun to talk to during the class breaks. Susan was a wonderful writer, and Jerry had that artist vibe and character going for him – which I loved and had missed so much being apart from my father.

Now, newly separated from Nasser after nine years of marriage, I was feeling rather desperate and felt that I needed to find work right away – even if it was temporary. While still at the college, I had talked to Jerry about his art

– and modeling. I had playfully volunteered myself as an artist model one time and he encouraged me to come by the house to see his studio. Now that Nasser and I were separated and the divorce was in process, I decided to give Jerry a call. He said he was happy to hear from me and we made an appointment for me to come over to his house.

When I visited them, the warmth and character of their charming turn-of-the century house with its fine, polished wooden floors and leaded glass windows matched that of Jerry and Susan. They met me at the door and welcomed me in as their guest, chit-chatting in the family room for a while before getting down to business. Jerry's art studio was behind the house, and he took me back there and showed me some of his works-in-progress. Then Jerry and Susan walked me upstairs to the large attic space where Jerry did most of his sketches with models. I felt warm and comfortable there – tucked away under the exposed rafters and surrounded by antique trunks, old wooden picture frames and draped storage, which all played a part in the backdrop of the set design for Jerry's artwork. It seemed a safe place to work and it was nice having Susan close-by.

I soon went to work modeling for Jerry, paid at minimum wage. After about a dozen sitting appointments, he ultimately produced several sketches. From one of the sketches he later created a single large watercolor painting – which once framed, would measure five feet by seven feet in size. The "watercolor incorrect" – as he coins his paintings, is a full length nude of me sitting on a pink satin comforter, glancing off to the side with a particularly moody stare on my face – (probably thinking of my divorce). *This painting now hangs over a gleaming black grand piano in the home of a prominent community figure in Sacramento. In addition to the portrait over the piano, there are a series of framed original sketches owned by private parties and professionally referred to as "The Dante Collection". . . . At the time I was modeling for Jerry, he was just beginning to gain strides within the art world, especially painting in that medium he referred to as "watercolor incorrect." He described them as "paintings in watercolor, not watercolors." Jerry would later become a well-known, successful artist, displaying over 900 paintings in art galleries and shows from London to New York to Beverly Hills.*

Meanwhile, I knew that being an artist model I would not make enough money nor would it establish me in a career. Luckily I saw a newspaper ad for another new business start-up. A young, commercial real estate broker had just moved to Sacramento from San Francisco and was in the beginning stages of building a new real estate company. He was still working out of his house – which by-the-way, was a beautiful mansion in one of the most established neighborhoods in Sacramento. How exciting I thought it would be just to work there!

His name was Bill Greer, and he and his brother Jim were busy with their new company – which was basically a marketing group for large subdivision builders and developers. "William Greer &Company" would come into a large housing development and subcontract a designer and landscaper to prepare the model homes, and then would staff them with salespeople. They would then sell the homes and have an escrow coordinator process the files. It was a full-service marketing and sales team – a brilliant idea that was catching on fast. In fact they had three new projects already set up down the road and needed to get things moving fast. I was hired as the Executive Secretary for Bill Greer. Within months the company quickly grew and moved into a nice large office building. I remember turning thirty in that office and everybody there celebrating with balloons and cake – then taking me out to dinner after work.

Working for the Greers was interesting and paid well enough. It was a fast-paced business and I started learning about real estate. Bill Greer was considered very successful and was written up in the real estate magazines as a young, up-and-coming businessman. When I saw how much money the project salespeople were making, I thought about getting into real estate sales myself someday. After working there for a while, I became good friends with the receptionist, and we ended up moving into a duplex together. Jan and I had some good times together, although she was about five years younger than me and hung out with a different crowd – who were into the drug scene. She would hardly eat anything all day and just maintain an adrenaline high on bennies. But she seemed very efficient at work, so it didn't seem to impair her abilities. I was always afraid of drugs, and while I smoked marijuana from time to time, I never got into the hard stuff. I had learned my lessons over the years, and felt that I needed to maintain control of myself and others.

I dated men on and off and had a few steadies – even a couple of marriage proposals – but I never got too serious with anyone. I felt I didn't need any more men telling me what to do. And besides, like my mom, I was becoming a bit of a party girl – (Nasser's biggest fear!).

Speaking of my mom, every now and then I would drive the three hours to spend the weekend with her and Richard in Pacific Grove. I remember on those trips, while driving my smoking hot 1968 Camaro sports car down the dark lonely highway, I would blast Manfred Man's "Blinded by the Light" on my state-of-the-art, eight-track player. Visiting my mom and Richard was always good times. I remember us going to the Officer's Club at Fort Ord one evening for a drink. When Richard got back from the Men's room he told us that one of the officers had stopped him in the hall. He told Richard that it looked like he might have a problem given that he was with two women, and suggested that maybe he could be of assistance. Richard laughed and said "No problem at all, one is my daughter and one is my wife!" Ha! Richard was *hardly* old enough to be my father!

Mom and Richard

Things went well for Mom and Richard until at the age of 37, Richard had a heart attack and was discharged from the military. Although he survived the heart attack, he became completely devastated, lost and depressed. Heart disease ran in his family – his younger brother had died from it at age 34. So, Richard knew he was on borrowed time. Not long after coming home from the hospital and starting his recovery, he and my mom began having financial troubles. Richard would sometimes be gone from the house all day – supposedly at the golf course. Eventually, after about six months, he seemed to finally pull himself together and was able to take on a night job as a desk clerk at one of the coastal hotels on Lover's Point. That seemed to help, but Mom began getting calls and visits from bill collectors and soon discovered that they were a couple of months behind in their rent. Richard said it was too expensive to live in the Monterey area anyway, and that he was going to apply for a job in Sacramento with a hotel chain there. Living there would be more affordable and my mom would be closer to me. (That sounded familiar.) He did apply and got the job (or so he said). Needless to say, I was thrilled that my mom was coming back to Sacramento to live!

Soon after being accepted for the new job, Richard surprised me one night by showing up at the door of my apartment in Sacramento. This seemed very odd, but then he told me that he was in town to meet with his new employer and that he needed to talk to me in person. Over dinner he told me about his new job and how excited he was to be moving to Sacramento. Then he opened up his soft side and related how hard it had been on him since having his heart attack and being released from service after he had expected a life-long career in the military. He said that while he was *trying* to make ends meet for him and my mom, things had been rough. Now he wanted to make a fresh start in Sacramento. My heart went out to him and I was happy to see his dedication and new-found enthusiasm, and wished him well.

Richard knew that I had received a small cash settlement from Nasser and asked if I would loan him and my mom some money to pay off part of their debt and help finance the move. He said they had already packed up their belongings and he just needed to go back to Pacific Grove to pick up my mom and all their stuff at the apartment. I actually felt proud that I had the money to help them out, and made arrangements to meet him at the bank the next day. I called and talked to Mom after Richard left the apartment. She said she was surprised that he had dropped by to see me, but knew that he had gone to Sacramento to meet with his new employer and was relieved and thankful for the news that I was going to help them out with a loan.

The following day Richard and I met at the bank. I remember us sitting down talking with a banker there and given the size of the loan, I even had Richard sign a promissory note to make the loan more official. The banker cautioned me that there were no guarantees that I would ever be paid back – I was forewarned. Richard left the bank as happy as could be. He said his plan was to go straight to the new Sacramento landlord to put the deposit down on the new apartment and then he would return to Pacific Grove to take care of business there and pick up my waiting mother.

I didn't talk to my mother the rest of that day or the next and assumed all was going well. But late the next night, I got a call from her. A feeling of dread washed over me when she asked me: "Where is Richard? I've been sitting here all day on boxes and he still hasn't returned!"

Once again we found ourselves involved in another emotional phone call. *Where could he be?* Maybe there was a car accident. We were both frantic. The following day continued to be filled with anxiety and panic until the answer finally came when I got a letter in the mail from Richard. You could tell by the messy handwriting that he must have been very upset when he wrote it. He said that he regretted having to tell me in this letter, but that he couldn't face up to my mother to tell her in person that he had taken my loan money and *gambled it all away*! He decided that since he couldn't possibly be forgiven, that it was best for him to *leave my mother altogether! He* was confident that "you will be able to work it all out together somehow." He went on to say how very sorry he was, and how he could never forgive himself, and wished us a good life in the future. *Imagine my having to call my mother with that news!*

Of course my mother was hysterical. We were both at a total loss about what to do. Now I didn't have enough money to help her – she was two months behind on the rent and the utilities were going to be turned off – and she said she didn't have a dime to her name. What *could* we do?

I'm not sure where I got the idea, but I called the military department where Richard had been working and told them the story. Perhaps I thought that they would know how to track him down or help out in some way. I remember talking to a very serious and stern man. He talked down to me like I was a child, but actually turned out to be very helpful, putting us in touch with someone who assisted military families in crisis. They paid my mom's back rent and utilities.

I was able to use the last of my money from Nasser's settlement to help Mom until she found a job in Monterey as a housekeeper for one of the hotels. She then moved to a smaller apartment nearby that she shared with a roommate to help with the rent. Things were at least more stabilized for her, but needless to say, she was devastated by Richard's abandonment.

Ironically Richard showed up a few months later to apologize to my mother and to ask her to take him back. Considering the circumstances, she said no – which she regrets to this very day. At the time, Richard also confessed to being an addictive gambler – a habit he said he acquired in Vietnam. He said the habit had gotten out of control after the heart attack when he started encountering financial problems.

Larry Drummond

With Richard now gone, I would occasionally come down to visit my mom and we would go out on the town, after all we were both single girls now. One time my mother went with me to the Hyatt House in Monterey, where they always had a live band – and I loved to dance. Mother was following a bit behind me when we passed the bar on our way to the Ladies room. When we got into the bathroom, she told me she had seen this handsome man turn around as I passed by and he had said "Whoa, I think I'm in love." Well, "this handsome man" would eventually turn out to be my second husband, Larry Drummond. He was visiting Monterey from San Francisco, for a golf tournament. He eventually asked me to dance and while he wasn't exactly my type (which was tall, *dark* and handsome – he had light colored hair), I slow-danced with him. He was a nice looking, tall, athletic guy – but the best part was that he was polite, charming and witty, and made me laugh. During the dance he asked me where I lived and worked. I told him I lived in Sacramento and was in real estate, but didn't give him my phone number. As my mom and I left that night, we saw him again outside and briefly spoke to him before we left . . . *and surprisingly a year later* I got a call from him! He had tracked me down in Sacramento. By then I had been taking night classes and was working toward a college degree in real estate (if there had been such a thing). I had since left the Greer Company and was an independent contractor working in real estate sales for Century 21 – yes, with the gold coat and everything. One afternoon Larry surprised me by coming into a house I was holding open – wearing a baseball uniform! (Well, yes, that got my attention.) He said that he was in a semi-pro baseball league and they happened to be playing in Sacramento that day.

Larry invited me to go to dinner with him and I took him up on it. We met at a restaurant later that night. He confessed to me that when he first met me he was in the middle of changing employers, and since he wanted to make a good impression on me he waited until he was settled into the new job. Well, that sounded like a good excuse and I believed him. While he was nice and charming and made me laugh on that first date, I felt we were somehow coming from two different worlds. I don't know if it was because he was from the big city, San Francisco and I was from what some people called "the hick town" of Sacramento, but as he talked he kept using insider innuendos and hip clichés, most of which I couldn't even understand. Also he talked sports, and while I had once been an athlete of sorts, I didn't really keep up with the teams, scores and players – so we didn't have *that* in common. Larry had just left the Bank of America headquarters to work as a sales manager for a smaller company in the City called Chartmasters, a media production company. This was before desk-top publishing had come out and while he tried to explain his business to me, I never quite caught on. All in all, we were finding it difficult to find something we really had in common.

After that Larry called from time to time, but we didn't meet up again until about six months later when a group of us from the office decided to go to San Francisco for a conference. We were going to go out on the town after our meetings, and so I called Larry and gave him a heads-up that I was in the City with my work associates – and would he like to join us for some fun. He did and we all had a blast. From then on it was hard-sell pressure: Larry would send flowers to my office with cards of romantic poetry he wrote. Once he even had me put my co-worker (whom he had met in San Francisco) on the telephone to get her to convince me that he was the guy for me. In addition, there was more pressure. My father's sister Doris, from Florida, came for a visit, and when we went to San Francisco, Larry toured us around and took us out to dinner. So then my Aunt Doris started in with this "wonderful, fun-loving guy" and why wasn't I taking him more seriously routine. I began to think that maybe my perception of him was skewed somehow. (Was I protecting myself from getting hurt?). In time I started treating him more seriously with the idea that he might be someone with long-term potential. He was very supportive of me and my career and didn't seem to need to control me like some of the other men I had met.

So, Larry and I started a long-distance romance – he'd come to Sacramento, I'd go to San Francisco. After about six months of that, Larry invited me to take a golf trip of several days with him to Monterey. Of course I couldn't pass that up, and I made provisions at work for someone to take over for me while I was gone. My trips to San Francisco from Sacramento always seemed to be eventful. One time they even closed the Bay Bridge down – with me on it – because of a warehouse fire. Fortunately this trip was uneventful and I arrived in San Francisco in the pouring rain. The next day it was raining hard too as we started our trek down Highway 101. I worried the whole way down about how we would be playing golf in a torrential downpour. To my knowledge we were staying at the Travel Lodge in Monterey, but as we drove into town Larry said that for sentimental reasons he wanted to stop by to visit the Hyatt House, where we had originally met. Of course I agreed and we drove up and parked in front of the Hyatt. I can remember sitting there in the car with the cold rain pouring down and commenting on how it was such a shame, that it could ruin our golf plans. Then we counted to three and quickly jumped out of the car and ran inside, trying to dodge the rain.

Once we were inside Larry led me by the hand into the bar. It was in the middle of the afternoon and no one was there except the bartender, polishing glasses. Larry directed me to the exact spot at the bar where he said he had first seen me "walk by with my mother on that fateful night" – and that's where he sat me down. Larry seemed nervous and after having a short conversation with the bartender – telling him that this was where we had first met – he ordered us both a round of drinks. This was rather unusual as we didn't normally drink in the middle of the afternoon. After the drinks came and we had taken a few sips and talked about the weather, he relaxed a bit. He then opened up his coat and took out an envelope and gently laid it on the counter in front of me. He had a shy look on his face I could tell by the stationery that it must be another one of his custom-made love letters. I smiled and when I opened the letter, it was a romantic proposal of marriage asking me to be his wife and the mother of his children. The note was so sweet that it made me cry. While it was totally unexpected, the timing was right; I was ready to settle down and get married – and so I said yes.

Larry was 38 years old by then and had never been married. So his family was surprised when they heard that he had made the commitment. Most of them lived in the East Bay – close to Walnut Creek where he had been raised. Since Larry's parents had divorced when he was about eighteen, his mother and father had long since gone their separate ways. His father, who lived in Concord, had married a woman younger than Larry and they had an eight-year-old daughter. I remember the first time I went to meet them – it was Thanksgiving 1979 – I was thirty-one. That first visit with them was similar to my first date with Larry. They were so into sports that was all they talked about. It didn't stop there. Our entire day was wrapped around football – I'm talking about foot-stomping, screaming, yelling, jumping up and down, high-five football. I was in foreign territory. I sat there and observed them as if they were part of a science project and I would have to turn in my report later. I was always seeking family connections, but I didn't know how I could possibly fit in here. *But they were kind and loving people and were always good to me. Fortunately our family relationship eventually took hold and developed into something very special over the years.*

Then there was Larry's mother, Betty Hill. Now she was in a class of her own. She was larger than life and twice as radiant. She had such character, personality and style, with her long skirts and flowing pearls and turquoise – no one could look at her without smiling. Besides, you couldn't just ignore Betty – her whole face would light up when she saw you as if you were the most fabulous and important person in the world! No one could escape her influence – not the postman, the grocery clerk, or the stranger standing in line with her at the store – she would just shine her light on them and they would soon be caught up in her spell, laughing and joking right along with her. What a hard act to follow.

Betty was working raising the three children of a wealthy widower – a well-known attorney living in the Piedmont hills. During the week, she lived in his mansion overlooking San Francisco Bay, and on the weekends she would drive with her fancy, groomed, little poodle Fonzie in the front seat of her red 1964-1/2 Ford Mustang convertible – a unique, limited model – with the Betty Boop bumper sticker ("Beep if you Boop") all the way to her home in Clear Lake – more than two hours away.

When I first met Betty, a few months after Larry and I started seriously dating, she seemed excited to meet me and was so gracious and warm. When she found out her son was planning to get married, she instantly took on the role of Wedding Planner. This was okay with me, as all that wedding stuff was foreign to me and I didn't have the least idea of what to do. Besides, it was hard for me to be very involved given that I was still living in Sacramento and we were planning the wedding for a few months out, in San Francisco. Larry had a good friend who was a member at the elegant and prestigious St. Francis Yacht Club – and so we booked the wedding there. This was turning out to be another fairy tale.

The wedding event was definitely something special for me, a dream come true – especially so, since my wedding to Nasser had taken fifteen minutes in a courthouse with strangers. This magical day, March 1, 1980, turned out to be a beautiful sunny day in San Francisco. We were married in a bright, scenic room looking out onto San Francisco Bay and the Golden Gate Bridge – the most spectacular sight I had ever seen! We had an intimate family ceremony with only Larry's immediate family, my mother (who came up from Pacific Grove), and my good friend Naomi (from the Senior Center) attending. Naomi, my bridesmaid, and I wore vintage-inspired dresses and hats. My dress was made of cream-colored chiffon and lace with pearl ribbing. We were married by a woman minister from the Unity Church in Sacramento, which I sometimes attended with Naomi close at my side. When Larry fumbled as he tried to put the ring on my finger, I broke out into nervous giggles and everyone joined in on the laughter.

The reception at the yacht club was amazing. About 80 people attended – maybe twenty of them were my friends and business associates, and the rest were Larry's extended family and friends. My mother was the only member of my family who attended. I was disappointed that my father and his family couldn't come from Florida. Nevertheless, it was a fabulous time and Larry and I made our escape from the Yacht Club on a small boat, with Champagne in hand. I remember that while we were motoring by restaurants and docks close-by, people were hanging over the railings and out the windows waving and taking pictures of us – Larry in his tux and me still in my big brimmed hat and gown. We waved back and toasted them with our champagne glasses. After our boat ride, we had a taxi deliver us to the funky, historic "Mansion Hotel" on Sacramento Street in the City, where we were staying that night. I remember us both being quite inebriated when we arrived. Then the next day we took our time and drove down to Monterey for our honeymoon – of course we stayed at the Hyatt House where we had met. We went to the elegant Lodge at Pebble Beach for dinner the first night and played golf at Spyglass the following day. We were living the high life – at least we started out that way – with great expectations for our future ahead.

Now, back to reality. I had become used to the quiet Sacramento suburbs and when I came to visit Larry in San Francisco before we were married, I never did find the crowded and hilly city dwelling very amusing. I had little interest in living there, especially since I would be practicing real estate and having to drive everywhere. So instead, Larry and I had located a modest two-bedroom apartment in the bedroom community of Lafayette, on the East Bay. It was simple – nothing special, but the apartment complex had a nice pool and big shady trees and was not too far from the BART station for Larry's commute to San Francisco.

I went to work for a real estate company named Fox & Carskadon. They were just opening up a new office in Lafayette. With my track record it seemed that I could go anywhere, and I chose that office (even though it wasn't ready to be moved into yet) because the manager, who was very pleasant (a "good 'ol local boy"), had similar training as me and we spoke the same sales language. Also, Larry's friends from the Peninsula across the Bay had told me that Fox & Carskadon was the premier real estate company for the Bay Area and that I should go there. I think that decision turned out to be a big mistake, and I found it tough-going. Not only had the economy gone into a slump – with interest rates close to twenty percent – but Fox & Carskadon was just breaking into the East Bay and no one was familiar with their hard-to-pronounce name – or mine either for that matter. (Although Dante Drummond has a certain ring to it.) Also, a lot of the agents in my office were from the upper crust of Lafayette society – some were even famous celebrities and retired athletes dabbling in real estate – they all seemed relatively rich and established in the community. I didn't know anyone or even how to get around the town. I found it all quite intimidating.

I also had to rethink my business practice. Inflation in the Bay Area was rampant, and it took me a while to remember to put the "hundred" before the "thousand" when discussing the prices of homes. In Sacramento where an average home might sell for sixty-thousand dollars, in Lafayette I had to remember to say "*one hundred* and sixty thousand dollars" – for the same quality house! The other thing I had to get used to was all the wealth in the area. One of my first sets of clients was a couple in their thirties who were buying a $500,000 house! That was a lot of money in 1980. While I was excited about selling an "expensive" house, I couldn't get over how everyone had so much money. I was in culture shock.

Given my description of the wedding, I might have misled you to think that Larry Drummond was a rich man. That would have been nice, but it wasn't essential to me. One of the reasons I was attracted to him in the beginning (apart from his romantic and charming ways – and the fact that he spoiled me) was that he had a good job and had been the head of the Audio/Visual department of Bank of America Corporate – a prestigious position. Given his modest San Francisco living arrangement, however, I could see right from the beginning that financial wealth did not appear to be part of the package. When I first met him he lived with two roommates in an apartment in the southern part of the city. He had few possessions to speak of (an old car and an old bed and dresser). I soon found out that he did not have much of a bank account to show for his hard work, partly because he was so generous to those around him. I also learned that he had borrowed money from his boss for our wedding and honeymoon.

So, we lived quite simply in our little Lafayette apartment, trying to pay off the loan. We both had big dreams though and shared optimistic views of our future together. I was studying for my broker's license and could see that when the economy turned around and I became better acclimated to the area, that my business would get better. Also, Larry's company, Chartmasters, was doing well and was getting ready to expand into the South Bay. Things were looking up and we had a bright future ahead.

Sure enough, something wonderful and truly amazing happened . . . I found out I was pregnant! Only seven months into the marriage and we were starting a family! From the beginning we had agreed that I would go off birth control in hopes of having a baby. Our wish had been granted. We were very excited and so were our parents – this would be the first grandchild. I will never forget when we invited Larry's family to our apartment for dinner to tell them – Larry's father literally fell off his chair! Larry's biological mother squealed with glee. *It's funny that I can't remember the long-distance reaction from my mother, or my father and Valora. It must not have been so dramatic.*

I continued to work while I was pregnant. The Lafayette area was pretty hilly, and I remember sitting in the back seat of another agent's car, driving through the hills of Happy Valley and breaking out into a sweat – hoping I wouldn't lose my breakfast. By-the-way, those office agents who I had referred to earlier as upper crust, snobby people, put on a fabulous baby shower for me and even loaned me some of their maternity clothes. I realized that they were all good people, just more educated and wealthier than I was – which brought out my foster child default mode of thinking – *I just wasn't good enough to be like everybody else.*

So, I took my broker's exam when I was eight months pregnant. I recall that right in the middle of the exam my baby kicked me so hard that I gasped and grabbed my side, taking people's attention away from their tests. I'm sure they must have wondered if I might deliver right then and there in the room. When I started labor a month later, I was on the phone making sure that the title company had the information they needed for a transaction scheduled to close escrow that day. The buyers of that property sent my daughter birthday cards for years to come.

Babies

I'm proud to say that I managed the delivery without any drugs. Our "little" baby, Ashley Elaine Drummond was born in Walnut Creek in June, 1981 – all 9 pounds, 8 ounces of her! She was a sweetie and as healthy as can be. Thank God for that. It was surely nice to have the

Drummond family close-by, and Larry's step-mom, "Nurse Nancy," was a huge help to us during those early months.

Larry and I met a nice group of people at the Lamaze parent training class we took. We kept in touch and I was part of a mothers support group. At one point I remember getting together with our husbands and babies for a potluck dinner and taking pictures of all the babies lined up on a blanket on the carpeted floor. A few of these Lamaze couples would later become my clients as they looked for new homes in which to raise their families. A nice added bonus.

There was nothing more wonderful for both Larry and me than having a child. Ashley was the center of our world and brought us such joy. So, it was so very hard when it came time for me to go back to work. I interviewed a couple of caregivers and found a nice older couple to care for her – though I could barely stand leaving her there. Betty was the most doting grandmother, always bringing something for both me and Ashley when she would come to visit. My mother in Monterey was too far away to really be involved. (Although she did lend moral support, I don't think she was ever into caring for babies or little children.) It was okay if they belonged to someone else, but she had little tolerance for them around her – that is unless they were being especially quiet, sweet and cute.

Ashley started out without a hair on her head, but would later grow the most beautiful thick and curly reddish-brown hair. While she looked a lot like me at that age, with her long arms and legs, she had her father's sunny disposition. She was an easy-going, happy-go-lucky child and took life in stride. She adored her "Grandma Betts" and Betts would spoil her so. Ashley really brought the Drummond family closer together. It also helped when Larry's older sister, Debbie had a little girl a year later. Then the family as a whole started drawing even closer together, especially during the holidays.

Larry would commute to work in San Francisco and I would make my way trying to sell a house or two around the "Lamorinda" area – Lafayette, Moraga and Orinda. It was certainly a challenge, but I was slowly becoming acclimated to the area. Larry and I both liked living in Lafayette, but it was a snoozy bedroom community and there was nowhere to go at night. For a little excitement, we would go to Bill's Drugstore book department and hang out there for a while. How boring was that?

Well, we weren't bored for long because the next thing I knew, I was pregnant again! While this was great news, it was a total surprise and sure changed things for us. In addition, around the same time, Larry got the good news that he was going to manage the new million-dollar Santa Clara facility that Chartmasters was opening up. But we would have to move! Again, this seemed to be a recurring theme running through my life. I can remember being six-months pregnant, driving an hour down into the unknown South Bay area looking for places to rent. That was no fun. I recall the first time I went down there I got off Highway 101 at the Palo Alto exit. I had heard that this was supposed to be an exclusive community, but when I got off the freeway I found a very run-down area with a liquor store and some old stores. It looked dangerous. I was afraid to even get out of my car to get my map in the trunk. But I waited until the coast was clear of suspicious-looking street people, then jumped out, grabbed my map, got back in and immediately locked my doors behind me. My intuition was right. Just after getting back into the car, a man approached my door and tried to open it. When that failed he leaned down and smiled his toothless smile at me. I ignored him and continued reading my map. He knocked on the window and yelled that he could help me find where I was going if I opened the window. I continued to ignore him, and he ended up pounding on the hood of my car before he ran off down an alleyway. I found out later that I was in East Palo Alto and the Palo Alto I was looking for was further down University Avenue. I had stopped too soon in "Whiskey Gulch" – an area that would eventually be torn down and replaced with a Four Seasons hotel!

The good news is that I eventually found a really nice single-story condominium for rent in Cupertino, just twenty minutes away from Larry's new office. While Cupertino was the home of Apple Computer – which was only about a mile down the street, its presence did not make an impact on me at the time. While I never quite got into the Cupertino community, I loved our little place. It was very private, at the end of a court, and was light and comfortable and even had a grassy backyard and a two-car garage. This would be where I would bring home our sweet little Chelsea. Grandma Betts happened to be visiting when my water broke, so she was able to stay and take care of Ashley while I was in the hospital and Larry was at work. Chelsea Anne was born in May, 1983. She had such a sweet face with her dark little eyebrows and long eye lashes – and she had hair – lots of it! I can remember Larry posing for the camera with her little head rested on his shoulder as he stood there on the front porch beside the pink, hanging flowers that Grandma Betts had bought for the homecoming. I was in total mother bliss for the next four months, just staying at home nurturing and bonding with my two babies.

Still, having the responsibility of two small children was a bit daunting. Given my childhood history and lack of continuity with relationships, I wanted to make every effort to prove myself a good mother . . . after all, it wasn't like I could just leave when things didn't go right – a pattern of my past. Most of all, I wanted my children to have no doubts that they were loved by their mother and father. To add to the tension of being a new mother, after Chelsea was born I ended up with a diagnosis of Graves disease – which is an autoimmune disorder that leads to over-activity of the thyroid gland (hyperthyroidism). While it turned out to be great for shedding the extra weight of pregnancy (I had gained 60 pounds!), it caused me to be very nervous and high-strung. After the problem was diagnosed, I was put on medication which evened out my anxiety.

The only real mothering experience I could call on from my past was that of Mamma Jo and her care of the foster babies – which worried me because even then I had to rely on her for the simplest of things, like keeping a baby from choking to death! As with most new mothers, I was so afraid of doing something wrong. But fortunately I had Grandma Betts and Nurse Nancy Drummond to call on when I got stuck in the realm of the unknown.

Ashley – then barely two – wasn't too sure about the new baby. She could see that Chelsea was getting a lot of attention from me, and Grandma Betts. In fact everyone who came to visit was making a fuss over the new baby. When Chelsea got older the girls played and became the best of friends, but there was always a sibling rivalry between them. Their personalities would soon develop into a competitive nature, each vying for attention in their own way. Ashley was very methodical, observant and intuitive. I have often called her the "old soul." Chelsea on the other-hand was very spirited, active, and early in her development. She was walking at nine months – trying to get to where the action was! I tried to give them balanced attention and have alone time with each one . . . but then you know how that goes.

Our Cupertino place was situated in a good location for a new family. There was a park right around the corner and we could stroller along a pathway through a big field (that later became Highway 85) to a small shopping center that had a grocery store and an ice cream parlor. I can remember putting the girls in a little red wagon and taking them to their first Pumpkin Patch, that was set up in a vacant lot a few blocks down the street from us. My days with the girls were wonderful and I really got into the mothering role – something so very foreign to me.

Meanwhile, Chartmasters opened their plush new office in Santa Clara with all the latest state-of-the art technology. They started off with a big open house – with the expectation that hundreds of people would come. All of their vendors, clients and prospective customers were invited. Unfortunately, I think that there were more employees and company executives in attendance than there were potential customers – it was nothing like the big event they had planned for and expected. Larry and Chartmasters found out the hard way that it wasn't going to be easy to break into a new market in Silicon Valley.

A few months later major changes started happening with Larry's job. First our company car was taken away. So we had to go out and buy a car, the last thing we needed to do at the time. Then his health insurance premiums were affected and we started having to pay for all dependants. Larry was noticeably demoralized and started to feel angry and resentful. It didn't take long before I had to face the reality that one income could not sustain us and I had to go back to work. I had fought this from the start, and at one point decided to take in other children and do daycare so I could continue to stay home with my girls. So, I interviewed a couple of mothers and was lining up that possibility, when I came to my senses and realized that it just wouldn't work out for me. I was a business woman and while I enjoyed my babies, I didn't think I had the patience to care for a house full of children. So, I resigned to the fact that I would have to go outside of the home to look for work.

I knew that I couldn't go back to selling real estate at that point when my children were so small. (Although I was already doing some phone consulting and referrals to other agents from home.) There were too many hours involved, especially having to work weekends and nights. I needed a job where I could clock in and clock out – and be done at the end of the business day. After some interviews, I was hired as the second employee for a technology start-up company which just happened to be located in the building next to where Larry was working at Chartmasters in Santa Clara. The company name was Inventory Transfer Systems. When I started working there I found it was so hard to be separated from my girls – and in the beginning I often found myself in tears. Ashley was going to a daycare center near our house (about 20 minutes away) and Chelsea was staying with a caregiver at her house during the day. My income barely made up for the costs of child care.

It wasn't long before my company moved to Palo Alto – which doubled my commute time. The pressure was on. I remember coming home from work one night and talking to Grandma Betts on the phone. I was at my wit's end. I had just gone through a horrendous commute and picked up the kids late – Larry wasn't home, the kids were hungry, the kitchen was still a mess from the night before and I was exhausted. Betts was on the phone trying to reassure me and told me to give it just one more year and things would be easier. *One more year!* At the time I wasn't sure how I would make it through *one more hour!*

But life with our babies made it all worthwhile. It was 1984 and after about a year of living and transitioning in Cupertino, Larry and I met with a CPA that Larry knew from back in his Bank of America corporate days. The CPA suggested I get back into real estate and start in Palo Alto. It just so happened that he knew a business associate there who was a developer, looking for an office manager – a good way to go back into the business without jumping right into sales. How perfect. The salary was also considerably more than I was making at the start-up company – which was on the verge of collapse due to its imminent loss of funding. Larry's company, by then, had decided to close the Santa Clara branch altogether, and instead expand the San Francisco corporate office where Larry would go back to work. This combination meant that we were either faced with longer commutes or yet another move – a costly proposition.

Palo Alto and Beyond

One day in 1985, Larry and I and the girls were taking a Sunday afternoon drive around neighborhoods in Palo Alto looking for places to rent. We had seen everything listed in the paper but could not find anything in our price range that we liked – and by then I was pretty sure that Palo Alto was outside of our financial reach. As we were passing through one of the finer neighborhoods, Crescent Park, we came upon a For Rent sign on Dana Avenue. It was a lovely older home with a painted white brick facade and heritage blue shutters. I noticed new homes were going up right across the street where a school had been torn down. Larry wanted to stop to take a look at the vacant rental, but I was so convinced that the price would be over our heads that I wouldn't even get out of the car! Larry got out and peeked in the windows and came back and said it was perfect. I reluctantly got out of the car and looked inside, and yes it was lovely – too good to be true – so I was even more certain that we couldn't afford it.

After we returned home to Cupertino, while I was fixing dinner, Larry called the number that was listed on the sign. Sure enough the rent was much too high for us. But Larry didn't let that deter him and over dinner he continued to talk about the house to the point where I finally called back and made an appointment with the agent to see it. The next day as Larry and I walked through the spacious house with the leasing agent, I felt that I didn't deserve such a wonderful house. While it needed to be updated, it was so elegant and spacious and had such character and charm that the condition didn't matter to me.

We agreed to at least give it a try, and I started right then to negotiate the rent with the agent. We continued the negotiations for several days until we finally settled on a price I thought we could afford. The agent was not familiar with the lease forms and sounded confused, so I went to her office and wrote up the lease myself. The owners accepted our price – and before we knew it we were living in Palo Alto!

The Dana house had happy vibes. After sitting empty for almost a year, I think it was glad to have our little family living there. I began to refer to it as the "Grandma House" – as it was sunny, warm and inviting. An added plus was that we were only a few blocks from Eleanor Pardee Park, and when we wanted to venture a little farther (pulling the girls along in their little red wagon) we could go to the Children's Library and Museum at the Lucie Stern Community Center. Also, Larry's commute to the City was cut by a third and I was now only seven minutes away from my office in town. We hired a live-in au-pair, who became like family to us, and she took care of the girls during the day. Things were looking up.

I loved my challenging job working for Bill Reller, who had developed many of the recent condominium projects on Forest Avenue in downtown Palo Alto, and who had also just completed the big development called "Palo Alto Central" on California Avenue by the train station. His office with five employees was right in the heart of town in a 1927 historic building – The Lanning Chateau. My job as Office Manager was primarily to act as Bill's secretary – and to update and automate the office. Apple was really breaking into the marketplace by that time, and I remember how exciting it was to switch from an IBM typewriter to an Apple computer. Being in the birthplace of Silicon Valley, I could feel the excitement in the air. *An interesting fact to note here is that at the time I worked for Bill Reller, he owned the Hewlett Packard garage at 367 Addison Street –*

dedicated as the "Birthplace of Silicon Valley." Bill Reller was an interesting man – kind, compassionate and generous. His philosophy on dealing with others changed my view on how the real estate business could be practiced. Unlike the intimidating and confrontational spirit I had experienced working with the guys at William Greer & Company in Sacramento, I found that Bill's cooperative and respectful approach produced the same or better results in the end.

Meanwhile, before Larry and I knew it, Ashley was starting school! At first we thought she would be going to kindergarten at Walter Hays School and I became involved in creating a new program there to help provide after-school daycare for working mothers. Then just before school started, she was assigned to Duveneck Elementary. I have to say that this whole experience – living in the exclusive Crescent Park neighborhood and interacting with the affluent parents at that school was initially quite intimidating for me. Everyone seemed so wealthy, heavily degreed and up on all the current world events, while I was still operating in survival mode. (Even the sixteen-year-old babysitter, who lived down the street from us and was taking special trips and workshops on the path to becoming an astronaut, probably had a higher net worth than ours!) It was easy for me to find evidence to support my acquired belief and default thinking pattern that "I'm not good enough." I had always felt like I had to strive to "keep up with the Joneses" – yet knew I never could. So I would just have to be me and give it my best.

One painful example of this disparagement was that it seemed that all these families had the time and money to travel to world-wide fabulous resorts and take extended vacations together. Even their children came home with glorious stories of fun and adventure. *Our* vacation consisted of a weekend drive to Grandma Betts' house in Clear Lake, where upon arriving, I was most likely to keel over from relief and exhaustion – knowing that my girls were in safe hands. Betty loved to explore the antique shops in small nearby towns, like Cobb Mountain, Lakeport, and Calistoga, or drive around the lake, which took several hours with stops along the way. Also, Larry's aunt and other distant relatives and friends of his mom lived up there, and we would sometimes stop in to visit with them. I remember on Easter Sundays we would have a large combined family luncheon at the Riviera Golf Course, where all the kids and cousins would run around the manicured lawns hunting for Easter eggs. Those were happy times. By then Larry's sister Debbie had another daughter, and our four girls, each about a year apart in age – who we referred to as the "staircase sisters" – would play together and entertain the adults. Betty's poodle Fonzie had since been sadly laid to rest and replaced by a grand white Standard Poodle named Jazbo. He was almost as tall as the girls and when we were at Betty's house he would gallop around like a small pony on his long furry legs, chasing the screaming girls around the yard, nipping at their bottoms. We would find the four girls all lined up giggling and squealing together on top of the propane tank and would have to call the dog off to let them come down. Happy times, but hardly equal to a week on the Riviera!

Also our family was fortunate to vacation a couple of times at Bill Reller's wonderful family "cabin" in Twain Harte, a little town in the Sonora Mountains not far from Yosemite. While he called it a cabin, it was three stories high and I think it slept sixteen people. The views were magnificent and there was a small lake just down the path from the cabin. It was a great get-away. We spent some of our most pleasurable times together there walking the woods and trails, going down to the lake, swimming – and challenging each other to table tennis. There were no TVs or computers to compartmentalize us. I have to admit that those family vacations are some of my fondest memories. I especially savored the feeling of being part of a real family with Grandma Betts; Papa Doug, Nancy and Karen; with Debbie, Ruby and Camille; and of course Larry, me, Ashley and Chelsea. That extended family was a dream finally come true for me.

But it was expensive to live in Palo Alto – then and now – and over time I found it impossible to save money. While we were living on Dana Avenue, the Palo Alto real estate market continued to climb. There was another cute little grandma house just two doors down from ours that came on the market for sale. Because it was small and had only two bedrooms, it was one of the most affordable houses recently available in the neighborhood. I would have liked to buy it despite the size, but it was still too expensive for us. It broke my heart when I found out it sold even higher than the list price. I was even more devastated when the new owners *tore the house down* and built a big two-story house in its place. This was at the beginning of the Palo Alto "McMansion" phase – which ultimately prompted a building moratorium and more restrictive size allowances in the zoning regulations.

Nationwide tax reforms in the mid-to-late 1980s had a big impact on investment real estate and caused a jarring spin for developers and investors alike. The environment quickly changed. And after working a couple of years with Bill Reller – helping to renovate and automate his office, assist with staff changes and sell a few of the family and company-owned properties – it was time for me to move on. So in 1987, with the advice of my CPA, I decided to take the scary leap into straight-commission sales again. After interviewing a couple of brokers, I decided to join the premier real estate company in Palo Alto at the time – Cornish & Carey Realtors. My troubled history as a care-free juvenile, had made me a stickler for the rules and the law, especially when it came to the serious business of practicing real estate. Since I was just getting back into sales as an independent contractor, I decided to begin in the smaller Cornish & Carey Midtown office – partly because the managing broker at the time was a real estate attorney and I felt safe under his wing. The Downtown Palo Alto office (where all the action was) seemed to me a less welcoming environment, especially with its gruff and grumpy office manager, John Lazar. I had been told by several people that the Palo Alto real estate market was impossible to penetrate because everyone in town knew at least two real estate agents. A wonderful surprise for me was that our Palo Alto-based CPA firm started to refer me to some of their clients who were clearing their trusts of investments. This luckily gave me an introductory kick-start into the marketplace. *It always helps to know somebody.*

I remember when I took my first big real estate listing. The house was being sold because of a divorce. It was a beautiful, updated and charming story-book home in the heart of Old Palo Alto – shark territory for agents. The husband-seller was a local architect who was well-connected with agents, builders and developers in the area. The divorce attorney, who just happened to be connected with my CPA source, had suggested that the couple interview three agents and then pick one – my name was suggested as one of the three. I knew my competition would be tough and I went in swinging with all I had. By then I was known to be well-organized and prepared in situations like this – being an analytical person coupled with my compulsion to always be "looking good." I was later told that the competition came out in full group-force – in the manner of the good ol' boys network – and that they were so confident they had the listing that they didn't even prepare any paperwork to present their case. On the other hand, I was far less confident, but well-prepared as I sat down at the dining room table with the husband and wife. It was the wife who spoke up on my behalf at the presentation – giving me a chance and defending me as the underdog. To everyone's surprise, including mine, I got this prime Old Palo Alto listing. The wife and I have been friends ever since.

On Being in Real Estate

It has been 35 years now and I still fly to the light and call of my profession. There have been good times and bad times, but overall the real estate business has been good to me. Above all it demands humility, endurance and most of all . . . change. It constantly challenges you to grow and develop and seems determined to put you in your place – having you question who you really are and what grit you are made of. So I guess it's not surprising that a person who has lived in so many homes would end up making a career out of real estate. If you stop and think about it, it's just a continuum of a foster child's lifestyle – people come into your life, you get close, interact – and for a while you are an important and integral part of their lives . . . *and then they go away.* So it is with real estate sales. Even now once a sale is completed, I sometimes experience a bit of a withdrawal as my clients move on with their busy lives and are no longer in my life on a day-to-day basis. (*A small reminder of what I must have felt like as a foster child.*) Of course, I stay connected with my clients after the sale – and in fact some of my clients are now my closest friends and supporters. Working together has given them a glimpse of my true, authentic nature, as we usually go through quite a lot together during the sale and escrow process. And they can see that I care about them, have the knowledge and skills to earn their respect – and will protect them and put their needs above my own. The experience bonds us together for years to come.

Based on my experience, aging foster children like to think of themselves as strong, independent and determined – and aren't those attributes needed to be successful in real estate? I have sometimes compared myself to a lone cowboy out on the desert, drifting along on his horse. While he may have a home base somewhere, during the day he is alone – independent of others as he faces down his own internal demons in his pursuit of success. All my teachers' mantras over the years echo: "The sky's the limit! Anyone can be successful if they work hard enough." I guess it's true, but I learned that in reality to be successful you also have to take risks, learn to alter your natural personality, restructure your belief system, overcome shyness, overcome the fear of rejection, and transcend the awkwardness of not always "looking good" . . . all terrifying prospects for me.

Fortunately, in real estate sales, you have strict guidelines, rules, regulations, and laws to abide by. If you are a Realtor® member (which I am), you also have a Code of Ethics. One of the benefits of working as a sales agent is that as long as you stay in legal compliance and conduct yourself as a competent professional, you don't have authority figures breathing down your neck – though you are still accountable to a managing broker. As a former foster child, this style of independence works well for me.

As a real estate broker I still find it an honor and a privilege to be able to go through people's houses every day. I look to find the positive and the potential in every house I see, no matter what its condition. As a buyer's agent I pay attention to those inherit defects that could negatively impact the pocketbook or life balance of the clients, who have trusted me to help them find their future home. Or if I'm the seller's agent, I am always looking for ways to present the property in its best light and to be sure to disclose, disclose, disclose – to keep us all out of trouble. Sometimes I even find myself talking people out of selling their home or backing off from the sale entirely, if I think something is not right. I would rather they be happy with their home in the long term and refer me along to others – knowing that I am not just focused on making that sale.

At times I resonate with a house so strongly that I imagine myself living there. It's usually a comfortable home full of sunshine, surrounded with views out to nature and lush mature gardens. I'm not attracted to big houses. In fact, they tend to intimidate me, as I wouldn't want to spend the rest of my years cleaning and spending my money maintaining it. Besides, I'm sure I would only wander around hoping to fill all that space with something of meaning and value so as not to feel lonely.

I frequently tour about 20 houses a week. After 35 years in the business, I have learned to take the time when possible to appreciate and admire the gardens, or the art, or the color choices, or that special carved chair, or Tiffany lamp, or creative shelving unit – or even the books in the library or stacked at the bedside. Most houses and gardens tell a story about the people who are living there or have lived there, and sometimes I think how wonderful it would be to meet them. Because sometimes the visual story is so intriguing, I expect the owners to be extraordinary. It's such details my mind takes in and enjoys, while also making mental notes – continuing to be the eyes and ears of my client. I'm feeling one with the house – is it light enough, big enough; does it have the right floor plan? Is there noise, a peculiar odor, deferred maintenance? Does it fit the client's description of what they want?

It is always fun to visit the home of a child. There is the artwork on the refrigerator and the trophies on the mantle and the posters on the walls in their bedrooms – not to mention the toys, toys, toys. Sometimes elaborate murals on bedroom walls take me back to when I was a child living in my father's house. Of course, recently in our area most buyers don't get a chance to see these active signs of home life, because by the time houses come on the market the owners have already moved out and have had the house "staged" by professional designers. In fact, one of the first rules of marketing a house for sale today is to *de-personalize* it so that while the buyer is there he can more easily visualize it as his own home – rather than being distracted by the seller's photographs and personal possessions.

Most often I am right in-sync with my client's needs and get very excited when I find them what they want in their price range. Finding the right home can sometimes be immediate, or may take years. One of the most frustrating things for me is, after looking for a long time and finding what I think is the *perfect* house for my client, to discover that the client is out of town or is just too busy to look at it – or (worst of all) doesn't even *call me back*. Then, that window of opportunity rapidly closes and the house is sold.

Sometimes people who are planning to sell their house are embarrassed to show it to you at first – before they can ready it for sale. (I think mostly it is because they worry that the things they always wanted to improve but never did will be obvious to everyone else.) Luckily I can easily see through the clutter and boxes and peeling paint and visualize the potential of how it can be. Sometimes after the owners have moved out and I have the house prepared and staged for sale, they come back to see it and can't believe their eyes! They often say, "Wow! I didn't know our house could look this way! Maybe we should move back in!" Fortunately, no one has so far. All in all real estate seems right for me and I can't imagine doing anything else.

Menlo Park

The prices in the real estate market in the late 1980s were moving up quickly, and when I saw the little two-bedroom granny house on Dana Street torn down, I knew my dream of owning our own home in the Palo Alto area could never be realized. Many of the buyers who had not yet acquired equity were able to finance their houses with the help of their parents, but we knew that neither Larry's parents nor mine would be able to help us. Then in 1989 our hand was forced when the Trust who owned our sweet little Dana house decided to sell. Unfortunately we were not in any position to buy it given its list price. But with house prices going up and since we were going to have to move, our CPA suggested that we consider teaming up with an investor to buy a house and "get on the train before it leaves the station." He happened to have such an investor who was willing to finance the down payment if we took on the mortgage payments – paying them interest-only payments on their investment. I was so desperate to own my own family home that we took him up on it.

We were given what was then a modest price range to work with and were able to start searching for our new home. Our primary criterion was good schools. We already knew we couldn't afford Palo Alto, so instead we ended up buying a house in the more affordable Willows neighborhood of nearby Menlo Park. I loved this area for its quaint, tree-lined streets and for the fact that it was walking distance to downtown Palo Alto. The neighbors, mostly young professionals starting families or original owners of 1940s houses, were friendly, and there were plenty of children on our block of Marmona Drive. Fortunately it was summertime so the girls were not interrupted in the middle of the school year and had time to get to know their new neighbors and acclimate to the change of environment.

Owning our own house was to prove more difficult than we thought. Soon after we made our move in 1989, a recession hit Silicon Valley and people started losing their jobs and the real estate market slowed down. Larry was demoralized at work – Chartmasters had not only closed the Santa Clara office but also began downsizing the main office in San Francisco, once again laying off people and reducing salary and benefits. Larry was lucky to even have a job. The invention of desktop publishing had changed the game for them. About this time our CPA suggested that perhaps Larry should quit his job and partner with me in real estate. Larry had good business experience and maybe by using a team approach we could make more sales and eventually exceed his income. Larry was good at managing others – keeping them motivated and supported – but I didn't feel like I needed to be managed. However, after some discussion we agreed that Larry probably could contribute by marketing and bringing in customers. So, he quit his job and joined me in the real estate business. I would like to say that this made a positive change for us, but right away we sensed that it was a big mistake. While his intentions were good and he tried, Larry was out of his element in real estate and we ended up arguing and bickering most of the time.

Not only was it not working out for us, but we no longer had Larry's steady income. After about a year of trying to make real estate work, Larry attempted to find new ways to bring in income. He put together his own start-up company, consulting with people in his field of computerized slide-show presentations. He also joined a Casino Night party outfit that would put on events for charities and corporate fun nights out. About three or four times a month he would dress up in a tuxedo and go out to work at those events in the evenings as a card dealer. While it didn't make a lot of money, it got him away from the stress and responsibilities at home, and he made new friends along the way. Still the tension was immense for both of us as we tried to meet what seemed monstrous mortgage payments and other financial obligations during those tough times. The stress of it began to wear on our marriage and our family's well-being. Given my childhood history, I tried to hang-in there – and when I felt like I couldn't, I tried to fix it through marriage counseling, even though we couldn't afford that either. That helped somewhat and we persevered another year or two. But perhaps by that point it was already too late. In retrospect it is easy to see how things got out of control. We placed too much faith in the future of my business, despite the warnings of the recession. And the business wasn't a good fit for Larry, though we thought that if we just worked harder, things would eventually turn around. But I was already working long hours, and wanted to be with my children. Then I found that when I *was* with my children, I became angry with myself for feeling guilty that I wasn't out working to support them! *I was tormented.* Our CPA encouraged us to keep going and even helped us out financially, adding to our debt – trying to just get us through the recession – then things would right themselves again.

~

What finally put me over the edge in everything including my relationship with Larry stemmed from a bad car accident we had on the way home from Clearlake. It was a rainy afternoon and we were stopped in traffic on the freeway in Santa Rosa when a Suburban plowed into the back of our car with such force to cause a four-car pile-up. The SUV hit us hard enough to collapse the trunk, forcing everything into the back seat where our sleeping children sat. I believe the only thing that saved their lives was the fact that we were in our sturdy Volvo sedan. Thankfully, at the time our injuries seemed somewhat minor – other than suffering from shock – and we all were able to get out and walk away. While there were no broken bones or deep lacerations, we worried that Ashley might have a concussion as her head had slammed into the front seat, leaving a big knot on her forehead and almost knocking her unconscious. I had a minor leg injury from hitting the glove compartment. Chelsea seemed okay, though by the time the ambulance arrived she had begun to hyperventilate. Perhaps because of our particular positions on the right side of the car, Chelsea and I both suffered from neck and back pain that would later evolve into more serious problems for us. Larry, who was driving, came out of it without a scratch – though he and Ashley also suffered from whiplash. Luckily we all had our seat belts on. Our Volvo was totaled – but it had saved our lives. Then on top of all that I had to fight with the insurance company to get a decent replacement value for the car.

As a result of the accident, even as the market was finally starting to strengthen, I collapsed in will and spirit – suffering from exhaustion and back pain. I just couldn't hang in there any longer. In 1995 I wrote a letter to our investors stating that I had had enough. Though the timing wasn't the best for us to fully recoup the equity lost from the declining market, it was decided that we would all cut our losses and put the house up for sale.

It just so happened that the lovely elderly lady who had lived on Robin Way, right behind our house, had passed away a year earlier. I knew her house was still sitting there vacant – so I contacted her family and said that I had a proposition to make. When I told them our housing story, and how we wanted to be able to keep our children in the neighborhood and in their schools, they agreed to rent the house to us. It was about half the size of our Marmona house – but it turned out to be the perfectly acceptable new home for us. Larry and I joked about throwing everything over the back fence to move in. But by then it was too late for us. After several months of trying to co-exist in the rental house, Larry finally moved out and I was left alone to raise our two teenage girls. For a while he remained in the picture – often coming to the house, and going to the girls' games and school events. A couple of years later he moved to Las Vegas to become a professional card dealer. We finalized our divorce several years later.

Robin House Memories

Many memories stand out for me in the Robin Way house. First, since I still lived in the neighborhood, I happened to witness our former family home on Marmona Drive being torn down to make way for a new and improved two-story model. It was a frightful sight.

Do you know that it only takes two men to demolish a house? One sits in a machine that is almost as tall as the house itself. The other is there just to hose down the dust from the debris. What was once your precious family home dissolves in minutes, as if it were made of Paper Mache. Once the roof is lifted off, everything is exposed to the light of day – revealing to the intimate observer the hidden history and memories of all those rooms. Rooms where you sat and laughed with your family over dinner; memories of tickling your children on the big bed – memories of reading stories to your babies before tucking them into their bed with a goodnight kiss, memories of chatting with beloved family members now long since gone; and in my case, memories of a family that once existed as a cohesive unit with all the hopes and dreams that never quite came true.

So it was a traumatic experience watching the house crumble. I stood across the street, sheltered by other neighbors standing close-by, tears streaming down my face. It was then, on that sunny spring morning, that everything became hushed and quiet. I held my breath. The birds no longer sang. The machine had paused, and I watched as the glistening snow of insulation floated gently down into my baby Chelsea's bedroom. I stared at the sight, and for a moment in time it seemed as if the world had stopped and I became the silent witness of a surreal and twisted fairy tale dream.

Perhaps what helps me gently take others through the daunting experience and process of change and transition – leaving their home and friends behind – moving from one house to another – is that I can relate to some of what they are feeling. I use my own past experience and expertise to clear a path for them so they don't have to worry about much other than taking care of themselves and their family.

~

The girls and I learned to love our modest little rental house. Robin Way was a small, quiet street that no one needed to cut through to get anywhere, so we mostly saw neighbors going by. The street was also protected by a canopy of Maple trees – an idyllic little paradise for the active squirrel population. I put a picnic table out in my side front yard and sometimes sat out there in the morning sun with my coffee, greeting neighbors as they passed by. The girls grew up and become women in that house. Of course there was always drama of some sort, but I prided myself for being able to manage and survive raising two teenage girls as a single working mom.

~

Ashley was a very active and popular girl in high school. She was involved in theater and was preparing to perform in another play. This time my mother had come up from Pacific Grove on the bus to see her opening night. Larry was there at the house too and we were all getting ready – everyone quite happy and pleasant as we looked forward to the big premiere.

Ashley was in the shower when the phone call came. It was Larry's stepmom, Nancy. Her first words to me were "We lost her. We lost our Betts." I couldn't imagine what she was saying. I didn't *want* to imagine what she was saying. She went on to explain that Debbie, Betty's daughter, had called to say that Grandma Betts had

233

unexpectedly passed away that evening from a heart attack. She told Nancy that Betts was on her way to Debbie's house – in the Mustang with Jazbo in the back seat – when according to witnesses, she suddenly pulled the car off the road and stopped near a ditch. Someone came to see if she was alright, but she was unconscious and the dog would not let anyone near her. By the time animal services had arrived to remove the dog, our Betts was gone. Once the shock had worn off, we all had to agree that it was just how she would have wanted it to be – all dressed to the nines in her party dress and pearls, in her Mustang, with her beloved Jazbo. No suffering, no hospitals, no doctors.

But how was I to tell Ashley? I stood at the bathroom door and listened to the sound of the shower running on the other side. At this moment in time, I decided Ashley need only to remember her lines for her play. So far she was shielded from the truth awaiting her on the other side of the door. Larry, Chelsea and my mother were still in the other room swooning from the news. I went back to join them, allowing Ashley time to finish up in the bathroom. There was no need to hurry to give her the words that would break her heart. Once she came out to go to her room, I guided her to mine instead and onto the "big bed." As I gently broke the news, we both cried together – her there with her dripping hair, our wet faces mirroring each other as if we could be washed clean from our pain. I thought, given the circumstances, that she would not go to the play that night. *But the show must go on*, she said and insisted that she would not let her friends down. Ashley got dressed for the play. Following her lead, the rest of us somehow managed to pull ourselves together. We attended the play as a united family, though I think we all sat there quietly weeping in the dark – despite that the play was a comedy. Ashley was a good actress – you would never know from her performance that night that anything had happened.

Betty's passing really affected me. I adored her. She was a strong woman with high self-esteem, and yet she managed to be kind and loving to all. She left us with some lovely memories along with her life's motto: "Live Love Laugh." That was indeed the true spirit of Betty Hill. My heart still cries out for her.

Dear Mother

My mom Helen has had her share of ups and downs over the years. After Richard left she worked as a housekeeper for several different inns and hotels in Carmel, Pacific Grove and Monterey. She told me about a harrowing experience at the Double Tree Inn while she was cleaning a bathroom in one of the guest rooms. Without any warning some crazy guy came in and attacked her, pushing her into the tub and wrecking her shoulder and hand – she was off on disability for a while before returning to work. Later on, Mom began experiencing heart trouble and I found out she had congestive heart failure. At one point I had to call Cliff and Fran to come to California because she was going in for heart surgery and they didn't know if she would make it or not. As it was, she pulled through fine and it gave us kids and Mom an opportunity to visit with one another – Fran coming from Missouri and Cliff from Virginia. It was during this reunion that I heard more stories about my step-father Charlie and what life was like for my sister and brother growing up with him and Mom – stories I wouldn't want to repeat. *In retrospect, I'm so lucky that I was cast out at the age of six.*

Then in 1997, I got a call that my mother had had a serious accident and was in the hospital. I rushed down from Menlo Park to Pacific Grove and found out when I arrived that she was having hip surgery. The accident had been innocent enough – my mom had walked out of her apartment and stepped onto the sidewalk and was instantly sideswiped by a teenage girl riding by on her bicycle. Mother was knocked down and her hip was broken. That accident marked the beginning of a series of operations, blunderings, infections and multiple hip replacements – one in which her leg bone was broken by the surgeon while putting in a press-fit implant. After years of on-going hospitalizations, repeat surgeries, nursing homes and painful procedures, Mom was finally stabilized to the point where, although disabled and using a walker, she is able to continue living alone in her own home with the assistance of a part-time care-giver.

Dear ol' Dad

After I left Tucson I had little direct contact with my dad over the years. Valora would call once or twice a year just to stay in touch and she would sometimes put him on the line to say "hi." I don't think he really knew how to treat me now that I was an adult woman, but when we connected, he always had sweet things to say that made me feel loved – I hung onto his every word. When I was still living with Nasser, I had gone to Florida to visit him and the family in 1972 – a year after they moved back there from Virginia. Dad and Valora divorced a year later.

I made another trip to Florida in 1974 and stayed with Valora in her new St. Petersburg apartment for a couple of days and then with my Aunt Doris who lived in Orlando with her sister Jean. During that time I had only a quick, one-day visit with my dad who, by that time, *had already married another woman.* Carol, a pretty blonde nurse with three children, was only a few years older than me!

Then in 1980, my dad – who had already been divorced from Carol by then – couldn't be convinced to come out to California for my wedding to Larry Drummond. The next time I saw him was at my sister Star's wedding in 1985. I had not seen Star since she was eight years old, so I was really excited to get an invitation to her wedding in Houston Texas, where both she and Valora had moved. She was twenty-one by then and it was interesting to meet her again as an adult. She was beautiful, and I thought she looked like Valora and had similar mannerisms. I stayed with Star and the groom-to-be and followed her around as she made last-minute errands in preparation for the wedding – which, incidentally was in a *boxing ring*. (She loved the old historic brick building.) I only saw my dad briefly during my stay.

Dad moved around a lot over the years, so we were not in contact with each other, but I would hear from Valora or Aunt Doris about his latest shenanigans. Once I got a newspaper clipping and a letter from a member of the family apologizing for, but wanting to let me know of my father's latest scandal. It turned out that at age sixty-five he had married an eighteen-year-old woman and they performed together as exotic dancers . . . there were photos . . . in the local papers.

Several years after I received that letter, Valora called to tell me that my Dad's mother had passed away and left him a little money. He had bought a small house with an in-law unit near where his sisters had moved to in Orlando. By then he was no longer married to the exotic dancer, and my brother Curtis who was forty-three years old by then, was living with him. Valora gave me their contact information commenting about how my dad and brother were an inseparable team – both doing handyman jobs and house painting for a living. Curtis was also a practicing rock musician.

I called my dad and I remember how exciting it was to reconnect with him again. After our initial long talk on the phone, trying to catch-up on our lives, I started making a habit of calling every few months, to try to rekindle the relationship. Dad and Curtis always seemed happy to hear from me. Sometimes I would also write long letters and send cards, which Curtis called "sappy." I can't recall getting much response from either of them.

In 1997 while I was living at the Robin house in Menlo Park and still married to Larry Drummond, I had an opportunity to attend an accredited business course at a conference Coldwell Banker was giving in Orlando Florida. I thought it was the perfect opportunity for me to visit my dad and family *and* write-off the trip on my taxes. Soon after I told Valora that I was scheduling a trip to Florida, I got a phone call from my sister Star. It had been a while since we had talked and she said that she wanted to see me and fly from Houston to Orlando to join up with me and visit with Dad while I was there. It was a great idea!

Star was the one who greeted me at the airport in Orlando. She was even more beautiful than in the pictures that Valora had sent, especially with her long red curly hair and infectious smile. She had high energy and seemed as excited to see me as I was to see her. I really liked my sister and felt a little guilty that we didn't stay in closer touch. She had rented a car and drove me to the hotel near the conference center to drop off my things. Since my classes wouldn't start until the next day, I checked in and we made our way to Dad's house to take him and Curtis out to a late lunch.

My dad's house was a real fixer-upper – dwarfed in size by a large, tired-looking, rusty red and white boat mounted up on blocks looming over the partially fenced backyard, which was filled with what appeared to me to be mostly junk. Dad was already coming out the door to greet us as we pulled up onto the dirt driveway. At seventy-four years old, he appeared much older and somewhat frail, but he still looked handsome to me, and I tried to hide my tears when he gave me a big hearty hug. Curtis, who also came out to greet us, was a big, tall guy with a long ponytail of red hair down his back. I found him to be like a gentle giant and very protective of his father. He was quick to warn me that Dad would start drinking around four in the afternoon and he didn't want any visitors after that. I was concerned that this could present a problem for me since my real estate classes didn't let out until early afternoon – but I didn't say anything.

After we posed for pictures, all four of us piled into the rental car and drove off to Dad's favorite buffet restaurant. I didn't have much appetite given my excitement, so I spent most of the time just staring into the face of my father. *It was really him. I was once again in the presence of my beloved father. How I adored him.* As I watched him I became concerned that my girls, now fourteen and sixteen, would never have an opportunity to meet their grandfather. I knew he would never come out to California, so later that night I called Larry Drummond, who was at the Robin house with the girls, and made arrangements for them to immediately fly to Orlando to join up with us, and . . . go to Disney World. (A crazy request.) They could then fly back with me. Ashley and Chelsea arrived in Orlando a couple of days later. I had forgotten how charming, funny and theatrical my dad could be, and he made a big impression on my girls. I was so excited that they were able to meet their grandfather.

At one point during my visit I was able to pry my father away from everyone and sit down in a cafe alone with him. Instinctively I felt the need to express how much he had meant to me over my lifetime and how much I had always adored him. While this seemed to make him a little uncomfortable, he was kind and receptive and said he loved me too and that I would always be his "little girl." I think it was an important exchange for us both to make at that time in our lives and was the highlight of my visit.

A year after my Orlando visit I heard from Curtis that Dad was quickly going blind from macular degeneration. Since he couldn't see well, he had walked into a sliding glass door and cut himself up pretty badly. During the hospital stay, they discovered that he had prostate cancer – for which he was being treated. I continued my calls and sappy cards and letters. After a while my telephone messages were no longer returned, and when I did get Curtis on the line he would tell me that I couldn't talk to Dad because he was asleep, or drunk, or at the doctors or something.

Then one day in 1999, when I was still at the Robin house, I got a panic call from Valora. She said that she had received a disturbing, emotional letter from Curtis that *alluded* to the death of his father. She was quite upset and was not able to reach Curtis, and wanted to read it to me to see what I thought. As I listened I thought that it was rather cryptic, *but it was clear to me that my dad had died.* One of my first thoughts went back to my trip to Orlando and the talk I had with him at the cafe. I realized that that might have been our final good-bye. After I hung up with Valora, moments later I got a call from Star. She had just heard the news from Valora and was extremely upset. My heart cried out to her with love. Like so many people, she had never had a chance to have that final conversation to express her deepest feelings, and say good-bye to her father.

After a few days of much conversation with Valora and Star, trying to figure out exactly what had happened, I finally received a call from Curtis. He said that Dad had passed away at the Veteran's Hospital from prostate cancer. When I asked about whether he would have a funeral or anything, he just said no, that he couldn't afford one and that the hospital had already disposed of the body. His conversation with me was brief and I could tell that he didn't want to talk about it. I offered my love and condolences and we hung up.

As the days went by, I began to process my grief and realized that I wasn't as brave as I thought – and the events of my father's death started to wear on me. It occurred to me that I had not been in touch with my favorite Aunt Doris for a long time and thought about how she and my dad's family must be taking this. She was in Orlando with her sister and a few cousins, and had been my main line of connection to my dad's family. Late one night, a few weeks after Curtis had called me, I wrote her an email to express my condolences for the loss of her brother.

The next day all Hell broke loose! *My dad's family was unaware that he had died*! I was shocked when Doris called me – grief-stricken and furious, with a million questions to ask me that I couldn't answer. I found out during our conversation that my dad and Curtis had some kind of feud going on with her side of the family and that they were not on speaking terms with each other. Later in the day, Doris called again and told me she had sent her daughter over to my dad's house to confront Curtis. He told her the same story about Dad passing away at the Veteran's Hospital. But when Aunt Doris subsequently called the hospital . . . they told her that my Dad had not been there recently – *and had not died there*! Now the question arose – *where was his body*! By then Doris, and other family members, were all trying to locate Curtis to find out the truth. But he was not returning their calls and was not at home.

Finally, late that night, Curtis called Doris back and said he was coming over to her house. There in front of his two aunts and a couple of cousins, Curtis confessed that Dad had died at home – of natural causes – and, *that he had buried him in the backyard*! With that confession, the police were called. It was ironic that in the days before the confession, my Aunt Doris was talking to me about scenarios as to what could have possibly happened to his body. I had jokingly said to her that maybe Curtis had done him in to put him out of his misery . . . *and buried him in the back yard!*

I will never forget that night when I was driving to a client meeting and got that call from Doris. *"You were right!"* she said, *"Curtis has buried your dad in the back yard! The police are over there now digging him up!"* I almost crashed the car pulling over to the side of the road.

Needless to say, when Curtis pointed out to the police where my father's body was buried in a laundry basket in the back yard, he was arrested – and made the six-o'clock news. The police also discovered that, due to their similar names, Curtis had been cashing my father's social security checks. Although that evidence provided a motive for murder, the autopsy couldn't prove any wrong-doing. Curtis' story to the police was that he had come into his room one morning and found him dead in his bed. He said he had buried him in the backyard because he didn't feel that his father's family and friends cared for him like he did, and he wanted his dad to be close. He also said that he didn't want to put up with all the drama of insincere visiting family and friends attending a funeral that he couldn't afford – and that my dad wouldn't have wanted. Curtis was eventually released from jail. It was noted in the newspapers that there was *"no law in Florida against burying someone in the backyard."* But I think Curtis is still paying back the government for the Social Security fraud.

My dad's body was cremated and I was glad to cover the expenses.

Rest in peace Dear ol' Dad.

Living in the Now

I was especially proud of being able to finance college for Ashley, although it was pretty heart-breaking when she went away to live in a dorm at the University of California, San Diego. While Chelsea wasn't as interested in academics, she was very social and always had a close-knit group of friends nearby. I vividly remember her driving off down Robin Way alone for the first time in the new used car that I bought her – a fresh driver's license in hand. And when it was time for *her* to move out and on her own, I felt so much anxiety. It was sad to see her go – my last little bird to leave the nest. Thank Heavens for my career.

I had a windfall at work in 1997 (just after my trip to Orlando). Several years earlier I had moved to the downtown Cornish & Carey real estate office, where I ended up working for John Lazar (*who I found was not so scary, once I got to know him*). With John as my managing broker, I represented a well-known developer in the listing and sale of nineteen new construction homes on Everett Avenue in the heart of downtown Palo Alto – a $15-million project at the time. This "new community" listing really put me on the map and was a great learning experience for me. At the end of my work there I received an incredible letter of reference from them.

After the project was sold out and my girls were living away from home, I looked to see what new venture I could take on. Through the encouragement from some of my colleagues, I became involved with the leadership side of organized real estate. The business had been good to me and I wanted to give back. So, I started volunteering at the local Board of Realtors, first with committee work and then in a leadership role.

There were close to 3,500 members in the regional trade association, Silicon Valley Association of Realtors.

243

This included Realtors from as far north as Woodside, Atherton, Menlo Park, and Portola Valley – all the way south to Los Gatos, including the areas of Palo Alto, Los Altos, Mountain View, Sunnyvale, Cupertino, and Saratoga. Palo Alto alone had about 300 Realtor members at that time. I started chairing the weekly Realtor meetings in Palo Alto, helping to bring in speakers to keep us up on important local issues, as well as introducing new technology, laws and matters necessary to successfully operate our business practice. Exhausting as it could sometimes be to juggle my business and the volunteer work, I really enjoyed chairing those meetings for several years – during which time I got to know most of the agents in our district.

Over the years I became the Chair of the Palo Alto District Council and was twice selected by my peers as "Palo Alto Realtor of the Year". I was also on the Board of Directors for the Silicon Valley Association of Realtors, where in 2004 I was named "Realtor of the Year" for the region. By that time I was also traveling the state as a Director for the California Association of Realtors. While I had been repeatedly asked to run for President of the Silicon Valley Association of Realtors, I never took them up on it. That would have been a huge commitment of time and energy. Not only did I need to work to support myself, I was still helping to support my daughters and my aging mother who had become disabled from a bicycle accident. Then in 2006, I was diagnosed with cancer – the treatment for which slowed me down considerably, making it necessary to curtail my volunteer activities and focus entirely on my business. I consider myself one of the lucky ones . . . a survivor.

My community volunteer work created life-long friendships with some of my hard-working peers – whom I always respected and admired. It also gave me a new sense of self-respect and confidence that has since continued to help me in my business and personal life.

For the past fifteen years now I have been in an exclusive relationship with a man whom I have grown to love dearly. It's funny – his name is *Larry! You can imagine how confusing that was at first.* While dating and *life between the Larrys* was eventful, my latest Larry is now the shining star in my life – full of wit, intelligence and compassion.

So life is good. *My health is good.* I'm still young enough to work and travel and I look forward to the future with hope and enthusiasm. While I can't say that I have graduated from MIT with a degree in Rocket Science, I can say that I have survived the odds. Perhaps I might have accomplished a great deal more in my life were it not for the low expectations that were planted in my head early on. I lacked direction and confidence and I let the seeds of doubt grow. It wasn't until later in life that I blossomed and realized that I was capable of more. Through time, and with the faith and encouragement from others, I began to believe in myself and found that I could accomplish more than I dreamed possible . . . and yes, I *was* good enough all along.

Epilog

**Inspiration, Motivation
and
Surprises**

Mamma Jo and Other Surprises

After I turned sixty years old, I felt that my mortality was on a short leash because people I knew and loved started dying. Attending funerals at an increasing frequency led me to wonder who would be next . . . and if it was me, what would they say at my funeral. Reviewing my past, I started thinking more about the people I used to know and things I did – as well as things I didn't do that I wished I had done, things I still wanted to accomplish and so on. I became curious about certain people in my life that I hadn't contacted or spoken to in decades. Perhaps the real need was just to confirm that they truly did exist as I remembered them. I wondered who I needed to thank before it was too late. I was motivated to contact them because they were getting older too and if I waited too long I might never have the chance to connect with them . . . and so it was with Mamma Jo.

I felt guilty that it took me so long to reach out to reconnect with her, but there was a reason for my long disconnection from the Buckner family. I left Mamma Jo's house to live with my father the summer of 1964, when I was sixteen. Two years later, after I had left my father's house and was living with Nasser in California, I did make a call to her home. And when I got Hershel on the phone I was so excited to make a connection with someone at the Buckner house! No one else was home at the time so I babbled on to Hershel – bringing him up-to-date on my new life in California and some of the more extreme adventures I had experienced since I left his house (although I left out the R-rated parts). I was also eager to tell him about my new relationship with Nasser, the man who would soon become my husband.

As Hershel listened – interrupting here and there with questions and comments, I felt his comments were judgmental and critical and I was hurt and angered by

248

them. Instead of feeling happy for me surviving these ordeals, he seemed focused on criticizing the choices I made that had endangered my life. Though his response may have been warranted, it upset me and I felt that he was not in my court at all and perhaps never had been. My mind flashed back to the time I lived at Mamma Jo's house and to the relationship I had with Hershel at the time. I remembered that he avoided me a lot, yet he had a real affinity for my arch nemesis, Sandi. I felt my old jealousy flare up again and I accused him of never really liking me – and hung up the phone.

I was (and still am) a very sensitive person when it comes to rejection and abandonment. For some time after that 1966 phone call with Hershel, I remained troubled. I thought about anything I might have ever done wrong at the Buckner house and why they would have reason to not like me and to be critical of me. I knew I had made my share of mistakes while living there – I couldn't help playing them out over and over again in my head. So for forty-plus years, I had harbored that self-inflicted pain of rejection, feeling that perhaps I had never really been accepted by or belonged as part of the Buckner family. I convinced myself that somehow I was not good enough to have ever lived up to their expectations and that I had failed them just like I felt I had failed everyone else. With this in mind, there seemed no reason for me to contact them again.

But then decades later, *time* had worked its magic and I had become a more forgiving, accepting and self-confident person. As I thought about Mamma Jo and Judy and the rest of the Buckner foster family and all the good times we had together, I started to worry that Mamma Jo might pass away without my ever having had an opportunity to thank her for all she had done for me during those formative adolescent years.

So in 2009, I decided to look up the Buckner family again. I first Googled Hershel Buckner and got a hit, but it was in Kansas City, Missouri, so I thought they must have moved back to Hershel's childhood home. I then Googled Rick Buckner and sure enough he popped up right there in Tucson. Since he was listed as a real estate agent, I found an email address and wrote him to ask if he was the son of Hershel Buckner who had run a foster home in the 1960s and told him who I was. When I didn't hear back from him I just figured he wasn't the same Ricky Buckner. Then several days later I received an email from a Kathy Wilson, a common enough name, but not anyone I was familiar with at the time. I'm so glad I didn't just delete it, as I would so often do with the 30 or more emails coming across my computer daily – *because* after opening the email I saw that *Kathy Wilson was Mamma Jo!* It totally blew me away!

My mind just couldn't grasp that this was really coming from *my* Mamma Jo after all these years. In fact, my reaction can't be explained. *I couldn't even reply.* It was just too much to take in – as if a ghost had just risen up from the dead. I had convinced myself that I had burned my bridges with Mamma Jo and the Buckner family and that they hadn't given me a second thought. However, the email from Mamma Jo didn't say that at all; instead she expressed her desperate search for me over the years – a search to find her "little red-headed *daughter*" that she "loved so much!" Sending me her phone number, she pleaded with me to call her right away to get back in touch. Strangely enough I didn't know what to do. Emotionally it was just *way* too much for me to take in. I had to think about this. I printed out her email and put it aside, but I couldn't look at it. The thoughts in my head were swimming around in circles. *Had I been wrong all these years, thinking I had been rejected by her?* What was I going to say to her? I felt stunned, conflicted and for some reason . . . afraid. I could not reply until I was able to sort out my thoughts and feelings.

250

Even as I write about this now, something has come over me and I feel myself shaking, needing to put my pen down to pause and regroup. I can't seem to put my finger on my exact feelings now – just as I can't seem to adequately describe exactly how I felt then when I read Mamma Jo's email for the first time. Is the feeling fear, shame, remorse, guilt? I didn't mean to punish Mamma Jo all those years by not being in touch with her – after I allowed my sensitive feelings to be hurt by Hershel. Why did I feel so stunned? Why couldn't I just pick up the phone and call her right then and there as her email requested? Could it be that those feelings of rejection I had all those years were just made up in my head? Could it be that I didn't feel good enough about myself to believe I deserved love from someone like Mamma Jo? Perhaps all those years that I had felt like I had been abandoned, it was really me who had abandoned Mamma Jo!

It was days before I could summon the strength inside to brace myself and pick up the phone to make the call to Mamma Jo. And then when she answered and heard it was me, she sounded so excited and her familiar Midwestern accent and the rhythm of her voice made me realize that this was truly my Mamma Jo – *and there was nothing to fear.*

Mamma Jo talked about how she had prayed for this day to come when she would once again hear my voice. She said she was 83 years old now and living in a retirement community in Kansas City, Missouri. She explained that in her new life she was doing the same thing she had done when she had the foster home – she was taking care of people! She told me with pride how she made the decorations and center pieces for the lunch and dinner tables and how she would get people up and out – singing, dancing and exercising – seeing to it that everyone was alright and as happy as they could be, given their circumstances. Mamma Jo was doing just as she had done for us kids so many years ago. She said her ankles and feet had pretty much given out, so she wasn't able to walk much and used a motorized wheelchair to take her to and from the dining and entertaining areas where she helped out.

Mamma Jo told me that forty years ago she had discontinued the foster care home, as it had taken its toll on her – continually having to give up kids that she had become so attached to. She said she even had wanted to adopt a couple of them, but in those days it wasn't allowed. Mamma Jo related that from 1961 to 1969, she'd had 41 foster children come to stay with her! Some would stay for days, some for months and some, like me, would stay for years. (I was at her home for three years.)

She went on to tell me that Judy and Ricky, her biological children, had both become teachers, and that after they moved out and started their adult lives, Mamma Jo and Hershel got a divorce. She said that several years later she met the "man of her dreams" and they were married for fifteen years before he died – just a couple of years before our call. I could still hear the grief and longing in her voice as she spoke of him. Mamma Jo said Judy had married her high school sweetheart and had also moved to Kansas City, not too far away from where she lived. Ricky had also married and lived with his wife not too far from Hershel and other family members in Tucson.

Soon after this heartening phone call, I finally did send that long overdue thank you letter to Mamma Jo. Here is how it reads:

> Dear Mamma Jo,
> How can one thank another for caring for their life? From the ages of 13 to 16 you were the safe harbor for me when I felt alone and afraid and missing my parents. You graciously offered me your own

home complete with a loving family, a warm bed to sleep in, food to fill my craving adolescent stomach, and hope to guide my yearning spirit. What more could anyone ever ask for?

People look at me crazy when I say I was a foster child, as if to say "how tragic!" But from my perspective, it is "how fortunate!" Some children are better off in a foster home.

I know I speak for your other foster children when I say how fortunate we were to have someone like you to be there to look out for us and to instill your good values, much needed discipline and structure during our formative years. With tender love, a great big THANK YOU!

Your scraggly little red-headed foster kid,
Dantie

For Mother's Day 2009, the year that Mamma Jo and I became reacquainted, I sent her flowers and she sent me a Mother's Day card. *Inside her card was a Mother's Day card that I had sent to her when I was sixteen years old!* Here is what it said:

Jo,
It's almost been three years since I first came here. It may not have been perfect, but I want to thank you for putting up with me. I may not have

been as good as Judy, but at least I can say I have tried! I won't ever forget no matter where I am. Just look around you and see how dull and quiet it is now, without me and just think, nobody to buy fat, huge, gigantic, tremendous shoes for. And nobody to take all the hems down for, and nobody to gripe at you all the time. I'm sort of sorry I have to leave even though I miss my folks. I just hope I'll have it half as easy as I did here. If you hear a knock on the door some day and I'm standing there (or lying there) you'll know what happened. Well, this is your last Mother's day with me, so I hope it will be the best you've ever had. I won't forget.
Love,
Dantie

A few months after that Mother's Day in 2009, Mamma Jo sent me a package in the mail. It was a large 10x13 inch envelope with a return address from Kathy Wilson. I still had to pause to think . . . *who* was Kathy Wilson? When I opened up the envelope there were sheets of photo-copied pictures of Judy, Ricky, Mary, Sandi and me as we had all looked back then in the 1960s when we lived together in the Buckner foster home. This was quite a thrill for me to see.

However, what came next, included with the copied photos of us kids, was a real surprise to me. There was a 5x7, color school photograph of me at the age of thirteen, when I had first come to live at Mamma Jo's house. As I looked at the girl in the photo, I had to find a place to sit down. *Seeing that picture explained it all.* It was a shock to my system to look upon the face of that young girl that had once been me. So this was the little girl who had caused all the trouble – the one who had been passed on from one home to another at least nine times by then – beaten, neglected, abused, and teased – the child for whom no one would take serious responsibility to protect and even more importantly, proudly claim as worthy enough to be their own . . . daughter.

It was true what my step-mother, Valora, had once said – I *was* a pathetic and pitiful-looking child – and as I looked at my picture I could see the pain in those eyes as if recalling a tragic flash-back. I experienced the memory of this awkward, fragile and gangly red-headed girl as she was stood up in front of a classroom of kids *every year* – being introduced as the *new kid* in school. Then the relentless questions that followed about her family history, and the lies she felt she had to tell to cover up the truth. I realized the teasing and cruelty that came later from the mouths of bullies had grown to be predictable and expected.

Something deep within my soul cried out to her. I wanted to hold her in my arms and tell her that she was loved and that she would be loved by many and that everything would turn out all right in the end. I took the photograph upstairs with me to the safety of my room and lay down on the bed with it held close to my heart. It was if I had taken her in my arms and hugged her and we cried together. For three days I hardly left my room. A heavy cloud of emotional grief hung over me and all I wanted to do was sleep away my feelings . . .

During that time it seemed that a metamorphosis was taking place – the child and the adult were blending together as one. Somehow I knew she had always lived there deep down inside me just waiting to be discovered, waiting to be reborn to someone who would fully understand and accept her for the valuable being that she was – someone she could belong to who was willing to give her the unconditional love that she so badly needed and deserved. *I would be that person* – the attentive parent she never had. *I* would love her for who she *was,* for everything she was *not,* for everything she had *done* and for everything that had *been done to her by others.* I would never abandon or neglect her or go away. I would always be there for her. I would understand.

After the days in my room had passed, my work and life called out to me. I ventured out, reluctant at first, with my movements slow and tentative as if I was so fragile that if someone said the wrong thing to me I might shatter into a million pieces. The photo of the little red-headed girl was put back and sealed in the envelope. I could not bear to look at her face. It was still too freshly haunting and emotionally disturbing. I needed more time.

~

Then in 2011, I took a trip back to Tucson to see the Buckner family: Mamma Jo, Hershel, Judy, Ricky (and Mary who lived in a town close-by). Mamma Jo had told me she was traveling from Kansas to Tucson with her daughter Judy to visit the rest of the family. It was going to be a family reunion of sorts. Mamma Jo called me and asked me to join them. I was so excited to get her invitation and made the three-day trip and stayed at a nearby hotel. It was quite an emotional experience seeing everyone again after so many years! More importantly, it was great to be able to say thank you, eye-to-eye, to both Mamma Jo and Hershel – whom I had long-since forgiven.

Then in early December 2013, Mamma Jo called me to say that she was taking another trip from Kansas to Tucson. (Unfortunately Hershel had passed away only months earlier.) She said Judy wouldn't be able to come this time, but asked me if I would like to meet her again there in Tucson. Of course I was elated and quickly cleared my schedule for the trip. This time I brought along my 32-year-old daughter, Ashley. It was great to see Ashley and Mamma Jo together – there seemed to be an instant bond created between them and we all connected in mind and spirit.

Several big surprises happened during that 2013 Tucson trip. One was that on Ashley's and my last day together with Mamma Jo, we searched out the house where I had lived when I was in Mamma Jo's care back in the 1960s. As we drove by it and stopped, I noticed that someone was home, so I decided to knock on the door. The nice lady who owned the house graciously let me, Mamma Jo and Ashley in! Though it looked just like I remembered it, everything seemed so much smaller. It was hard to believe that four of us teenage girls had survived living together in a ten-by-eleven foot room, and that there had been 41 foster children through that little 1,200 square-foot house. When we went to leave, the owner told us that she had considered taking in foster children as well. Now she said she was even more inspired to do so.

The other remarkable thing that happened on that same impactful day was that I decided to drive by Catalina High School. It was after school hours and I parked the rental car in the lot in front of the school so that Ashley could take my picture. As we approached the front steps, a group of people about my age were coming out the main door. I noticed that one of them was wearing a Stanford University sweat shirt, so I started up a conversation with her. It turned out that they were the CHS Foundation Board of Directors! When she found out that I was an alumnus from 1966, the woman with the Stanford sweat shirt suggested she take me on a tour of the school. What an exciting treat! She was like the Mayor of Catalina High – at her request people quickly came to help us unlock doors throughout the school. I was able to get into the auditorium where I had performed in plays, into the cafeteria (where all the *real* drama had happened), and into the library – and down the other halls of my past. It was so surreal. (*Later when I got back home to California I looked up my hostess in my 1966 Catalina year book and found that she had been one of the most popular girls in school at the time – a student body officer, who at seventeen already had a long list of grand awards and achievements. She had gone on to graduate from Stanford University – just down the street from where I now live! What luck that we connected!)*

That night was Ashley's and my last night with Mamma Jo. We had a delicious pasta dinner at Rick and his wife Pat's house. As we were getting into the car to leave and Mamma Jo and I were saying our good-byes, it warmed my heart when she looked me straight in the eyes and said that she didn't consider me her foster child, but a member of her family. She hugged me and called me her "Baby Girl." It brought up such a warm feeling of acceptance in my heart – that continues to envelop me even to this day.

On our final day in Tucson, before getting on the plane to go home, Ashley and I took an early morning drive through the desert to Old Tucson – which still stands as a movie location and popular tourist destination. When we arrived the first person I met there was the Old Tucson historian and he and I talked of old times and people we both knew from days gone-by. He said Bob Shelton – who was turning ninety-three – was still alive and well. All-in-all that trip to Tucson was an amazing adventure and I'm so happy to say that my daughter shared in my love of the Sonora Desert.

~

Toward the end of writing this memoir, amazing things started to happen. At the urging of my partner Larry, I hunted down my old high-school friend Lisa. Her last name had changed and she lived far away from Tucson, but I eventually found her through the Internet. Though we have talked on the phone, texted, emailed and exchanged photos, as of this writing we have not yet met face-to-face. She seemed as thrilled as I was to finally reconnect, but she said her family does not know of our escape to California and the dramatic events that took place there. Understandably she prefers that I not use her real name.

She told me that when she was returned from the Los Angeles Juvenile Hall back to the Arizona girls' home, she was put in solitary confinement for running away. There she encountered our long-lost traveling companion, Susan! Susan told Lisa that she had *turned herself in* to the police that night when we were at the Pike in Long Beach! Lisa also told me that Susan was only *fourteen years old* when we ran off to California; I didn't remember her being so young. It is such a relief that after almost fifty years, *that* mystery has been resolved!

~

My step-mother Valora passed away while I was writing this memoir. It was quite painful for me because we had become good friends in her later years. She knew I was writing my memoir and supplied me with as much information as she could remember. As I continued to write what I felt during earlier times with her – and I know I did not always paint a rosy picture of her – I wanted to be honest and to tell it like it was for me then. I wrote a poem about her a few weeks before she died which I have included here.

~

Now, let's discuss the matter of my name. I was sixteen years old when I finally decided that I wanted to change my name – though it wasn't officially done until I was nineteen. I can still remember those awkward times when I was stood in front of new classrooms of gawking students and was introduced as "Dantie Sauer," – the kids could hardly contain their outbursts of laughter. I heard all kinds of teasing over the years, such as "Dantie's panties" and "I'll have a Dantie Sauer on the rocks please." When I was in my teens, someone must have suggested I drop the "i" and make it Dante. (I don't think I would have ever thought of that myself – not yet knowing about the "Divine Comedy" and Dante Alighieri.) I have yet to discover the origin of the name Dantie – *other than that it was my grandmother's given name and I was named after her.* It's too bad that no one thought to ask her about it before she died. Now no one remains of that generation to ask. *Actually my Nana Dantie died with lots of secrets.*

During the last visit I had with Nana, back when I was still in my early thirties (before meeting Larry Drummond), she was living in a trailer behind my Great Aunt Elsie's farmhouse in Virginia. During my short stay there, Nana insisted that I *not talk* with my aunt in the front house – she said they were having a feud. So, out of respect for my grandmother I didn't talk to Aunt Elsie, who was just a few yards away – even though I really wanted to.

As I was driving past the farmhouse to leave (with my boyfriend of the time) Aunt Elsie came out of her house – and shocked us both by her ghostly, skeleton-like appearance. She walked onto the road like a zombie in front of our car to wave us down. When we stopped, she bent over and looked into the window at my surprised face and asked that I come inside. My boyfriend was quite impatient and by then wanted to leave, but I begged him to let me go inside with her for a brief visit. He agreed, but stayed in the car.

After I sat down with Aunt Elsie in the parlor, she attempted to tell me something "important" about our family history – but she was having difficulty coming to the point. It is unfortunate that I don't remember much about that conversation because I was so distracted by her changed appearance and the horn honking outside for me to hurry up. So I left and was never able to reach her again to talk with her. It occurs to me now that the feud between her and Nana likely had to do with her wanting to tell me some secrets of the family – part of which might have been the fact that my *Nana really wasn't my grandmother after all* – something I later learned. My mother didn't find this out herself until she was forty-two years old and needed her birth certificate to go with her husband Richard overseas.

The County would not release it to her because *she had been adopted* – a total shock to her! By then Nana and Aunt Elsie had both passed away and she had no one left in the family to ask about it. To this day it remains a mystery as to who my mother's parents really were. My mother thinks her mother may have been Nana's other sister – someone she never met, but had seen in old family pictures. Mom thinks she might have died or was disowned by the family, because no one ever spoke of her.

~

Memoir writing is an emotionally trying experience. It's a wonder that anyone ever finishes it. From the beginning questions arise: why are you writing it – who cares? *Why do you think of yourself as so important that people would want to read about you?* Then all along the way you continue to fight the battles in the thick shrubs of doubt – will you be offending others – will they never forgive you for including them – or for *not* including them? And, oh, the exposure. Do you want the general public to read it – if so should you use a pen name and/or change other people's names? Will you be shamed by revealing your past? Will it adversely affect your career or business? So many considerations.

Then there's the editing. I realize now that a memoir is never really finished. Every time you think it's done, it needs to be gone over again – there is always that urge to re-write, add or delete portions. And even after all that, I have to believe that anyone who has ever written a memoir is sure, once it goes to print, that there is *something* in there that they wish they had changed.

~

Other than wanting the family (or in my case, *families*) to know about my life journey, the other inspiration to write this memoir came from my desire to reach out to foster youth. I want to contribute to them in some way – to give back for help I got along the way. I

261

hope by telling my story I might be able to gain their trust to work alongside them. I hope that my story offers a more inspiring view than the one presented in the sad and depressing TV commercials with their statistics about foster kids and their dismal fate. I want to give encouragement by showing that, while there is much to learn and *unlearn*, life can be good and we can all make a positive contribution to our world. *And my limited but real success can serve as an example.*

I feel that in my case there were very low expectations set around me as a foster child. In looking back, I wish I had reached out to more people outside of home to teach me, to have faith in me, and help show me that I was capable of more. Over time I have somehow found the strength to reach within and find a way to eventually grow out of my cocoon of distrust and self-restraint and shed it on the pathway to a new life. A path that has allowed me to use my childhood experiences to be of help to others. Through my story I especially want to give hope to the foster teens aging out of the system – which for me seemed to be the darkest time. I found that the most difficult part of that time was my inability to let go of the rage over injustices done to me as an innocent and vulnerable child – to let go and believe in myself enough to know that I deserved better. Once I started to accomplish that, I felt I was on the road to self-acceptance and was able to gain insight into my own authenticity.

~

My 86 year-old mother Helen still lives alone in her apartment down in Pacific Grove. I support her and provide a caregiver who visits on a regular basis. Since her disabling 1997 accident my mother has learned to depend on me and I guess, to some degree, I also depend on her. We usually get together on holidays, and every month or so I make the 90-minute trip down to the Monterey area to visit with her. We love to take a little drive to Carmel

Valley to get out of the fog and have lunch. When we come back to Pacific Grove, we park by the water near Lover's Point and talk for hours and watch the sunset together before driving through Cannery Row and back to her apartment. That's our usual routine. There have also been times when I have visited her in the hospital or during her stays in convalescent care homes after numerous surgeries.

I realize the little girl who resides within me still wants her mother. Now that she is near I don't want to lose her again – no matter what our relationship has been in the past. We have had some good times together as adults and we still relive those memories over and over again. Especially memories that make us laugh, like the pillow fight we had one night when I was visiting with her back in the 70's. We were lying on the guest bed talking in her apartment – giggling over the gyrations of her lava lamp – when we got into a pillow fight. During the fight she fell off the side of the bed. I couldn't see her on the floor and since there was complete silence, I thought I might have killed her or something. I jumped up and ran over to the side of the bed to see what was wrong. She was lying there laughing so hard she couldn't catch her breath. We still laugh about it today. Another great time, before her accident, we took a Spring excursion to beautiful Yosemite together. We have talked many times about it, reliving the happy memories of that special trip.

Now that my mother is older and less mobile, we are limited in what we can do together. Occasionally I will give her advanced warning that I am going to come by and "kidnap" her to go on a "little adventure" together. I tell her to pack her bags. This always tickles her and as long as she is feeling well, she is game to get out of the house. I have to admit that I'm not getting any younger and these little adventures – which usually just consist of going away to a small town close-by (like Santa Cruz) and spending the night at a luxury beach hotel with views to the ocean – can take their toll on me and my body. It is trying for me to manage the physical transport of my mom and her walker, but I find every minute of it is worthwhile.

It is comforting to know that my mother is only a phone call away. I count my blessings that she is near and find that it is her that I call when I need a calm reassuring voice to tell me that everything is going to be all right. We always end our visits and phone calls with "I love you" – because we never know when we might lose one another again.

~

I have found that in the end, Katharine Hepburn has nothing on my real mom. For despite all our differences and history together, my biological mother is still my mother and without her I wouldn't be here – driven forward to my destiny as the mother of my two wonderful daughters.

So, best to you Katharine Hepburn! Thanks for being there when I needed you. See you at the movies!

Cindy, Valora, a friend and Me

Valora

Flaming hair, flaming spirit,
Loving and kind, yet harsh and crude –
She can be all things . . . love and joy one day, tyrant the
next
Apologetic, not quite at peace with the world.
She wants the simplest of things – love, affection, attention
from all.
She is a seeker of truth and God
Her quest to be continued . . .

She is my historian, the one who knew me when and sees
me now,
The one who knows my journey like no other,
Never expecting those dreams to come true –
Humbled and proud, my biggest fan when they did.

My unpredictable, part-time guide through space and time,
No longer there for me on those quiet lonely mornings
A long distance call away to boost her spirits as much as
mine,
Bringing laugher, hope, encouragement and love,
Receiving in return praise of life's exceeded expectations.

Holding on to the last delicate fiber of life
She passes the baton and I rise to the top, the historian –
Poised to observe
Not without the imprint of the one I love.

Dante Drummond

Acknowledgements

If you told me in 2006 that I would ever write my life story and publish it, I would have said "Yeah right . . . just after I win the lottery!" Although I have enjoyed journaling over the years, letting the skeletons out of one's closet is not a great career move for someone in the public eye. And yet, unusual events have conspired over these past few years to make me undertake recalling a past that few people, not even close family, knew about.

The one person most instrumental in the completion of this work is my editor Phyllis Butler, who has held my hand on the roller coaster ride of emotions and conflicts that this expedition has uncovered. If it were not for her support, perseverance, and expertise my memoir would never have emerged from the cavernous depths of my memory out into the glaring light of day. Phyllis should get a medal for keeping me focused and on track, guiding me through the assembling of my childhood, jig-saw puzzle memories. She knows me now better than anyone, and we have developed a wonderful friendship along the way.

Next there has been no greater friend, supporter and midnight editor than my partner, Larry Fretto. He has been the slayer of demons, insecurities and doubts that still present themselves on a regular basis as I struggle with the realities of exposing a life story much different from what most would have expected.

Love and thanks to both my darling daughters: Chelsea, for her encouragement along the way, and Ashley for her support, feedback and creative design of this book cover.

Others who have helped make this book possible are Kaethe Langs and Ann Richardson who through their bravery in sharing *their* stories, encouraged me at the outset to share mine.

Finally, I am grateful for the role the foster care system played in my journey to adulthood. My hope is that my story may encourage other foster children to realize that they are not bound by their circumstances or negative expectations of others. They can reinvent themselves and find their own way and must never give up on their dreams. Along the way there will be people standing by to help and mentor them to grow and discover their inner power and potential.

Dante Drummond is a dynamic and successful Silicon Valley business woman working in Palo Alto. After recovering from a bout with cancer in 2006 she felt compelled to share with her family and friends, secrets from her past – including her adventurous escape to California – that helped forge her strong and willful character. So she took a memoir class and started writing it all down with the encouragement of her teacher and the small writing group that evolved from that class. The experience was both revealing and surprising – particularly to those who thought they knew her.

~